T0272934

DRINK:LOS ANGELES

The Beverage Lover's Guide to Los Angeles

PROSPECT PARK BOOKS

Published by Prospect Park Books
prospectparkbooks.com
eat-la.com

Distributed to the trade by
Consortium Book Sales & Distribution
cbsd.com

SPECIAL SALES
Bulk purchase (10+ copies) of Drink: Los Angeles is available to companies, organizations, mail-order catalogs and nonprofits at special discounts, and large orders can be customized to suit individual needs. For more information, contact Prospect Park Books.

Library of Congress Cataloging in Publication Information
The following is for reference only:
Bates, Colleen Dunn
        Los Angeles / Colleen Dunn Bates
                p.cm.
        Includes index.
        ISBN: 978-1-938849-38-1
        1. Los Angeles (Calif.) – Guidebooks. 2. Los Angeles County
(Calif.)
    – Food / Restaurants.
        I. Bates, Colleen Dunn. II. Title.

First edition, first printing

Production in the United States of America
Design by Renee Nakagawa & Joseph Shuldiner
Printed in China on sustainably produced paper

DRINK **LOS ANGELES**

The Beverage Lover's Guide to Los Angeles

EDITOR
Colleen Dunn Bates

CONTRIBUTING EDITORS
Miles Clements
Pat Saperstein
Alex Sayles
Elina Shatkin
Garrett Snyder

WITH
Jean T. Barrett, Jennifer Bastien, Sascha
Bos, Ben Muller, Renee Nakagawa, and
Sylvie Ramirez

PROSPECT PARK BOOKS

[TABLE OF CONTENTS]

[ABOUT THE AUTHORS]

COLLEEN DUNN BATES (editor and publisher) was the American editor of the Gault Millau guides and the restaurant critic for *L.A. Style*. Now she writes about restaurants for *Westways* and heads up Prospect Park Books, which publishes *Eat: Los Angeles* and award-winning cookbooks (including *Das Cookbook, The Auntie Em's Cookbook, Who Wants Seconds?, and Little Flower*), as well as fiction, humor, and regional books. A sixth-generation Southern Californian, Colleen lives in Pasadena.

MILES CLEMENTS writes about drink and food for *Westways* and *Orange Coast*; he has also written about drink and food for *Eat: Los Angeles*, the *Los Angeles Times* and many others. The Long Beach resident (and native) also roams the South Bay—and, indeed, all of Southern California—for his blog, *Eat Food With Me*.

PAT SAPERSTEIN is the intrepid drinker and eater behind *Eating L.A.* (eatingla.com), one of L.A.'s most respected food blogs. The Silver Lake resident is also a senior editor at *Variety* and a contributing editor to *Eat: Los Angeles*.

ALEX SAYLES is the former social media director for *Eat: Los Angeles* and was a regular writer for Eat-LA.com. The Hawaiian native scours Southern California in search of the best craft beers, happy hours, and, for balance, fresh-pressed juices. He lives in West L.A.

ELINA SHATKIN is a senior editor at *Los Angeles* magazine who often focuses on drinking and eating. She was born in the Ukraine, educated at UCLA, and has worked as an entertainment-industry reporter/editor and food and drink writer for *Eat: Los Angeles*, the *L.A. Weekly*, and *Squid Ink*. She lives in West L.A.

GARRETT SNYDER is the editor of *Tasting Table Los Angeles* and a former writer about drink and food for *Squid Ink* and *Los Angeles* magazine. He fell in love with writing about food and drink while an undergrad at Loyola Marymount University in Westchester, not so long ago; today he lives in Chinatown.

[THE REST OF THE TEAM]

CONTRIBUTORS: Jean T. Barrett, Darryl Bates, Sandy Gillis, William Goldstein, Susan LaTempa, Melody Malmberg

ART DIRECTOR: Joseph Shuldiner

COVER DESIGNER: Renee Nakagawa

PRODUCTION DESIGN: Amy Inouye

MANAGING EDITOR: Sascha Bos

EDITORIAL ASSISTANTS: Jacqueline Abelson, Willa Zhang

DATABASE DESIGNER: Anton Anderson

INDATA GENIUS: Joe Matthia

WORDPRESS GURUS: Jesse McDougal & John Stephens

DISTRIBUTOR: Consortium Book Sales & Distribution

[PLEASE CHECK OUT OUR WEB SITE AT: Eat-LA.com]

SPECIAL THANKS to L.A.'s passionate and interconnected drink-and-food-writing community, especially Jeff Miller at *Thrillist LA*; our own Garrett Snyder at *Tasting Table LA*; Russ Parsons, Jonathan Gold, and S. Irene Virbila at the *Los Angeles Times* Food section; the gang at the *Times*'s Daily Dish; Amy Scattergood and friends at the *L.A. Weekly* and its blog, *Squid Ink*; Patrick Kuh, Lesley Bargar Suter, and our own Elina Shatkin at *Los Angeles* magazine; Evan Kleiman and *Good Food* (KCRW); Krista Simmons at LAist; Kat Odell at Eater LA; Merrill Shindler; the *Hometown* books and their authors; and, of course, the Chowhounds. Finally, heaps o' gratitude and a generous pour of aged whiskey for our radio pals John Rabe and Kevin Ferguson at 89.3 KPCC.

[ABOUT DRINK: LOS ANGELES]

SEEMINGLY OVERNIGHT, LOS ANGELES has become a fantastic drinking city. We've had great eating for decades, but no one would have put us first in the beverage department, except perhaps for horchata. Seattle had better coffee, Portland had better beer bars, Boston had better pubs, San Francisco and Chicago had better neighborhood bars, and New York had better cocktail lounges. Boy, have times changed.

This explosion in good drinking inspired us to take the *Eat: Los Angeles* concept to a new place and create this curated pocket guide to find the best drinking across the greater L.A. area, whether you're thirsty for a boba or a beer. This is by no means a comprehensive guide—that would be so massive you couldn't lift it. *Drink: Los Angeles* is, however, a broad-ranging book, in terms of geography, styles, and price points. Most of all, it's a discerning one—we don't have every single karaoke bar in Koreatown, for instance, but we point you toward our favorites. Our goal is to give you interesting, thoughtful, tasty choices in every category across L.A. County.

Here you'll find the Why, What, and Who for L.A.'s best beverage sources, from cocktail bars and coffeehouses to craft breweries and cold-pressed juiceries. But we don't know it all, not by a long shot. So if we've missed your favorite dive bar or wine shop or tea room, please let us know at Eat-LA.com, the shared home of Drink & Eat LA.

Colleen Dunn Bates
Editor

P.S. DESPITE OUR BEST EFFORTS . . .
Please forgive us if a business has closed, if management has changed, or if your experience does not match ours. We labored mightily to verify every scrap of information in this book, but some places will close, change, or misbehave, and we can't do a thing about it.

HOW WE DECIDE WHAT TO INCLUDE: *Drink: Los Angeles* has more than 500 listings, but of course the L.A. Basin has gazillions more places to drink. Our job is to steer you to the best. If we don't like a place, we simply don't include it.

Most importantly, we celebrate the places that are mom 'n' pop in spirit—individual businesses and local chains with hands-on ownership and enthusiasm for whatever is being cooked, sold or served. So you'll find loads of smaller pubs, bars, and coffeehouses, but you won't find every high-end hotel restaurant, say, or the sort of MBA-managed club-restaurants that run rampant in Hollywood.

SPEAKING OF CLUBS: We ignore them. This is a book about drinking, not about clubbing. So you won't find bottle-service clubs, doorman-intensive, exclusionary places, or nightclubs that are really about live music or dancing.

A NOTE ABOUT CHAINS: In general, we eschew corporate chains. This isn't because we think they're inherently evil—we aren't going to judge—but everyone knows about them, and you don't need us to help you find Starbucks or the Yard House. Occasionally we'll make an exception, as with Peet's, which has an indie sensibility and is sometimes your only choice for good coffee in certain parts of town.

BAR CRAWLS: This chapter brings you 12 profiles of drink-lovers' neighborhoods. Some are walkable and some require driving, but each has a strong sense of place and a vibrant drink community. Once you explore them all, you'll be a true Angeleno.

ESSENTIALLY L.A.: In each chapter, we recognize some places as "Essentially L.A." Perhaps it makes a killer margarita, or roasts coffee worth driving out of your way for, or has the best selection of Spanish wines in town. Or perhaps the food and drink aren't exactly remarkable, but its atmosphere or history or people are, well, essentially L.A.

DRINKING & DRIVING: We're not your dad, or the CHP. You know the drill. We'll just say that the Metro, Uber, Lyft, and an increasing number of pedestrian-friendly neighborhoods are making it easier and easier to hoist a few without driving.

[THE ICONS]

You'll see little icons scattered around the pages that follow. Here's what they mean:

🌴 **ESSENTIALLY LA:** The places that define L.A., or that are worth going out of your way for.

⊼ **DIVE BAR:** "Dive" is in the eye of the beholder, so this is kind of a loose category, but in general it's a place where it doesn't matter what you wear, where the floors might be less than sparkling clean, and where the drinks are relatively cheap.

👂 **QUIET:** This can vary a lot; some bars are quiet at 6 p.m. and deafening at 11. We generally use it when it's relatively quiet most of the time. And since we brought this up: L.A. bar and restaurant owners, unless you own a dance club, please, please turn down the music. We all want to have fun, but fun involves talking to other human beings, and it's getting harder every day.

💲 **GOOD VALUE:** Again, a relative quality. Yelp is full of people griping about a place that charges $10 for a craft cocktail, while others find that reasonable. We use this to connote a good value for what it is—so if the French Champagne is inexpensive compared to other places serving French Champagne, then it's a good value.

🏛 **GOOD FOR GROUPS:** It can be tough to find a place to go out with a gang of friends, so we tag ones that have private rooms or good areas for a posse.

🎤 **KARAOKE BARS:** Self-explanatory, but note that some with this icon have karaoke every night, and some just on certain nights, so read the review and double-check the website.

☼ **PATIO:** It's a crime how few places in our sunny corner of the States have outdoor seating, so we point you toward the ones that do.

♥ **ROMANTIC:** Charm, atmosphere, coziness...you get the idea.

[THE REGIONS]

It's not easy to break massive L.A. County into manageable chunks, and it requires some semi-arbitrary decisions. Here's how we did it:

CENTRAL CITY: The city of L.A.'s modern core, encompassing Los Feliz, Hollywood, Koreatown, Hancock Park, Beverly/Third, the Mid-City area, Melrose, Miracle Mile, Fairfax, and West Hollywood.

EASTSIDE: The city's original core: Downtown, East L.A., Highland Park, Echo Park, Silver Lake, Eagle Rock, and environs. Okay, fussy folks, we know it's sacrilegious to some to call Silver Lake "eastside," but that's the way things are evolving in L.A., and we're going with the flow.

SAN GABRIEL VALLEY: A huge swath of the east county, ranging from Monterey Park to the Covinas and encompassing Pasadena, San Gabriel, Sierra Madre, and beyond. Yes, we know Glendale and La Cañada aren't technically in the SG Valley, but for simplicity's sake, we're pretending they are.

EAST VALLEY: The San Fernando Valley from Burbank to Sherman Oaks, including Studio City and North Hollywood.

WEST VALLEY: From Encino and the 405 way out northwest and west to the Ventura County line.

WESTSIDE: CENTRAL: The heart of the westside, including Beverly Hills, Culver City, Century City, Rancho Park, and Westwood; the 405 is the western border.

WEST OF THE 405: Pretty self-explanatory. Brentwood to the Palisades, Malibu to Venice.

SOUTH BAY TO SOUTH L.A.: Another huge swath of the county, from the South Bay beach towns (Playa del Rey, Manhattan, Redondo), along the coast from Torrance to Long Beach, and across the south basin from Downey to Inglewood.

INLAND EMPIRE: The Far East, including San Dimas, Claremont, Pomona, and Redlands.

Bar Crawls

[YES, WE DO WALK IN L.A.]

Not only are Angelenos increasingly moving around by foot, but we're also taking advantage of our growing Metro system. So a bar crawl L.A.-style might mean walking a pedestrian-friendly 'hood, like Little Tokyo or Old Pasadena or Venice, or it might mean a night of hopping off and on the Gold Line or the Red Line.

In this chapter, you'll find our dozen favorite bar crawls in the greater L.A. area, all of which include suggestions for good food to complement the liquid sustenance. And thanks to Metro, Uber, Lyft, taxis, and/or your cool friend who's volunteered to be the designated driver, it's easy to make the rounds without even thinking about getting behind a wheel. Sláinte!

[THE CRAWLS]

[DOWNTOWN L.A.]

Downtown has no shortage of bars—there are so many good ones that you've got to be selective or you'll reach your alcohol limit in no time flat. Here's an edited list of some of our favorite spots in the few-block radius between the Pershing Square and 7th Street metro stations. Start off early at Josef Centeno's Bar Amá (1) to take advantage of Super Nacho Hour. Grab a seat at the bar, order some inventive nachos, and watch as cool, unpretentious bartenders mix fun drinks against a lovely blue-tiled backdrop.

The party continues a couple of blocks southeast, where you can grab a French dip sandwich at historic Cole's (2). Or get your sandwich to go and head through the speakeasy-style door to the Varnish, a mixology spot of modern legend. Another two blocks down is Peking Tavern (3), a hip underground spot for Chinese bites and drinks. Two and a half blocks west on 8th Street, you'll be drawn in by the iconic neon signage of the Golden Gopher (4), a fun spot with arcade games and kitschy gopher lamps. Hungry? A right on Olive and a left on 7th will get you to Mo-Chica (5) for Peruvian ceviche and a great cocktail, too. Across the street is the bustling Más Malo (6) and the quieter Bar Jackalope (7), a speakeasy inside the Seven Grand bar. The former's a great spot for tequila; the latter, a chill haven for sipping small-batch whiskeys. Try both if you're feeling daring.

1. **Bar Amá,** 118 W. 4th St.
2. **Cole's & the Varnish,** 118 E. 6th St.
3. **Peking Tavern,** 806 S. Spring St.
4. **Golden Gopher,** 417 W. 8th St.
5. **Mo-Chica,** 514 W.7th St.
6. **Más Malo,** 515 W. 7th St.
7. **Bar Jackalope (Seven Grand),** 515 W. 7th St.

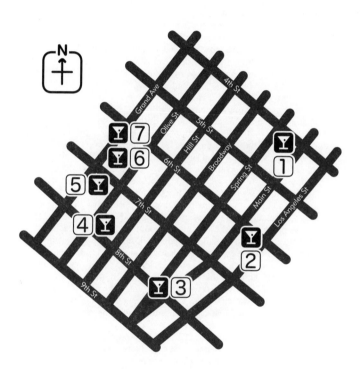

[ECHO PARK]

Drinkers have found several clever ways to attack a bar crawl
down Sunset Boulevard in Echo Park and Silver Lake, from a
literary-themed tour to a walk called "the El Train" that stops at El
Compadre, El Chavo, and El Condor. No matter what the theme,
Sunset is the perfect street to cruise for cocktails or craft beers.
It's only two and a half miles from Dodger Stadium to the Vista
Theater, so hardy types can walk off an IPA or two and go the
whole distance. For a more reasonable crawl, concentrate on either
the Sunset Junction area (see the Silver Lake bar crawl) or this one
in Echo Park, which is packed with bars, music venues, and, yes,
guys with man buns and girls with fedoras.

Start on the western end with a brew and a nosh at Mohawk
Bend (1), a locavore gastropub in an old movie theater. A vegan-
friendly menu and 72 taps of mostly Californian beers are served
all day long in the airy back room or the patio along Sunset. A few
blocks east, Taix 321 Lounge (2) has an atmosphere reminiscent
of grandpa's den, but it's a surprisingly cool place to see an
acoustic band or comedy show, and you could do worse than the
happy-hour frites. If you're more serious about your music, stop
at the Echo (3), where L.A.'s coolest bands show up. Otherwise,
keep heading east to El Prado (4), a groovy beer bar with vinyl
on the turntables and lesser-known Belgian ales and cheese plates
on the menu. Just make sure to save room for the locals' fave,
the Tacos Ariza truck, which usually parks on Logan just north
of Sunset. For a break from the drinking, stop for a pick-me-up
coffee and to shop for a new book at Stories (5) or browse for a
record at Origami Vinyl (1816 W. Sunset Blvd.), then move on
to Sunset Beer (6), a must for connoisseurs of the brew. It's a
happy combination of a retail store, stocking hundreds of hard-to-
find varieties, and a laid-back bar with board games and several
rotating taps.

Next, head to Little Joy (7), which has a solid cocktail
selection, a good happy hour, and a pool table. Those who haven't
eaten yet can bring in a juicy brisket sandwich from Trencher
next door. Finish up the crawl with either a flaming margarita at
El Compadre (8), because by then it's all about the fire, or hit the
dance floor at the Short Stop (9) until the Uber arrives.

1. Mohawk Bend, 2141 Sunset Blvd.
2. Taix 321 Lounge, 1911 Sunset Blvd.
3. The Echo, 1822 Sunset Blvd.
4. El Prado, 1805 Sunset Blvd.
5. Stories, 1716 Sunset Blvd.
6. Sunset Beer, 1498 Sunset Blvd.
7. Little Joy, 1477 Sunset Blvd.
8. El Compadre, 1449 Sunset Blvd.
9. Short Stop, 1455 Sunset Blvd.

[GOLD LINE]

Metro's Gold Line covers a swath of the city that stretches from east Pasadena through Downtown into the heart of East Los Angeles. It's also the cleanest and smoothest of the city's trains, which makes for a pretty sweet bar-hopping experience. Here's our favorite Gold Line crawl.

Start at Del Mar Station at the Otis Bar (1) in Pasadena, a wood-paneled, leather-chaired bar next to La Grande Orange restaurant inside the historic and handsome former Southern Pacific train station; Monday through Friday, there's a swell happy hour until 7 p.m. Hop on the southbound train, get off at the Mission Station in South Pasadena, and head for Griffin's of Kinsale (2), a proper Irish pub with Guinness on tap and, if you're lucky, live music; if you're hungry, the shepherd's pie and bangers and mash will satisfy. Next, continue the southbound journey to increasingly happening Highland Park, where the Greyhound (3) is packing 'em in every night; the locals know to go early for the happy hour. A few more stops south is Chinatown Station, where you'll find Hop Louie (4), a Chinese restaurant and bar inside a pagoda with an old neon sign and a cigarette machine. Or keep going one more stop to landmark Union Station, where you should absolutely get off just to stroll through the main hall; a martini at the small art deco Traxx Bar (5) is just a bonus.

Continuing southbound, the next stop is Little Tokyo, where Far Bar (6) is a must-stop for Asian-inspired drinks: it's right in front of the station, and your TAP card will get you a discount. Then it's back on for your final destination: Mariachi Plaza/Boyle Heights Station, where you'll find Eastside Luv (7) about a block away—that's the funky-cool spot to go for a Michelada, sangria, or a sobering espresso and live entertainment.

1. **Del Mar – The Otis Bar at La Grand Orange, 260 S. Raymond Ave.**
2. **South Pasadena – Griffin's of Kinsale, 1007 Mission St.**
3. **Highland Park – The Greyhound, 5570 N. Figueroa St.**
4. **Chinatown – Hop Louie, 950 Mei Ling Way**
5. **Traxx Bar, Union Station, 800 N. Alameda St.**
6. **Little Tokyo/Arts District – Far Bar, 347 E. 1st St.**
7. **Mariachi Plaza – Eastside Luv, 1835 E. 1st St.**

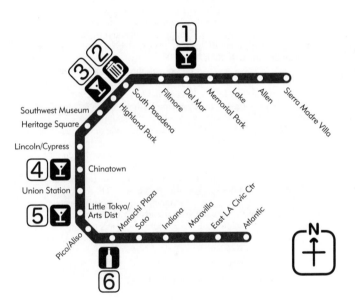

[KOREATOWN]

The combination of cool old apartment buildings, lots of good Korean restaurants, and a central, accessible location has made K-town one of the most desirable places for young Angelenos to live—and it's a fun place for a drinker's ramble. (This crawl starts and ends near the Wilshire/Normandie Metro stop.) To do it right, open and close the evening with karaoke. First stop is Café Brass Monkey (1), a dark little dive bar whose stage is packed with singers every night; start your crawl here before it gets too crowded, and if it's a weekend, make a reservation (karaoke starts at 4 p.m. on weekdays and 8 p.m. on weekends). After you've belted out Bohemian Rhapsody, cross Wilshire, head a block east, and settle into a booth at the HMS Bounty (2), one of L.A.'s great old-school bars. The décor is nautical, the drinks are cheap, and the baseball-cut steak is pretty tasty. Last stop on Wilshire, a few blocks west, is Pot Lobby Bar (3), the newest project from star chef Roy Choi in the chic Line Hotel. It's loud, it's a scene, but you should check it out and try a kimchi cocktail.

Now it's time for a stroll to walk off some of the booze. Head west on Wilshire, walk about six blocks, and turn right on Western. Just past 6th you'll find Beer Belly (4), a craft-beer haven with great local brews and terrific food (like the duck French dip). It's a nice place to chill after the action at the Pot Lobby Bar. When you're ready to sing again, head east on 6th several blocks to Gaam (5), where if you've planned properly you've reserved a private room for you and your friends to karaoke to your heart's content, while nice waiters ferry in drinks to keep you all lubricated.

1. **Café Brass Monkey,** 3440 Wilshire Blvd.
2. **H.M.S. Bounty,** 3357 Wilshire Blvd.
3. **Pot Lobby Bar,** 3515 Wilshire Blvd.
4. **Beer Belly,** 532 S. Western Ave.
5. **Gaam,** 3909 W. 6th St.

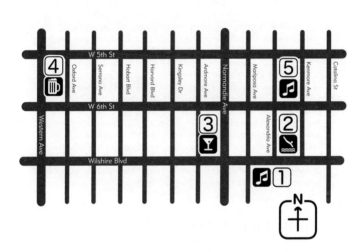

[LITTLE TOKYO/ARTS DISTRICT]

The Arts District and Little Tokyo area may be part of Downtown, but it really has its own culture—a funky mashup of old-school Japanese influences and the hipster loft-dweller scene. Luckily, it's a great place to walk around, making it perfect for an offbeat bar crawl. Skip the car and take the Metro instead—the Gold Line will plop you right in front of the Geffen Contemporary and your first destination: Far Bar (1). On the patio behind an unremarkable fusion restaurant you'll find excellent Japanese beers, sakes, and tasty house cocktails. Show them your TAP card for 10% off the bill.

Now that you've wet your whistle, you might be ready for some chow. Ramen is a excellent choice for drinkers, and you won't go wrong at Daikokuya (327 E. 1st St.), which is worth the wait in line. If you're more in the mood for high-end pub grub, head to Lazy Ox Canteen (2), which also has an impressive list of draft beers, wines, and sakes. Next, walk south on San Pedro and make a quick left onto Boyd to find the Escondite (3), an unmarked spot with wacky burgers, good drinks, and live music most nights. A few blocks away is Angel City Brewery (4), a big old brick warehouse that's now a popular but chill taproom; while you're there, check out the always-interesting art on display in the gallery area. Want more beer? Walk east on 3rd and you'll see Wurstküche (5), which serves excellent German and Belgian beers with equally excellent bratwurst and fries.

1. Far Bar, 347 E. 1st St.
2. Lazy Ox, 241 S. San Pedro St.
3. The Escondite, 410 Boyd St.
4. Angel City Brewery, 216 S. Alameda St.
5. Wurstküche, 800 E. 3rd St.

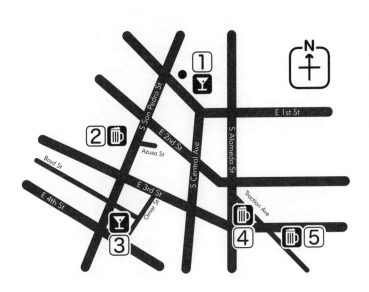

[LONG BEACH]

Downtown Long Beach, whose nightlife once solely comprised sports bars, is now home to enough worthy spots—including a destination brewery and a pioneering whiskey bar—for a full-on crawl. Strap on your walking shoes (Long Beach isn't exactly compact) and get ready for a diverse night on the town that hits all the cool new spots while still paying homage to classic institutions. Start on the tiny slice of pedestrian heaven that is the Promenade, a grass-lined, car-free street in the heart of downtown. If you're travelling on two wheels, park your bike at the ultramodern Bikestation on 1st Street. Your first stop should be happy hour at the legendary Beachwood BBQ & Brewing (1), where you can hang out on the patio with one of the 22 rotating craft beers on draft and munch on a $6 pulled-pork sandwich. Barbecue not your thing? After you've had a beer or two, grab a pizza at Michael's Pizzeria next door and unwind by the fire pit.

Just along the Promenade you'll find the Stave (2), a serious whiskey bar boasting more than 100 varieties. Next, walk one block down to the Promenade Square and turn right on 1st Street to reach the Federal (3), an upscale gastropub housed in a former bank, where you can sip classic cocktails and snack on mussels and blue cheese sliders. (Note that its location right in front of the Blue Line stop makes this crawl a great option for those taking the Metro.)

Walk off the food and drink you've imbibed thus far with a trip down 4th Street, Long Beach's hipster haven. If it's before 10 p.m., you can grab an excellent coffee at Berlin Bistro (4), an offshoot of Portfolio located inside a fantastic record store called Fingerprints. Keep heading east until you reach the V Room (5), a beloved dive with pool tables, a jukebox, and cheap drinks. Across the street is the Stache (6), another divey spot—but its drink menu features organic cocktails anchored by housemade ginger beer. If you need to sober up, stroll down Alamitos Avenue toward the old neon signage of Roscoe's House of Chicken N' Waffles (730 E. Broadway), which is open until 2:30 a.m. on weekends.

1. Beachwood BBQ & Brewing, 210 E. 3rd St.
2. The Stave, 170 The Promenade N.
3. The Federal Bar, 102 Pine Ave.
4. Berlin Bistro/Fingerprints, 420 E. 4th St.
5. V Room, 918 E. 4th St.
6. The Stache, 941 E. 4th St.

[OLD PASADENA]

Called "Old Town" by locals, this pedestrian-friendly area of bars, shops, and restaurants is a bar crawl every night. There are so many places to go that it can be hard to choose; here are our favorites, and we give you a few choices to suit your mood and tastes.

Start on the southern end of Old Town at the beautiful former Santa Fe train station that's now a restaurant called La Grande Orange and a separate bar, the Otis (1), which has a fine happy hour until 7 p.m. on weeknights. This also happens to be the Gold Line's Del Mar Station, so for Metro bar-crawlers, it's a great starting spot. For a light, refreshing start to your drinking, try Sara's Aperol Spritz. Next, head north on Raymond and cross to the west side of the street to find Lucky Baldwin's (2), an English pub with 63 beers on tap and a relaxing patio atmosphere; the folks sitting next to you might be Caltech geniuses taking a break from research. If you need a little caffeine to counteract the alcohol, cross Raymond and backtrack a short block to elegant Copa Vida (3), the new coffee kid in town with fantastic espressos, lattes, and teas.

If there's a game you want to watch, make your next stop Freddie's 35er (4), a no-frills sports bar with low prices and no attitude. If sports aren't your thing, walk north a couple of blocks to the Blind Donkey (5), a slow-sippin' kind of place with the best whiskey selection for miles around. If you're just learning about bourbons or single-malts, the friendly bartenders are happy to advise. By now you should be ready to eat, so walk a block or so to the popular Slater's 50/50 (6), where the house burger is made of 50% ground bacon (hence the 50/50 name) and the selection of draft beers is incomparable. If there's a good game on, lots of folks will be watching. If you're more a Malbec-and-mussels kinda person than a beer-and-burger kind, head instead for Vertical Wine Bistro (7), an elegant lounge with a fantastic selection of wines and excellent small-plates bar food. End your night a few doors west on Union to linger over a glass of Champagne and a chocolate soufflé under the crystal chandeliers at POP Champagne Bar (8). If you're taking the Metro home, the Memorial Park station is just a couple of blocks to the east.

1. Otis Bar, 260 S. Raymond Ave.
2. Lucky Baldwins, 17 S. Raymond Ave.
3. Copa Vida, 70 S. Raymond Ave.
4. Freddie's 35er, 12 E. Colorado Blvd.
5. The Blind Donkey, 53 E. Union St.
6. Slaters 50/50, 61 N. Raymond Ave.
7. Vertical Wine Bistro, 70 N. Raymond Ave.
8. POP Champagne & Dessert Bar, 33 E. Union St.

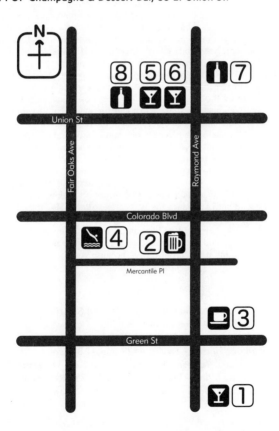

[RED LINE]

A Red Line bar crawl is a great way to check out a host of different spots without a car. Just remember to bring your TAP card! Start at whichever stop is closest to you, and hop on and off the train until it's time to go home.

You can mix up your order of stops, but we like to start at Civic Center for the Edison (1), which is almost equidistant from the station you just got off on and the next, Pershing Square. In the 1920s building that once housed an Edison power plant is a dazzling multi-level bar with a bit of steampunk flair, an absinthe fairy, aerialist shows, and swank cocktails; dress up a bit if you're coming here. Next, walk a few blocks down Hill Street to get to Perch (2), a stylish rooftop bistro where you can sip Côtes du Rhone as you look down at Pershing Square. A ride just one more stop to 7th Street puts you a block and a half from the cozy, book-lined Library Bar (3), next to the fabulous Los Angeles Central Library. Hop back on at 7th Street and continue on until Vermont/Sunset. Walk about three blocks east to the tiny, gloriously kitschy Tiki Ti (4), where you can get a mai tai the way God intended it to be made (note: cash only). Another stop will take you to Hollywood/Western and Harvard & Stone (5), a brick-walled bar with all the craft cocktails, beers, and burlesque you could want.

You can get back on the Metro and take it to the next stop, Hollywood/Vine, or take the opportunity to stroll down Hollywood Boulevard until you reach the W, home to Station Hollywood (6) and the Living Room, two swank hangouts within the same hip hotel. Get back on the Red Line until you reach the end of the line, North Hollywood Station. Tiki No (7) is a good twenty-minute walk away, but it's totally worth it, because you should never pass up the chance to go to a tiki bar.

1. **Civic Center** – The Edison, 108 W. 2nd St.
2. **Pershing Sq** – Perch, 448 S. Hill St.
3. **7th St** – Library Bar, 630 W. 6th St.
4. **Vermont/Sunset** – Tiki Ti, 4427 Sunset Blvd.
5. **Hollywood/Western** – Harvard & Stone, 5221 Hollywood Blvd.
6. **Hollywood/Vine** – Station Hollywood, 6250 Hollywood Blvd.
7. **North Hollywood** – Tiki No, 4657 Lankershim Blvd.

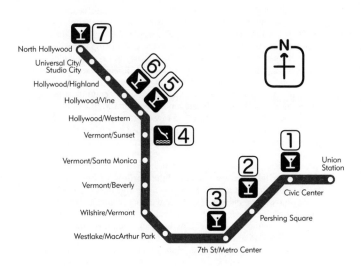

North Hollywood
Universal City/
Studio City
Hollywood/Highland
Hollywood/Vine
Hollywood/Western
Vermont/Sunset
Vermont/Santa Monica
Vermont/Beverly
Wilshire/Vermont
Westlake/MacArthur Park
7th St/Metro Center
Pershing Square
Civic Center
Union Station

[SANTA MONICA]

If you like to inhale brisk salt air while cruising from bar to bar, this is the crawl for you. You'll pop in and out of several oceanfront bars, from the fancy to the divey and back again, on foot or on bike.

Start at the Bungalow (1), a cocktail lounge that feels like a friend's house—if your friend lives on the beach and has a pool table in her living room. When it gets closer to sunset, head to the Hotel Shangri-La's rooftop bar (2), which has twinkly lights, and a little fire pit; it's the California dream and then some. Next, move a few blocks inland to get some good Spanish food in your belly at Bar Pintxo (3); the wines by the glass are as tasty as the tapas. Across the street is the famed Ye Olde King's Head (4), which may be touristy but is nonetheless a gem: it's a proper English pub (complete with darts), a bakery, and a "shoppe" for British wares and candy. God save the Queen!

For a true Santa Monica experience, you need to cleanse, so go to the Marketplace in the renovated Santa Monica Place mall and look for M.A.K.E. (5), a raw-food restaurant. Alcohol is apparently allowed in a raw-food diet, because the bar makes such living-food cocktails as the Heartbeat, with blood orange, strawberry, beet, basil, and white wine. Too precious? Head back toward the ocean for Chez Jay (6), a beloved dive bar where the Christmas lights are always on and the martinis are honest, if pricey (but this is a pricey 'hood, even for dive bars). If you'd rather have some more action, keep walking along Ocean until you reach the Viceroy Hotel, where you can get glitzy at the Cameo Bar (7), which is well stocked with cabañas and DJs. Finally, head a block down Pico toward Shutters, the gorgeous hotel plopped right on the beach. In the upper lobby you'll find the Living Room (8), where you can sink into a white-linen-covered chair with a nightcap and a plate of calamari and stare out at the moonlit ocean until you get sleepy. At that point (if you've got the means), you might just want to get a room upstairs.

1. The Bungalow, 101 Wilshire Blvd.
2. Hotel Shangri-La, 1301 Ocean Ave.
3. Bar Pintxo, 109 Santa Monica Blvd.
4. Ye Olde King's Head, 116 Santa Monica Blvd.
5. M.A.K.E., 396 Santa Monica Place
6. Chez Jay, 1657 Ocean Ave.
7. Cameo Bar, Viceroy Hotel, 1819 Ocean Ave.
8. Living Room, Shutters on the Beach, 1 Pico Blvd.

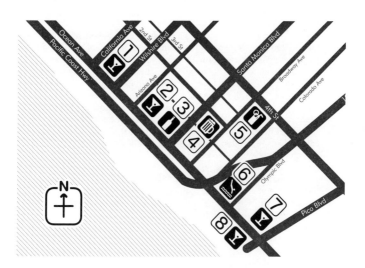

[SILVER LAKE]

The stretch of Sunset Boulevard that runs through Silver Lake has one of the best concentrations of worthy drinking spots in L.A. Just keep walking straight down Sunset for an all-night party with something for everyone, from posh to divey and from tequila to tiki. Don't get us in trouble and hit them all; just pick a selection from the 10 on our list.

First, get warmed up on the east end of Sunset at Cliff's Edge (1), a sexy spot where the patio wraps around a massive ficus tree and the garden theme continues into the drinks, which have herby garnishes like borage and lavender. Next stop is the Black Cat (3), a great spot for upscale pub snacks, cocktails, or a glass of wine. On your way, pop into Bar Keeper (2) and check out the selection of vintage barware and spirits. At Café Stella (4), just a few doors west of the Black Cat, you can have a lab-coated bartender whip you up one of the carefully crafted cocktails from the tiny but superb menu. A block and a half away is 4100 Bar (5), where you can take a shot with pickle juice (for real) and maybe grab a tamale or some barbecue from a food truck parked outside. Next up is El Cid (6), where you can catch live music or flamenco dancing or just chill out on the patio. On the next block you'll find Malo (7) and Jay's Bar (8) across the street from each other— Malo has a great tequila selection and Mexican bites, whereas Jay's is more of a gastropub. What do they have in common? Jukeboxes. On the corner of Fountain and Sunset you'll find Akbar (9), an inclusive gay bar with inexpensive drinks and a fun crowd. Bonus: another jukebox.

Hopefully you didn't hit every bar on Sunset, so to conclude the evening you can handle a nightcap at Tiki Ti (10), a tiny, old-school tiki bar with character to spare and the best mai tai in town (bring cash). If you're riding the rails, the Sunset/Vermont Metro stop is just a couple of blocks west.

1. Cliff's Edge, 3626 Sunset Blvd.
2. Bar Keeper, 3910 Sunset Blvd.
3. The Black Cat, 3909 Sunset Blvd.
4. Café Stella, 3932 Sunset Blvd.
5. 4100 Bar, 4100 Sunset Blvd.
6. El Cid, 4212 Sunset Blvd.
7. Malo, 4326 Sunset Blvd.
8. Jay's Bar, 4321 Sunset Blvd.
9. Akbar, 4356 Sunset Blvd.
10. Tiki Ti, 4427 Sunset Blvd.

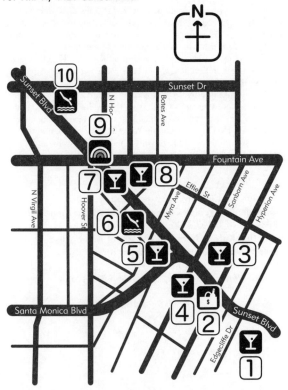

[VENICE]

Abbot Kinney is one of the coolest streets in L.A., if not the country; thanks to that street, the boardwalk, the ocean air, and the fabulous hipster people-watching, Venice is bar-crawl heaven. If you start out early at the Tasting Kitchen (1) you can beat the crowds to enjoy such sexy, well-made drinks as the Golden Ticket, with pisco, passion fruit, honey, and lime. If you're hungry, by all means order some food—after all, you're at one of the best restaurants in the city. Next, perk up with a little caffeine at the oh-so-Venice Intelligentsia (2), a coffee bar so precious that you'll feel like you're in an episode of *Portlandia Goes to Venice*.

Duly energized, head west on Abbot Kinney until you reach the Roosterfish (3), a longstanding gay dive bar with cheap drinks and plenty of local flavor. Or, if you want to get as clean and healthy as many Venice locals are, stop by Kreation Kafé (4), just one block west, and recharge your body with a cold-pressed juice on the Astroturf-lined, wood-paneled patio.

Keep walking down Abbot Kinney toward Primitivo Wine Bistro (5), where you can sample from the extensive wine list and snack on Spanish tapas. Finish the night on the beach with a beer at Venice Ale House (6) or On the Waterfront Café (7), both great options for casually winding down with a draft beer and a nice session of boardwalk people-watching.

1. The Tasting Kitchen, 1633 Abbot Kinney Blvd.
2. Intelligentsia Venice Coffeebar, 1331 Abbot Kinney Blvd.
3. Roosterfish, 1302 Abbot Kinney Blvd.
4. Kreation Kafé & Juicery, 1202 Abbot Kinney Blvd.
5. Primitivo Wine Bistro, 1025 Abbot Kinney Blvd.
6. Venice Ale House, 2 Rose Ave.
7. On the Waterfront Café, 205 Ocean Front Walk

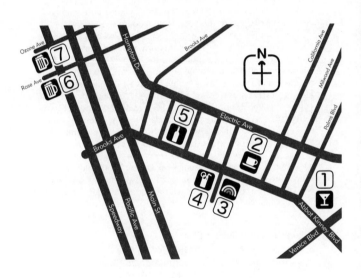

[WEST HOLLYWOOD]

West Hollywood isn't exactly known for its walkability, but there are a surprising number of excellent bars nicely grouped together between the Sunset Strip and La Brea, making for a fun, car-free night out, as well as a great taste of the neighborhood. Start the night early at Skybar (1), where you can beat the crowds out by the pool for a fantastic view of the city. Then head east on Sunset toward the infamous Château Marmont. Pretend you're a movie star at Bar Marmont (2), where you can sip on a well-crafted cocktail and fancy bar snacks (like comté cheese puffs and duck confit deviled eggs) at this total Hollywood scene.

Walk a few blocks downhill (south) on Crescent Heights to begin the Santa Monica Boulevard portion of the crawl. Start with Laurel Hardware (3), the hippest of the hip WeHo watering holes, where you'll find seriously inventive craft cocktails and beautiful people. The former hardware store boasts a full menu if you're hungry; just be prepared for a line unless you get there early. Once you've had enough of the see-and-be-seen scene, pop over to the Surly Goat (4) across the street, where you can choose from 27 taps at this more relaxed, beer-focused pub. Next, continue east on Santa Monica Boulevard a few blocks until you hit Bar Lubitsch (5), a Russian-themed spot with a (crowded) dance floor in the back and a classy vibe up front. Finally, sop up all that vodka at Astro Burger (7475 Santa Monica Blvd.; open until 4 a.m. on weekends) just a few blocks east, then order your Uber home.

1. Skybar, 8440 Sunset Blvd.
2. Bar Marmont, 8171 Sunset Blvd.
3. Laurel Hardware, 7984 Santa Monica Blvd.
4. The Surly Goat, 7929 Santa Monica Blvd.
5. Bar Lubitsch, 7702 Santa Monica Blvd.

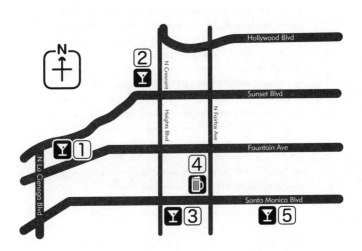

Bars + Cocktail Lounges

L.A. drinkers have never had it so good. The craft-cocktail craze has led to dozens of places where foraged herbs are muddled into small-batch liquors by men in suspenders and Civil War–era beards. But people who'd rather go dry than pay $15 for a "crafted" cocktail have plenty of places to get a pint of Guinness or a no-fuss martini. We've got fancy rooftop bars with views, grungy bars with music, Korean bars with karaoke, and casual beach bars with patios. We've got lounges that are good for conversation and bars that are good for partying. And contrary to New York perception, we've even got history—L.A. has some great bars with stories to tell. The pages that follow describe our favorites, and the next five pages in particular will point you toward particular favorites of many types, from karaoke to good food, quiet conversation to live music.

🍸 ESSENTIALLY L.A.   ↘ DIVE   🎵 QUIET   🐷 VALUE

[ESSENTIALLY L.A.]

CENTRAL CITY
326, Fairfax District (PAGE 44)
The Abbey, West Hollywood (PAGE 44)
Bar Centro, West Hollywood (PAGE 45)
Bar Marmont, West Hollywood (PAGE 45)
Café Brass Monkey, Koreatown (PAGE 46)
The Cat & Fiddle, Hollywood (PAGE 46)
Dan Sung Sa, Koreatown (PAGE 47)
The Dresden, Los Feliz (PAGE 48)
Formosa Cafe, West Hollywood (PAGE 49)
The Frolic Room, Hollywood (PAGE 49)
Good Luck Bar, Los Feliz (PAGE 50)
La Descarga, Hollywood (PAGE 52)
Laurel Hardware, West Hollywood (PAGE 52)
Musso & Frank Grill, Hollywood (PAGE 56)
Petty Cash Taqueria, Beverly/Third (PAGE 57)
The Prince, Koreatown (PAGE 58)
Ray's & Stark Bar, Miracle Mile (PAGE 59)
Tom Bergin's Public House, Miracle Mile (PAGE 62)
Windows Lounge, West Hollywood (PAGE 63)

EASTSIDE
Bar Amá, Downtown (PAGE 66)
The Echo, Echo Park (PAGE 71)
The Edison, Downtown (PAGE 71)
Golden Gopher, Downtown (PAGE 75)
Hop Louie, Chinatown (PAGE 76)
King Eddy Saloon, Downtown (PAGE 77)
Lazy Ox Canteen, Little Tokyo (PAGE 78)
Mo-Chica, Downtown (PAGE 81)
Mohawk Bend, Echo Park (PAGE 81)
Perch, Downtown (PAGE 83)
Red Lion, Silver Lake (PAGE 83)
Rivera, South Park (PAGE 84)
The Standard, Downtown (PAGE 85)
Taix 321 Lounge, Echo Park (PAGE 86)

GROUPS KARAOKE PATIO ROMANTIC

[ESSENTIALLY L.A. cont.]

EASTSIDE (cont.)
Tam O'Shanter, Atwater (PAGE 86)
Tiki Ti, Silver Lake (PAGE 86)
The Varnish, Downtown (PAGE 87)
The York, Highland Park (PAGE 89)

SAN GABRIEL VALLEY
1886 Bar, Pasadena (PAGE 89)
The Tap Room, Pasadena (PAGE 96)

EAST VALLEY
Laurel Tavern, Studio City (PAGE 98)
Red Door, Toluca Lake (PAGE 99)
Sardo's, Burbank (PAGE 100)
Tonga Hut, North Hollywood (PAGE 100)
Tony's Dart's Away, Burbank (PAGE 100)

WESTSIDE: CENTRAL
Akasha, Culver City (PAGE 101)
The Bar & Lounge, Hotel Bel-Air, Bel Air (PAGE 103)
Boardwalk 11, Palms (PAGE 104)
Picca, West L.A. (PAGE 106)

WEST OF THE 405
Abuelita's, Topanga (PAGE 109)
The Bungalow, Santa Monica (PAGE 111)
Chez Jay, Santa Monica (PAGE 112)
Father's Office, Santa Monica (PAGE 113)
Harvelle's Blues Club, Santa Monica (PAGE 114)
The Living Room, Shutters, Santa Monica (PAGE 115)
Roosterfish, Santa Monica (PAGE 117)
Suite 700 (Shangri-la), Santa Monica (PAGE 118)
Venice Ale House, Venice (PAGE 119)
Ye Olde King's Head, Santa Monica (PAGE 120)

🌴 ESSENTIALLY L.A.   ⚲ DIVE   🍸 QUIET   Ⓢ VALUE

[ESSENTIALLY L.A. cont.]

SOUTH BAY TO SOUTH L.A.
Joe Jost's, Long Beach (PAGE 121)
Nelson's, Palos Verdes (PAGE 122)
Observation Bar, Queen Mary, Long Beach (PAGE 122)
Tony's on the Pier, Redondo Beach (PAGE 124)

[A FEW BEST BETS FOR:]

CONVERSATION
The Bar & Lounge, Hotel Bel-Air, Bel Air (PAGE 103)
Big Bar, Los Feliz (PAGE 46)
Caña Rum Bar, South Park/Fashion District (PAGE 69)
Edendale, Silver Lake (PAGE 71)
The Living Room, Shutters, Santa Monica (PAGE 115)
The Parlour Room, Hollywood (PAGE 56)
Sadie Kitchen and Lounge, Hollywood (PAGE 60)
Tam O'Shanter, Atwater (PAGE 86)
The Tap Room, Langham Hotel, Pasadena (PAGE 96)
Ten Pound, Beverly Hills (PAGE 108)

FUN & GAMES
Eighty Two, Arts District (PAGE 71)
Golden Gopher, Downtown (PAGE 75)
The Short Stop, Echo Park (PAGE 85)
Spare Room, Hollywood (PAGE 61)
West 4th and Jane, Santa Monica (PAGE 119)

GOOD FOOD, TOO
Baco Mercat, Downtown (PAGE 66)
Drago Centro, Downtown (PAGE 70)
Mo-Chica, Downtown (PAGE 81)
Picca, West L.A. (PAGE 106)
Simmzy's, Manhattan Beach (PAGE 124)
Son of a Gun, Beverly/Third (PAGE 61)
Tasting Kitchen, Venice (PAGE 118)

🏯 GROUPS 🎤 KARAOKE ☼ PATIO ♥ ROMANTIC

[A FEW BEST BETS FOR:]

KARAOKE
Café Brass Monkey, Koreatown (PAGE 46)
Gaam, Koreatown (PAGE 50)
The Good Nite, North Hollywood (PAGE 98)
Oil Can Harry's, Studio City (PAGE 99)
Sardo's, Burbank (PAGE 100)
Smog Cutter, Silver Lake (PAGE 85)
Tattle Tale Room, Culver City (PAGE 108)
Ye Rustic Inn, Los Feliz (PAGE 64)

L.A. HISTORY
1886 Bar, Pasadena (PAGE 89)
The Bar at the Culver Hotel, Culver City (PAGE 103)
Bar Marmont, West Hollywood (PAGE 45)
Boardner's, Hollywood (PAGE 46)
Formosa Cafe, West Hollywood (PAGE 49)
The Frolic Room, Hollywood (PAGE 49)
King Eddy Saloon, Downtown (PAGE 77)
Musso & Frank Grill, Hollywood (PAGE 56)
Observation Bar, Queen Mary, Long Beach (PAGE 122)
Taix 321 Lounge, Echo Park (PAGE 86)
Tom Bergin's Public House, Miracle Mile (PAGE 62)

LGBT
The Abbey, West Hollywood (PAGE 44)
Akbar, Silver Lake (PAGE 65)
The Black Cat, Silver Lake (PAGE 68)
Oil Can Harry's, Studio City (PAGE 99)
Roosterfish, Venice (PAGE 117)

LIVE MUSIC
1642 Beer & Wine, Echo Park (PAGE 64)
The Auld Dubliner, Long Beach (PAGE 120)
The Echo, Echo Park (PAGE 71)

🌴 ESSENTIALLY L.A. ↘ DIVE 🕊 QUIET ⑤ VALUE

The Escondite, Arts District (PAGE 73)
Ireland's 32, Van Nuys (PAGE 101)
Old Towne Pub, Old Pasadena (PAGE 95)
Redwood Bar & Grill, Downtown (PAGE 84)
Taix 321 Lounge, Echo Park (PAGE 86)
Villain's Tavern, Arts District (PAGE 88)

OUTDOOR DRINKING
Abuelita's, Topanga (PAGE 109)
The Bungalow, Santa Monica (PAGE 111)
The Cat & Fiddle, Hollywood (PAGE 46)
Cliff's Edge, Silver Lake (PAGE 69)
Dog Haus Biergarten, Pasadena (PAGE 92)
Edendale, Silver Lake (PAGE 71)
Goldie's, Beverly/Third (PAGE 50)
Library Alehouse, Santa Monica (PAGE 114)
The Library at the Redbury, Hollywood (PAGE 53)
Lucky Baldwin's, Old Pasadena (PAGE 94)
On the Waterfront Café, Venice (PAGE 116)
Ray's & Stark Bar, Miracle Mile (PAGE 59)
The Tap Room, Langham Hotel, Pasadena (PAGE 96)
Venice Ale House, Venice (PAGE 119)
Verdugo, Glassell Park (PAGE 87)

VIEWS
Living Room, Santa Monica (PAGE 115)
Nelson's, Palos Verdes (PAGE 122)
Observation Bar, Long Beach (PAGE 122)
Perch, Downtown (PAGE 83)
The Roof on Wilshire, Miracle Mile (PAGE 60)
Skybar, West Hollywood (PAGE 60)
The Standard, Downtown (PAGE 85)
Suite 700 (Shangri-la), Santa Monica (PAGE 118)

GROUPS   KARAOKE   PATIO   ROMANTIC

CENTRAL CITY

[The 3 Clubs Cocktail Lounge] 1123 N. Vine St., Hollywood, 323.462.6441, threeclubs.com. Nightly 6 p.m.-2 a.m. Full bar. **WHY** Because you're in your 20s and you don't cotton to all. **WHAT** It may bill itself as a lounge, but 3 Clubs is a dark and divey rock 'n roll bar where the gin and tonics are usually strong and the beer selection is solid. The rowdier back room, which sometimes requires a cover to get into, is where you'll find bands playing or DJs spinning. But if you just want to sit and sip, stick to the front room. **WHO** People who want to drink in Hollywood without being part of some trendy Hollywood scene.

[326] 🌴 Farmers Market, 6333 W. 3rd St., Fairfax District, 323.549.2156, farmersmarketbars.com. Mon.-Fri. 9 a.m.-9 p.m., Sat. 9 a.m.-8 p.m, Sun. 10 a.m.-7 p.m. Beer & wine. **WHY** This quaint beer and wine bar hidden inside the Original Farmers Market is one of the best people-watching bars in L.A. **WHAT** Local craft beer by the pitcher and pint, as well as a surprisingly decent selection of wines by the glass. **WHO** Thirsty international tourists and well-seasoned regulars who make a habit out of the daily happy hour deals. 🗫 ☼

[The Abbey] 🌴 692 N. Robertson Blvd., West Hollywood, 310.289.8410, sbe.com. Mon.-Thurs. 11 a.m.-2 a.m., Fri. 10 a.m.-2 a.m., Sat.-Sun. 9 a.m.-2 a.m. Full bar. **WHY** Owned by SBE, Sam Nazarian's nightlife empire, this is West Hollywood's premiere gay bar. **WHAT** WeHo longtimers still remember when the vaguely gothic venue was a cheerful neighborhood coffeehouse. These days it's a vast, thumping nightclub with four bars and plenty of bodies to line up at them. There are occasional ladies' nights, but this is mainly a nightlife hub for men where the music is loud, the drinks are strong, and the party always seems to be on. **WHO** Various clubs and themed events draw different crowds on different nights, but hunks with six-pack abs are never out of style. ☼

[Acabar] 1510 N. Stanley Ave., Hollywood, 323.876.1400, acabar-la.com. Tues. 6 p.m.-midnight, Wed.-Thurs. 6 p.m.-1 a.m., Fri.-Sat. 6 p.m.-2 a.m. Full bar. **WHY** Bartenders Julian Cox and Josh Goldman designed a menu that reads like a roadmap of cocktail history, from Colonial-era punches to slick modernist creations. **WHAT** The stunning Moroccan architecture and ambitious drinks make for an entertaining night out in Hollywood. Acabar is a good

🌴 ESSENTIALLY L.A.　🌂 DIVE　🎵 QUIET　🗫 VALUE

place to entertain out-of-towners, who'll be wowed by the setting. **WHO** A fashionable Hollywood crowd that loves a scene but wants top-notch food and drink to go with it. ♥

[Bar Centro at SLS] 🍴 SLS Hotel, 465 S. La Cienega Blvd., West Hollywood, 310.246.555, sbe.com. Sun.-Wed. 5:30 p.m.-12:30 a.m., Thurs.-Sat. 5:30 p.m.-1:30 a.m. Full bar. **WHY** For the Philippe Starck décor, the witty and tasty cocktails and nibbles, and the Beverly Hills comedy writ large. **WHAT** Sure, it's crazy expensive and pretentious, but you've got to visit at least once to experience the setting, the crowd, and the showy cocktails (a mojito poured over cotton candy, an actually smoking scotch drink called Smoke on the Water) are great fun to try. Bring your sense of humor and your best credit card. **WHO** Rich young Persians on dates, empty-nester couples from the Valley celebrating a big anniversary, cougars/manthers, German tourists, ICM agents, plastic-surgery victims, young women trying desperately to walk in five-inch heels... in short, a highly entertaining crowd.

[Bar Lubitsch] 7702 Santa Monica Blvd., West Hollywood, 323.654.1234, barlubitsch.com. Mon.-Fri. 7 p.m-2 a.m., Sat.-Sun. 8 p.m-2 a.m. Full bar. **WHY** With Putin stepping it up as America's #1 archenemy, it's time to experience a little Soviet kitsch. **WHAT** West Hollywood is filled with bona-fide Russian establishments and the mono-browed babushkas who patronize them. This is not such a place. It's a classy lounge (dress appropriately) with a sexy, red, chandelier-adorned room in back and a small bar in front. The place gets packed, and though the dance floor is tiny, that doesn't stop people from grooving. **WHO** Dancers, prancers, birthday partiers, anyone who wants a bar in which to feel special without trying too hard. ♥

[Bar Marmont] 🍴 Chateau Marmont, 8171 W. Sunset Blvd., West Hollywood, 323.650.0575, chateaumarmont.com. Nightly 6 p.m-2 a.m. Full bar. **WHY** For the eternal Hollywood scene. **WHAT** You're probably not cool enough to enter this dark, atmospheric faux chateau—we're certainly not—but you might want to come anyway, just to check out the never-ending scene, have an overpriced cocktail, and taste the rustic food (taleggio mac 'n' cheese, avocado carpaccio, charcuterie), which is much better than it needs to be, given that nobody comes here just to eat. **WHO** People who are younger, richer, better looking, and more gregarious than you—or at least appear to be in the moment. ☼

🏠 GROUPS 🎤 KARAOKE ☼ PATIO ♥ ROMANTIC

[Big Bar] 1927 Hillhurst Ave., Los Feliz, 323.644.0100, alcovecafe.
com/bigbar. Mon.-Wed. 10 a.m.-midnight, Thurs.-Sun. 10 a.m.-1 a.m.
Full bar. **WHY** How many craft-cocktail bars have a happy hour that
starts at 2 and goes until 7 p.m. every weekday? **WHAT** This cozy
bar (the name is tongue-in-cheek) adjacent to popular Los Feliz
café the Alcove is known mainly for its cocktails and sophisticated
bar snacks like lamb sliders and bacon-wrapped dates stuffed with
goat cheese. The wine-by-the glass menu is better than at many
restaurants. If that isn't enough to get you in the door, happy hour
starts at 2 p.m. and features $7 cocktails (they're normally $12 to
$14) and a couple of craft beers for $5 a glass as well as discounted nibbles and vino. **WHO** Cocktail aficionados, stylish twenty-
and thirtysomethings with well-paying jobs. 🜪 ♥

[Boardner's] 1652 N. Cherokee Ave., Hollywood, 323.462.9621,
boardners.com. Sun.-Wed. 5 p.m.-2 a.m., Fri.-Sat. 4 p.m.-2 a.m. Full
bar. **WHY** This classic has seen it all, from the days of Raymond
Chandler to the nights of Guns N' Roses. **WHAT** Since the 1940s,
Boardner's has survived with few pretensions and a divey yet
historic vibe. Said to be the last place the Black Dahlia was seen
before she was murdered, the classic bar has an adjoining dance
club offering everything from goth to house music and a patio with
a tiled fountain. At the bar up front, a parade of nightcrawlers meet
up for straightforward cocktails, decade after decade.
WHO Rockers, old-timers, bridge and tunnelers. 🜪 ☼

[Café Brass Monkey] 🌴 3440 Wilshire Blvd., Koreatown,
213.381.7047, cafebrassmonkey.com. Mon.-Thurs. 10 a.m.-2 a.m.,
Sat.-Sun. 4 p.m.-2 a.m. Full bar. **WHY** Dive-bar karaoke at its best.
WHAT Make sure to reserve a table at this quintessential L.A.
karaoke bar in the heart of Koreatown—it's small, and competition gets fierce for the mic on the stage. It's dark, it's divey, and
they don't even have any beer on tap, but it's an experience every
Angeleno should have at least once. **WHO** People ready to party
and sing. 🎤

[The Cat & Fiddle] 🌴 6530 Sunset Blvd., Hollywood,
323.468.3800, thecatandfiddle.com. Mon.-Fri. 11:30 a.m.-2 a.m., Sat.-
Sun. 10 a.m.-2 a.m. Full bar. **WHY** English-pub warmth mixed with
California style, with excellent housemade bangers, crisp pasties,
hilariously decadent Scotch eggs, and a sherry trifle with fresh
sweet cream. **WHAT** Founded in 1982 by the late British rocker
Kim Gardner and his wife, Paula, a fashion retailer, this landmark

Sunset pub has been a music- and movie-industry hangout since the beginning. Outside is a courtyard with a friendly vibe and a real California feeling; inside the 1920s Mission Revival building is a cozy fireside seat and a dart room. **WHO** An after-work crowd of creative types from studios and music-biz offices nearby; British ex-pat rockers. 🏯 ☼

[The Churchill] Hotel Orlando, 8384 W. 3rd St., Beverly/Third, 323.655.8384, the-churchill.com. Sun.-Thurs. 7 a.m.-midnight, Fri.-Sat. 7 a.m.-2 a.m. Full bar. **WHY** On the "café corridor" stretching along West Third from La Cienega to Fairfax, you'll find more cutesy breakfast and lunch spots than you can shake a red velvet cupcake at. But people need to drink, too! **WHAT** The Hotel Orlando was smart to revamp its in-house eatery into a hip gastropub and cocktail bar. Even if the drinks (herbs, citrus, quality booze) and food (charcuterie, roasted brussels sprouts, wood-fired pizzas) aren't quite worth the price, the patrons are stylish and the scene is buzzy. **WHO** Fairfax District residents who want to walk home after a few too many hand-muddled libations. ☼

[Dan Sung Sa] 🍸 3317 W. 6th St., Koreatown, 213.487.9100. Nightly 4 p.m.-2 a.m. Beer & soju. **WHY** Stop in for late-night drinks after a night of karaoke or an AYCE Korean barbecue feast. **WHAT** This late-night Korean pub is famous for its imposing mural of Korean heads of state, including the late North Korean dictator Kim Jong Il. The interior is just as provocative: Tables are set inside dark wooden nooks, in which smoking is allowed. Bottles of beer and soju are cheap and plentiful, but those in the know opt for *makkegoli*, a milky, fermented rice drink that tastes a bit like high-proof kombucha. **WHO** Chain-smoking Koreatown salarymen arguing over grilled-meat skewers and groups of young partiers pounding soju and Hite beer. 🎤

[Delancey] 5936 Sunset Blvd., Hollywood, 323.469.2100, delanceyhollywood.com. Mon.-Fri. noon-2 a.m., Sat.-Sun. 6 p.m.-2 a.m. Full bar. **WHY** When you want a pizza or a bowl of pasta to go with that glass of wine. **WHAT** In the earlier part of the evening, this is more of a restaurant scene, where folks come to nosh and drink with friends. Later at night, it turns into a loud, buzzy bar, where they come to hit on each other and hook up. The patio is a good spot for an after-work meetup. **WHO** Millennials who have dollars to spend on dough. ☼

🏯 GROUPS   🎤 KARAOKE   ☼ PATIO   ♥ ROMANTIC

[The Dime] 442 N. Fairfax Ave., Fairfax District, 323.651.4421, thedimela.net. Sun.-Mon. 6 p.m.-1:30 a.m., Tues.-Sat. 7 p.m.-1:30 a.m. Full bar. **WHY** Hookup central for young Mid-city dwellers. **WHAT** Always popular for its central location, the Dime has gotten even hotter with the addition of more restaurants and trendy boutiques on Fairfax. It doesn't seem like there'd be enough room to dance to the mostly hip-hop soundtrack, but although it gets packed on weekends, the patrons still groove. Cocktails are fairly standard. **WHO** Twenty- and thirtysomethings looking to avoid the Hollywood Boulevard scene.

[The Drawing Room] 1800 Hillhurst Ave., Los Feliz, 323.665.0135. Daily 6 a.m.-2 a.m. Full bar. **WHY** Love it or hate it, this mini-mall dive attracts everyone from bona-fide movie stars to garrulous, ancient barflies. **WHAT** The Drawing Room manages to be both on the hipster radar and timeless, with cheap, basic drinks, a dragon mural that looks smoke-encrusted, and convivial potlucks during big game days—it's everything a dive bar should be and then some, and the jukebox isn't bad either. **WHO** Off-duty nurses and film crews at 6 a.m. and devoted drinkers at night. 🎋 💲

[The Dresden] 🌴1760 N. Vermont Ave., Los Feliz, 323.665.4294, thedresden.com. Mon.-Sat. 4:30 p.m.-2 a.m., Sun. 4 p.m.-11 p.m. Full bar. **WHY** The ideal backdrop for living out your own film noir or pretending you're an extra in Swingers. **WHAT** Opened in 1954, the Dresden is a "classic Continental" restaurant, but you don't come here for the food, you come here to sit in the lounge and sip a martini (or three) while reveling in the vintage vibe: leather booths, dim lighting, swinging tunes. Tuesday through Saturday evenings, husband-and-wife duo Marty and Elayne are the star attraction; he plays the drums and upright bass while she sings in a breathy falsetto. They may get older, but their act never seems to. **WHO** Angelenos yearning for some Old Hollywood glamour. ♥

[El Carmen] 8138 W. 3rd St., Beverly/Third, 323.852.1552, elcarmenla.com. Mon.-Sat. 5 p.m.-2 a.m., Sun. 7 p.m.-2 a.m. Full bar. **WHY** A small, cramped, boozy haven with a charm all its own. **WHAT** You don't have to be into Mexican wrestling to appreciate the colorful *luchador* masks that line the ceiling; you can't miss them, even though the place is dark as night. This local institution is best known for its menu of more than 100 tequilas, as well as for its margaritas. You can get a standard one or try it with muddled jalapeños for some kick, or with cucumber and mint for a

🌴 ESSENTIALLY L.A.   🎋 DIVE   🍸 QUIET   💲 VALUE

refreshing summer cooler, or with cilantro and ginger if you want to feel like you're drinking a garden. As a bonus, the place has a full kitchen, and the guacamole is great (and only $2 during happy hour). **WHO** Tequila fans, Fairfax District denizens.

[El Chavo/El Chavito] 4441 W. Sunset Blvd., Los Feliz, 323.664.0871, elchavorestaurant.com. Mon.-Thurs. 4 p.m.-midnight, Fri.-Sat. 4 p.m.-2 a.m., Sun. 11 a.m.-2 a.m. Full bar. **WHY** An old-school Mexican restaurant with psychedelic décor gave birth to a hopping bar next door. **WHAT** The Sunset Junction crowd gets its fiesta on here, either on the large back patio or in the packed El Chavito bar next to the original restaurant. The food may be bland, but plenty of tequila selections, a happy hour until 9 nightly, and lots of good-looking scenesters make up for any lack of spice. **WHO** Bar-hopping hipsters, birthday groups. 🏠 ☼

[Formosa Cafe] 🌴 7156 Santa Monica Blvd., West Hollywood, 323.850.9050, formosacafe.com. Mon.-Fri. 4 p.m.-2 a.m., Sat.-Sun. 6 p.m.-2 a.m. Full bar. **WHY** A piece of lovingly preserved L.A. history. **WHAT** Open since 1925, with part of the bar made from an old train car, the kitschy Formosa, patronized by generations of Hollywood folk, has long been a treasure although the Chinese food varies in quality. Cocktails have been updated with more modern selections, but it makes it easier to forget the Target next door if you order a classic martini or a manhattan while you peruse the celebrity photos and nestle into a dark booth. **WHO** Tourists, history buffs, refugees from the Hollywood bar scene. ☼ ♥

[Frank 'n Hank's] 518 S. Western Ave., Koreatown, 213.383.2087. Nightly 6 p.m.-2 a.m. Full bar. **WHY** Because it's Koreatown's best dive bar. **WHAT** Some bars are divey; this place is a true dive. It's small and narrow, with low ceilings. The Pabst Blue Ribbon is served unironically. There's a dart board, a surprisingly good jukebox, and a pool table. The drinks are cheap, though their strength may depend on how much the woman who runs the bar likes you. (She reportedly owns the place.) The service is quick and attentive, but bring cash; credit cards aren't accepted. **WHO** Everyone from twentysomethings who want to get smashed on the cheap to middle-aged regulars. 🐿 📷

[The Frolic Room] 🌴 6245 Hollywood Blvd., Hollywood, 323.462.5890. Daily 11 a.m.-2 a.m. Full bar. **WHY** It has one of the most gorgeous neon signs above its door, and it's even better

inside, where Al Hirschfield caricatures cover the walls.
WHAT The historic Hollywood dive dates back to the 1930s and
reportedly got its start as a speakeasy, but no one can confirm that.
It doesn't matter. These days you go to sink into a barstool and sip
stiff, cheap drinks. **WHO** Hardcore drinkers, patrons of the Pantages, dive-bar aficionados, occasional wide-eyed tourists. ⟍ 🏷️

[Gaam] Dan Sung Sa Plaza, 3909 W. 6th St., Koreatown,
213.908.5581. Sun.-Thurs. 6 p.m.-2 a.m., Fri.-Sat. 5 p.m.-2 a.m. Full
bar. **WHY** For karaoke that rocks. And for drinks. And for private
rooms in which to drink and sing karaoke with your friends.
WHAT The essential K-town karaoke destination, Gaam has lots of
private rooms (reserve in advance, especially on weekends), good
sound systems and song selections, a proper bar, fair prices, and
$2 valet parking. It's ideal for groups of five to about 40.
WHO Birthday partiers, bachelorettes, and other posses of friends
in the private disco-lighted rooms. 🏸 🎾

[Goldie's] 8422 W. 3rd St., Beverly/Third, 323.677.2470, goldiesla.
com. Mon. 6-11 p.m., Tues.-Fri. 11 a.m.-3 p.m. & 6-11 p.m., Sat. 10
a.m.-3 p.m. & 6-11 p.m., Sun. 10 a.m.-3 p.m. & 6-10 p.m. Full bar.
WHY Glasses of rosé and perfectly made Aperol spritzes make it
feel like summer even in February. **WHAT** This eco-cabin-esque
restaurant offers wines and cocktails that are all about refresh-
ment, served with a flourish of classiness. They go well with the
Cal-elegant dishes: kale salad, avocado toast, burrata with watermelon. Good bar seating; if you're eating, reserve a patio table
and you won't be sorry. **WHO** Fashionable 3rd Street shoppers
stopping in after a day of boutique hopping. ☼ ♥

[Good Luck Bar] 🌴1514 Hillhurst Ave., Los Feliz, 323.666.3524.
Mon.-Fri. 7 p.m.-2 a.m., Sat.-Sun. 8 p.m.-2 a.m. Full bar. **WHY** Equal
parts dive bar and kitschy classic, this bar is an easy crowd-pleaser. Fun jukebox, too. **WHAT** This Mandarin-theme lounge has
the feel of a kung fu movie set, with its red booths and hanging
lanterns. Such strong cocktails as the Potent Potion keep the theme
going; some are served in coconuts or tiki glasses. There's a good
buzz in the air, but it's typically not too loud to converse. **WHO**
Nostalgia-loving Los Feliz couples, along with the occasional
celebrity. ⟍ 🏷️ 🏸

[Good Times at Davey Wayne's] 1611 N. El Centro Ave., Hollywood, 323.962.3804, goodtimesatdaveywaynes.com. Mon.-Fri. 5 p.m.-2 a.m., Sat.-Sun. 2 p.m.-2 a.m. Full bar. **WHY** Like partying in your dad's den in 1976. Except a lot more expensive, of course. Oh, and for the roller-disco show every night on the patio roof. **WHAT** Enter through a garage sale (for real), open the door of the old refrigerator, and discover a '70s wonderland, complete with console TV, shag carpeting, snow-cone cocktails, and a DJ spinning Deep Purple and disco. It's all so much fun that within weeks of opening it became mobbed, so there's a long line most nights after 8 or 9. Do like the folks who were actually alive in the '70s and come early to enjoy the set design and sip a Tiny Dancer or Cisco Kid. Not nearly enough people wear striped pants and vests and platform shoes, so you should. **WHO** Young people who were not alive when guys like Davey had dens like this. ☼

[Harlowe] 7321 Santa Monica Blvd., West Hollywood, 323.876.5839, harlowebar.com. Nightly 5 p.m.-2 a.m. Full bar. **WHY** A roomy, comfortable hangout with tasty crafted cocktails and a good patio. **WHAT** Does this part of town need another bar with $14 mixology concoctions? Apparently, because this new place found an immediate fan base. Large and airy, with early 20th century style décor, it's able to handle a lot of people without becoming uncomfortably loud and crowded. A few of its house cocktails are "on draft" (premade) and just $7 during the nightly happy hour, and they're all excellent. Eric Greenspan designed the food menu, which suits the drinks just fine. **WHO** In the early evenings, quiet couples and small groups of friends conversing over a drink; later it's more packed with WeHo thirtysomethings. 🏠 ☼

[Harvard & Stone] 5221 Hollywood Blvd., Los Feliz, 323.466.6063, harvardandstone.com. Nightly 8 p.m.-2 a.m. Full bar. **WHY** The East Hollywood nightspot has a risqué vibe and superior cocktails. **WHAT** Don't wear shorts to this wildly popular brick- and wood-paneled lounge, which also bans baseball caps and flip-flops. Burlesque shows on the weekends and bands or DJs on most nights keep the scene rocking; there's often a line out the door. The mixologists have won numerous cocktail competitions for their concoctions, like the Viejo Fashioned, with tequila, vanilla, Armagnac, and orange bitters, or the Rabbits, with vodka, lime, carrot, and cucumber soda and cayenne. **WHO** Westsiders and eastsiders who are a touch more discerning than the usual Hollywood drinkers.

[HMS Bounty] 3357 Wilshire Blvd., Koreatown, 213.385.7275, thehmsbounty.com. Mon.-Thurs. 11 a.m.-1 a.m., Fri.-Sat. 11 a.m.-2 a.m., Sun. noon-1 a.m. Full bar. **WHY** Order the "Three Wise Men" shot and beer special, or class it up with a glass of wine and the famous "baseball cut" steak in the dining room—but skip the rest of the food. **WHAT** This nautical themed bar, attached to the Gaylord Apartments in Koreatown, is rife with historic charm. A couple of decades ago it got "discovered" by yuppies, who later left it for other trendy spots, leaving the barflies and old ladies in peace. A hipster invasion could happen at any minute, but for now, it's one of L.A.'s great old-school bars. **WHO** Koreatown regulars who have lived in the neighborhood since long before it was Koreatown. ➘ 💲

[The Hungry Cat] 1535 N. Vine St., Hollywood, 323.462.2155, thehungrycat.com. Mon.-Wed. noon-10 p.m., Thurs.-Fri. noon-11 p.m., Sat. 11 a.m.-11 p.m., Sun. 11 a.m.-10 p.m. Full bar. **WHY** The upscale seafood restaurant is a hidden gem in touristy Hollywood. **WHAT** Though it's known for its oysters and fruits de mer towers, this gem of a restaurant takes equal care with its libations. Grey-hounds are made with fresh squeezed grapefruit, and the Bloody Mary, made from tomato juice that's pressed in-house, is one of the best in town. Slurp a couple of oysters and down a pug burger while you're toasting. **WHO** Hollywood hotshots, foodies.

[La Descarga] 🌴 1159 N. Western Ave., Hollywood, 323.466.1324, ladescargala.com. Tues.-Sat. 8 p.m.-2 a.m. Full bar. **WHY** A hot Hollywood bar that takes speakeasy chic to new heights. **WHAT** It's hard to believe such a classy joint hides behind such a grimy exterior. That's the idea. This dim bar, perfumed with the scent of cigars, is a paean to bartender Pablo Moix's sweet and fancy rum cocktails. Floor shows, featuring flapperish burlesque dancers and hot-to-trot jazz bands, make it seem like Hollywood's idea of an underground Havana nightclub. Dress to impress, and on weekends, make a reservation. (At a bar? Yes, really.) **WHO** Cocktail hipsters, upscale party people, the occasional celeb, and Silver Lake residents slumming west of Hyperion.

[Laurel Hardware] 🌴 7984 Santa Monica Blvd., West Hollywood, 323.656.6070, laurelhardware.com. Mon.-Fri. 5 p.m.-2 a.m., Sat.-Sun. 11 a.m.-2 a.m. Full bar. **WHY** A popular hang with well-made cocktails and a lovely back patio. **WHAT** Gorgeous people serving elegant drinks in a repurposed hardware store brimming with even more beautiful people—this is the L.A. of television brought to life. Get there early Thursday through Saturday or prepare to wait in line. That is, unless you're truly beautiful, too. **WHO** Good-looking, gregarious, fit, and fashionable—you should be at least two of those. ⌂ ✿

[The Library at the Redbury] 1717 N. Vine St., Hollywood, 323.962.1717, theredbury.com. Wed.-Sat. 8 p.m.-midnight. Full bar. **WHY** This boutique hotel in Hollywood has a bar that's worth visiting even if you haven't booked a room. **WHAT** As its name implies, the indoor portion of this bar feels like your sophisticated uncle's reading room, thanks to its bookshelves, oversize leather armchairs, and pool table. It opens into a large and lovely patio where you can sip a crafted cocktail while you gaze upon Holly-wood below. Summer nights when DJs spin tunes are an especially nice time to visit. **WHO** The young and elegant who have plenty of rock 'n' roll edge. ✿ ♥

[Library Bar at Hollywood Roosevelt Hotel] 7000 Hol-lywood Blvd., Hollywood, 323.466.7000, thompsonhotels.com/hotels/hollywood-roosevelt. Nightly 5:30 p.m.-2 a.m. Full bar. **WHY** For those ready for a next-level mixology experience. **WHAT** The historic Hollywood Roosevelt has no stuffy bars—instead it's a veritable theme park of drinking spaces, including this intimate, speak-easy-style spot that helped bring L.A. into the modern age of cock-tail alchemy. There's no drink menu, just super-knowledgeable barkeeps who take full advantage of the bushels of fresh herbs, berries, and fruit on display to craft a distinctive drink for each patron. Prices reflect the personalized attention. **WHO** Hollywood drinkers who don't need pounding music to have fun. ♥

[Little Bar] 757 S. La Brea Ave., Miracle Mile, 323.937.9210, littlebarlounge.com. Nightly 5 p.m.-2 a.m. Full bar. **WHY** An unpre-tentious watering hole in an area that doesn't have tons of options. **WHAT** It's not quite a dive, not quite an Irish pub, and not quite a sports bar, but it's a convenient place to meet up in the Miracle Mile area. With a full liquor license, 18 taps of beer, a wide-rang-ing jukebox, and darts, there's a little something for everyone, and it's not even all that little inside. Birthday gatherings that reserve ahead get a free bottle of Champagne. **WHO** Office workers from the Wilshire corridor, nearby apartment dwellers. ⌂

[Little Dom's] 2128 Hillhurst Ave., Los Feliz, 323.661.0055, littledoms.com. Mon.-Thurs. 8 a.m.-3 p.m. & 5:30-11 p.m., Fri. 8 a.m.-3 p.m. & 5:30 p.m.-midnight, Sat. 8 a.m.-midnight, Sun. 8 a.m.-11 p.m. Beer & wine. **WHY** This Italian restaurant looks like it was born in 1930s New York and has a bar area that seems tailor-made for wise guys and good fellas. **WHAT** The front room gets crowded, but it's worth it—the cocktails are top-notch and inventive, from the Butternut Old Fashioned, to the Rosemary's Baby (tequila, toasted rosemary, and peach shrub), to the Garden of Earthly Delights (gin, celery, and atomized fennel). Wines, including the restaurant's own well-priced Dago Red and Dago White, are just right with the updated takes on old-school Italian dishes. **WHO** Though the setting is casual, there's nearly always a well-known director or actor sampling the drinks. ☼

[Littlefork] 1600 Wilcox Ave., Hollywood, 323.465.3675, littlefork-la.com. Sun.-Thurs. 5-10 p.m., Fri.-Sat. 5-11 p.m. Full bar. **WHY** Barman Dino Balocchi likes his drinks boozy yet balanced. He may even pour you a shot of Chicago's famously harsh Malört liquor. **WHAT** Pair elevated Atlantic-inspired seafood dishes with top-notch stirred cocktails or a glass of wine, and you've got Littlefork, a terrific restaurant and bar in the heart of Hollywood. Happy hour here is called "oyster hour"—every day from 5 to 7 and Friday and Saturday from 10 until closing, they serve oysters for $1.50, good house wines for $5, an excellent cocktail for $7, and a good bar menu. **WHO** Down-to-earth Hollywood couples and well-to-do East Coast transplants. ☼♥

[Lock & Key] 239 S. Vermont Ave., Koreatown, 213.389.5625, lockandkey.la. Tues.-Sat. 7 p.m.-2 a.m., Sun. 2 p.m.-10 p.m. Full bar. **WHY** You'll find some of the best craft cocktails in Koreatown, and a story to tell your friends about the hidden door. **WHAT** Behind a secret entrance covered in antique door handles lies this art deco–inspired speakeasy, offering elegant, easy-drinking cocktails and street food from a takeout window outside. **WHO** Korean-American couples out on dates and groups of young single drinkers looking to mingle. ♥

[Los Balcones] 1360 N. Vine St., Hollywood, 323.871.9600. Mon.-Thurs. 11:30 a.m.-11 p.m., Fri. 11:30 a.m.-2 a.m., Sat. 4 p.m.-2 a.m., Sun. 1-9 p.m. Full bar. **WHY** For a serious cocktail program that makes use of authentic Peruvian ingredients, including some 30 piscos. **WHAT** After bringing in a couple of cocktail consultants, the drinks at this excellent Peruvian restaurant are now every bit as good as the food, if not better. You can enjoy them at the bar or at a restaurant table; at either location, accompany your Pisco Punch, Tamarind & Smoke, or Martini del Peru with a ceviche, and you'll be very happy indeed. **WHO** A hip crowd of folks going to or coming from an ArcLight movie. ☼

[Magnolia] 6266 1/2 Sunset Blvd., Hollywood, 323.467.0660, magnoliahollywood.com. Sun.-Thurs. 11:30 a.m.-10:30 a.m., Fri. 11:30 a.m.-11 p.m., Sat. noon-11 p.m. Full bar. **WHY** Something for everyone, served into the wee hours, and convenient to the ArcLight and the Hollywood club scene. The weeknight happy hour is good. **WHAT** A handy place to know about, especially for a $5 Malbec or $6 cocktail and a few $5 small plates before a movie down the street (weeknights only for happy hour). The food isn't remarkable, but it's satisfying, and the drinks are properly made. **WHO** Hollywood business folk by day, moviegoers in the early evening, and a club crowd late at night. ☼

[Melrose Umbrella Co.] 7465 Melrose Ave., Melrose, 323.951.0709, melroseumbrellaco.com. Sun.-Wed. 4-11 p.m., Thurs.-Sat. 4 p.m.-2 a.m. Full bar. **WHY** A temple of modern cocktail culture with a rustic post-Prohibition apothecary theme. **WHAT** The mixology obsessed proprietors of this fairly new spot have a lot of ideas about drinks: they're "farming" their own ice, offering five cocktails on draft, and making their own cordials and tinctures. Each month's drink menu pays tribute to a different classic cocktail book. Bar snacks are by grilled-cheese maestro Eric Greenspan. Though prices are on the higher side, there's live music some nights. **WHO** A festive Hollywood-meets-hipster group packs the place after 10; go earlier to be assured a seat.

[MessHall] 4500 Los Feliz Blvd., Los Feliz, 323.660.6377, messhall-kitchen.com. Mon.-Thurs. 11:30 a.m.-3 p.m. & 5-11 p.m., Fri. 11:30 a.m.-3 p.m. & 5 p.m.-midnight, Sat. 10 a.m.-3 p.m. & 5 p.m.-midnight, Sun. 10 a.m.-3 p.m. & 4-11 p.m. Full bar. **WHY** A multi-purpose restaurant with a creative cocktail list and an approachable, rustic menu. **WHAT** This large space that cheekily references a woodsy summer camp appears to be just what Los Feliz needed, with a fire pit and separate bar that combine to heat up a patio that's well protected from busy Los Feliz Boulevard. Sit at the long bar inside the wood-trussed space that was once the Brown Derby's hat, where skilled bartenders lovingly char the orange peel for Old Fashioneds and plop enormous square cubes into glasses of whiskey. With cocktails like Stripper Perfume and Baby It's Cold Outside, it's hard to choose between the expertly mixed drinks and the huge selection of whiskeys. **WHO** An east-side cross-section of neighborhood couples for dinner and young drinkers later at night. 🔭 ☼

[Mission Cantina] 5946 Sunset Blvd., East Hollywood, 323.469.3130, themissioncantina.com. Mon.-Fri. noon-2 a.m., Sat.-Sun. 6 p.m.-2 a.m. Full bar. **WHY** A no-muss, no-fuss place that's good for meeting friends after work. **WHAT** Don't expect liquid alchemists behind the bar, just regular bartenders who can mix a standard margarita and a few funky variations on the drink. The venue is dark and long with lots of dark wood, a small patio, and a few fantastic stained-glass windows. The tacos are pretty meh, but that's why you have the Twins Sliders takeout window right next door. **WHO** Hollywood twentysomethings, margarita fans.

[Musso & Frank Grill] 🌴6667 Hollywood Blvd., Hollywood, 323.467.7788. Tues.-Sat. 11 a.m.-11 p.m. Full bar. **WHY** Martinis, atmosphere, flannel cakes, atmosphere, and atmosphere. **WHAT** God knows it isn't the cooking that makes this place an essential L.A. restaurant—it's the rich blend of traditional architecture and Hollywood history, faded smoke and legendary lies, all aged to an irresistible patina. (Okay, the cocktails are part of the draw, too.) Don't eat the vegetables or try to chat up the old-school waiters, but do get a martini and linger at the bar as long as possible. **WHO** Crusty old showbiz men, young bucks. 🍸

[No Vacancy] 1727 N. Hudson Ave., Hollywood, 323.465.1902, novacancyla.com. Nightly 8 p.m.- 2 a.m. Full bar. **WHY** Though it's in the heart of Hollywood, this super-popular spot is swanky without being stuffy. **WHAT** The décor of a Victorian house adds an antique elegance to a speakeasy-style space with a deceptively blank exterior. Tightrope walkers cross the patio, and fire dancers might also be on the program, along with gussied-up cocktails conceived by the city's top mixologists and served at two bars, both inside and outside. **WHO** Those who like to see and be seen. ☼

[The Parlour Room of Hollywood] 6423 Yucca St., Hollywood, 323.463.0609, vintagebargroup.com. Sat.-Thurs. 8 p.m.-2 a.m., Fri. 7 p.m.-2 a.m. Full bar. **WHY** You want to feel like a movie star in a Hollywood of decades past. **WHAT** With its plush leather seats, marble bar, chandeliers, and dim candle lighting, the Parlour Room is a dark and quiet retreat in the heart of Hollywood. (The only modern-looking device is a neon-lit computer jukebox.) It's the perfect place to impress a date or catch up with friends, whether you sit by the fire in the outdoor patio or at one of the room-length leather banquettes. The wide variety of cocktails more than makes up for the meager beer selection; the Parlour Trick (Casamigos tequila, agave nectar, jalapeño, and grapefruit juice) is particularly delicious. **WHO** Hollywood wanderers, couples, and small groups of twenty- and thirtysomethings with relatively deep pockets. ☼♥

[Petty Cash Taqueria] 🍸 7360 Beverly Blvd., Beverly/Third, 323.933.5300, pettycashtaqueria.com. Sun.-Mon. 5-10 p.m., Tues.-Sat. 5-11 p.m. Full bar. **WHY** New-wave margaritas, made with "good shit" tequila, and savory house-made Micheladas. **WHAT** Julian Cox developed the cocktails for this rocking, Tijuana-inspired taqueria, which boasts artisanal mezcal flights and Baja-imported craft beer. **WHO** Happy-hour office workers and young couples cutting loose with tacos and tequila shots.

[The Pikey] 7617 Sunset Blvd., Hollywood, 323.850.5400, thepikeyla.com. Mon.-Fri. noon-2 a.m., Sat.-Sun. 11 a.m.-2 a.m. Full bar. **WHY** An upscale British-inflected bar restaurant with an elevated pub menu. **WHAT** Red booths, dark wood paneling, and aged portraits on the wall give this spot the raffish look of a bar that's been around forever, yet the Pikey has been completely upgraded from its divey predecessor. The restaurant side is more French bistro, while the dark bar side is rock and roll. An intimate room in back can be reserved for parties. The scotch and bourbon selections are deep, and there's a solid cross-section of bottled beers, but only a few on draft. **WHO** Patrons fall somewhere between the cast of *Entourage* and the members of Spinal Tap, but in a good way. 🏚

[Plan Check Fairfax] 351 N. Fairfax Ave., Fairfax District, 310.288.6500, plancheck.com. Sun.-Thurs. 11:30 a.m.-11 p.m., Fri.-Sat. 11:30 a.m.-1 a.m. Full bar. **WHY** If you think that a burger topped with ketchup leather should pair with an equally wacky beverage. **WHAT** The second branch of Ernesto Uchimura's burger hangout features local craft beer and off-the-wall drinks created by cocktail chef Matthew Biancaniello, including ones made with strawberry-infused gin and balsamic, or aloe liqueur and truffle salt. Snaps for the great happy hour, with $3 to $5 snacks and good drink deals. **WHO** Burger fiends who have a taste for hoppy craft beers and outlandish cocktails.

[Pot Lobby Bar] The Line Hotel, 3515 Wilshire Blvd., Koreatown, 213.381.7411, eatatpot.com. Sun.-Tues. 11 a.m.-11 p.m., Wed.-Sat. 11 a.m.-2 a.m. Full bar. **WHY** For Roy Choi and Matt Biancaniello's throwback cocktails—imagine a Long Island iced tea with blood orange soda or a kimchi cocktail. **WHAT** Roy Choi crams fun tidbits of Koreatown culture into a blender and flips the switch—his bar/restaurant in the middle of the Line Hotel lobby always provides a lively evening. It's crowded, it's loud (especially when the DJ really gets going), the food and drink are fun, and the crowd is a happy multiethnic L.A. melange. **WHO** The Line Hotel guests, Koreatown locals, and stylish club-goers bobbing to the DJ's beat.

[Pour Vous] 5574 Melrose Ave., Melrose, 323.871.8699, pour-vousla.com. Tues.-Sat. 8 p.m.-2 a.m. Full bar. **WHY** When you want a dose of extra fancy to go with your cocktail. **WHAT** The elaborate drinks take time to craft, but they're worth it; they are exquisite. While you're waiting, perhaps you can catch one of the brief, not-too-racy burlesque-style shows. It's a nice place. That means gents are required to wear a jacket (loaners are available), and patrons of all stripes should show up looking they put some effort into their attire. That vintage trolley in the parking lot? It's the smoking patio. **WHO** Anyone who wants to impress their date or needs an excuse to wear flapper garb; escapees from the Paramount lot. ♥

[The Prince] 🌴 3198 1/2 W. 7th St., Koreatown, 213.389.1586. Nightly 4 p.m.-2 a.m. Full bar. **WHY** A time-warp treasure with a camera-ready original retro decor that's incongruously also a Korean restaurant and lounge. **WHAT** *Mad Men* is just one of the shows that uses the Prince's red-leather booths and kitschy paintings as a backdrop. It's also a hardcore Korean spot, with seriously spicy fried chicken and kimchi fried rice. Choose a Korean Hite beer to cool down the fiery appetizers, a soju cocktail, or stay in vintage character with a manhattan. Drinks aren't really the point, but they're a welcome half-off at the happy hour every evening until 8. **WHO** History buffs, Korean businessmen, and young bar crawlers. 🏯

[R Bar] 3331 W. 8th St., Koreatown, 213.387.7227, facebook.com/rbarktown. Nightly 7 p.m.-2 a.m. Full bar. **WHY** Who'd expect such a cool little neighborhood bar to be hiding in plain sight? **WHAT** This divey joint really is the kind of place where you can let it all hang out. It's louder and more raucous up front, but the area in the back is good for hanging out and chilling. Some nights there's karaoke, some nights there's a dance party, some nights there's comedy. But the jukebox is always free. A password is needed for entry: "Don't cross the streams." **WHO** In-the-know Koreatown and Hollywood residents. ✎

[Ray's & Stark Bar] 🍸 LACMA, 5905 Wilshire Blvd., Miracle Mile, 323.857.6180, raysandstarkbar.com. Mon.-Fri. noon-10 p.m., closed Wed., Sat.-Sun. 11:30 a.m.-10 p.m. Full bar. **WHY** Finally, a stylish cocktail lounge that complements the high-style architecture of the Los Angeles County Museum of Art. **WHAT** Tucked behind the photo-friendly Chris Burden Urban Light lamp posts, Stark Bar is the outdoor cocktail area next to the museum's upscale restaurant, Ray's. The decor is midcentury but the drinks are thoroughly modern, often flavored with elixirs of fruits and herbs, like Rose Wishes & Lavender Dreams. The bar menu is equally sophisticated, with creative flatbreads and snacks. **WHO** In-the-know tourists, chic collectors, and the occasional well-known artist. 🍸 ☼

[Rockwell Table & Stage] 1714 N. Vermont Ave., Los Feliz, 323.669.1550, rockwell-la.com. Mon.-Tues. 11 a.m.-midnight, Wed. 11 a.m.-1 a.m., Thurs.-Fri. 11 a.m.-2 a.m., Sat. 10 a.m.-2 a.m., Sun. 10 a.m.-1 a.m. Full bar. **WHY** A fabulous outdoor space, a good happy hour, and flatbread pizzas to share with friends. **WHAT** In front, there's a supper club that offers jazz and musical performances, while hidden behind is a sleek two-level, mostly outdoor lounge space built around a coral tree. Cocktails are skewed toward the crowd-pleasing vodka variety but with enough fresh creations to please more discerning drinkers, while an affordable wine list complements bar snacks and a full menu. **WHO** Quiet conversationalists for happy hour and a more convivial and celebratory crowd in the later hours. 🍸 🏯 ☼♥

[The Roger Room] 370 N. La Cienega Blvd., West Hollywood, 310.854.1300, therogerroom.com. Mon.-Fri. 6 p.m.-2 a.m., Sat. 7 p.m.-2 a.m., Sun. 8 p.m.-2 a.m. Full bar. **WHY** A semi-secret speakeasy on busy La Cienega with impeccable drinks. **WHAT** If circus performers had their own secluded bar and didn't mind paying upwards of $14 a drink, they might hang out at this intimate, clubby spot decorated with a giant circus mural next to the Largo. The menu throws around such in-the-know ingredients as cucumber foam and mezcal rinse, which go into the carefully concocted drinks, and sampling the three absinthe creations could make it a night that's hard to remember. **WHO** Convivial twenty- and thirtysomethings.

[The Roof on Wilshire] Hotel Wilshire, 6317 Wilshire Blvd., Miracle Mile, 323.852.6002, theroofonwilshire.com. Sun.-Thurs. 7 a.m.-11 p.m., Fri.-Sat. 7 a.m.- 1 a.m. Full bar. **WHY** The views don't get any better in this part of town. **WHAT** It's sometimes said that people in L.A. don't enjoy enough outdoor dining and drinking, but this pool and terrace atop the Hotel Wilshire is just the place to change that. Sunglasses are available for really bright brunches, but a sunset view is even better. Cocktails and other drinks are a little pricey, but a custom Mule section is a nice touch, with house-made ginger beer and variations like the Wilshire Mule and the El Diablo, made with tequila and cassis. **WHO** A Hollywood-ish crowd, but it's still more low-key than at the Sunset Strip hotels.

[Sadie Kitchen and Lounge] 1638 N. Las Palmas Ave., Hollywood, 323.467.0200, sadiela.com. Tues.-Sat. 6 p.m.-1:30 a.m. Full bar. **WHY** It's classy, lively, and grownup without trying too hard. **WHAT** One of the better cocktail joints in Hollywood, this is really three spaces in one. The front room is like a parlor and is mainly used for private events; the middle room is centered around a large square bar and can feel intimate or raucous depending on the crowd; and the gorgeous back patio with its glass ceilings is where you want to eat and converse. **WHO** The back patio is filled with people on dates or people who wish they were. 🏛 ☼♥

[Sassafras] 1233 N. Vine St., Hollywood, 323.467.2800, sassafras-saloon.com. Nightly 5 p.m.-2 a.m. Full bar. **WHY** Imagine if Disneyland's Blue Bayou served booze. **WHAT** Through the wrought-iron gates you'll discover a large bar that's halfway between a Gilded Age cathouse and an Antebellum plantation. There's a vine-covered smoking patio, an upstairs alcove where bands perform, and a small back room where you can spin the roulette wheel to get your drinks for free. **WHO** Anyone who likes campy charm and good cocktails and wants to escape the Cahuenga Corridor scene. ☼♥

[Skybar] Mondrian LA Hotel, 8440 Sunset Blvd., West Hollywood, 323.848.6025, morganshotelgroup.com. Daily 10 a.m.-2 p.m. Full bar.

WHY The view, the pool, and the Sunset Strip scene. **WHAT** The drinks are crazy expensive, the crowd can be bougie-douchey, the vibe is Vegasy, and you need to call ahead to get on the "guest list" to get in at prime times. And yet it can be worth a visit at least once, to sip a cocktail by the pool and soak in the view. (This is not actually a rooftop bar, but on the Strip, the city views are swell.) Come early to avoid the circus. **WHO** Hollywood show-offs, moneyed young tourists, and reality-show wannabes. ☼

[Son of a Gun] 8370 W. 3rd St., Beverly/Third, 323.782.9033, sonofagunrestaurant.com. Mon.-Thurs. 11:30 a.m.-2:30 p.m. & 6-11 p.m., Fri. 11:30 a.m.-2:30 p.m. & 6 p.m.-midnight, Sat. 6 p.m.-midnight., Sun. 6-11 p.m. Full bar. **WHY** Pretend you're Jimmy Buffett and throw back such craft cocktails as mai tais, daiquiris, and boozy snow cones crafted with upgraded spirits and liqueurs. **WHAT** Jon Shook and Vinny Dotolo's nautical-inspired seafood restaurant hides a tiny but adorable bar counter serving lush beach-style cocktails that are big on flavor. If you're feeling celebratory, the wine list is also rich with Champagnes, and if you order one of the wee lobster rolls to accompany your drink, you won't be sorry, although you might still be hungry. **WHO** Boat-shoe-wearing westsiders who enjoy a fun, tropical cocktail without too much seriousness.

[Spare Room] Hollywood Roosevelt, 7000 Hollywood Blvd., Hollywood, 323.769.7296, spareroomhollywood.com. Sun.-Mon. & Wed.-Sat. 8 p.m.-2 a.m. Full bar. **WHY** A fun place for a special night, with bowling lanes and superior cocktails. **WHAT** The Spare Room at the Hollywood Roosevelt Hotel is no ordinary bowling alley; instead it's a swank bar in the guise of a vintage wood-paneled gentleman's game room, with excellent cocktails, table games, and two gleaming lanes that can be reserved by the hour (handmade bowling shoes included). Drinks continue the playful theme, like the Mickey Mantle, with crackerjack syrup, and the Fernet egg cream, served with a pretzel rod. Several punchbowls are perfect for groups of bowlers. **WHO** A smattering of famous faces and Hollywood kids dressed to impress. 🏠

[Station Hollywood/Living Room] W Hotel, 6250 Hollywood Blvd., Hollywood, 323.798.1360, stationhollywood.com. Daily 11 a.m.-2 a.m. Full bar. **WHY** Two sleek spaces offer a respite from busy Hollywood Boulevard. **WHAT** Hollywood has gotten very glam in the past few years, and the W Hotel is part of the reason.

🏠 GROUPS 🎤 KARAOKE ☼ PATIO ♥ ROMANTIC

Outside, the Station offers jazz and movie screenings on an airy patio supplied with sofas and fire pits, while the Living Room bar inside is essentially the hotel's spacious lobby. Drinks tend to be sweet and yes, there's bottle service. **WHO** Hotel guests and groups of friends looking for a Hollywood patio experience. ☼

[The Surly Goat] 7929 Santa Monica Blvd., West Hollywood, 323.650.4628, surlygoat.com. Mon. 5 p.m.-2 a.m., Tues.-Fri. 6 p.m.-2 a.m., Sat.-Sun. 1 p.m.-2 a.m. Full bar. **WHY** A lively West Hollywood tavern for discerning beer enthusiasts. Both the Monday trivia night and the Wednesday karaoke sessions are worthwhile. **WHAT** Ryan Sweeney knows his beers, and his place has an impressive array of more than two dozen taps and a rotating brew on cask. Rare and fascinating beers are the norm, from the Bruery's locally made Marron Acidifie (sour chestnut) to a few choice Belgian ales, with the focus on the west coast. It's chill in the early hours, with people playing shuffleboard and tasting beers; later it can get louder. There's no kitchen, but regulars order in from Baby Blues BBQ next door. **WHO** Diehard beer aficionados and young drinkers looking for a more casual alternative to the Hollywood club scene. ⌦ 🏛 🔎 ☼

[Tom Bergin's Public House] 🌴 840 S. Fairfax Ave., Mlracle Mile, 323.936.7151, tombergins.com. Mon.-Thurs. 5 p.m.-2 a.m., Fri.-Sat. 11 a.m.- 2 a.m., Sun. 11 a.m.-7 p.m. Full bar. **WHY** A dose of L.A. history with an Irish accent. **WHAT** Since 1936, drinkers have been hoisting pints at L.A.'s oldest Irish outpost, and some of the cardboard shamrocks with regular's names affixed to the ceiling date back many decades. In the front room, a horseshoe-shaped bar is the perfect place for kibitzing with fellow drinkers, while the homey back room serves up pub grub. Irish coffee, Irish ale, and Irish whiskey are the drinks of choice. **WHO** Lots of longtime regulars as well as Wilshire corridor office workers.

[The Village Idiot] 7383 Melrose Ave., Melrose, 323.655.3331, villageidiotla.com. Mon.-Fri. 11:30 a.m.-2 a.m., Sat.-Sun. 10 a.m.-2 a.m. Full bar. **WHY** A fairly deep and thoughtful tap-beer selection, excellent fish 'n chips and spinach pie, and a pretty normal crowd for Melrose, especially midweek. **WHAT** The crush is too much for us on weekend nights, but otherwise we're always happy to stop into this brick-walled pub and restaurant for a Guinness and a steak sandwich or some fish 'n chips. The wine selection isn't nearly as good as the beer, but sometimes there's a good buy by the bottle. **WHO** Beer boys and girls seeking Boddingtons or Craftsman beers, something good to eat, and a jovial time.

[The Virgil] 4519 Santa Monica Blvd., East Hollywood, 323.660.4540, thevirgil.com. Nightly 7 p.m.-2 a.m. Full bar. **WHY** The world needs more comedy clubs that don't have a two-drink minimum *and* that serve good drinks. **WHAT** It's hard to know whether the Virgil, which is divided into a performance space and a smaller lounge area, is a neighborhood bar that happens to host comedy, or a comedy club with shockingly good cocktails. Either way, it's a win. Most nights it hosts some sort of laugh riot, dance party, or other form of entertainment (perhaps a movie screening). Pair that with a killer happy hour (all night on Tuesdays and 7 to 9 p.m. every other night), during which craft cocktails are only $6 and craft beers (a small but tasty selection) are $5, and you've got a terrific neighborhood bar on the edge of Silver Lake. **WHO** Comedians and the people who love to laugh with (or at) them. 🍸

[The Well] 6255 Sunset Blvd., Hollywood, 323.467.9355, vintagebargroup.com. Nighly 5 p.m.-2 a.m. Full bar. **WHY** You want to meet some friends for a burger and a brew without a lot of drama. **WHAT** With a blink-and-you'll-miss-it entrance just off Hollywood Boulevard, this casual bar is a welcome hideaway. The daily happy hour lasts until 9 p.m. and features $6 well drinks, $3 PBRs, and $6 Moscow Mules served in copper mugs. The drinks are strong and the menu is varied, though you're best off sticking to simple bar food like burgers and potato skins. Even when it gets busy on weekend evenings, the vibe is unpretentious. **WHO** Refugees from the Palladium, Hollywood denizens who don't care about craft cocktails and just want to booze it up with their friends. 🍸

[Windows Lounge] 🌴 Four Seasons Hotel, 300 S. Doheny Dr., West Hollywood, 310.273.2222, fourseasons.com. Mon.-Sat. 11 a.m.-1:30 a.m., Sun. 5 p.m.-12:30 a.m. Full bar. **WHY** Four Seasons' elegance, perfect cocktails, and highly entertaining people-watching. **WHAT** Ground zero for the good life, Beverly Hills–style, this lobby bar at the Four Seasons is luxurious but not pretentious—the staff is warm and friendly. It's not uncommon for journalists to interview movie stars or TV producers here, but the people sitting next to you might be just ordinary folks with seven-figure retirement accounts. Be warned that cigar-smoking guys can make the otherwise-fabulous patio pretty stinky in the later evening hours.

🏛 GROUPS 🎤 KARAOKE ☼ PATIO ♥ ROMANTIC

WHO Tea-takers by day and wine-sippers by night, with some amazing plastic surgery on display and the occasional movie-star sighting. 🦻 ☼♥

[Wood & Vine] 6280 Hollywood Blvd., Hollywood, 323.334.3360, woodandvine.com. Tues.-Thurs. 5 p.m.-midnight, Fri. 5 p.m.-2 a.m., Sat. 4 p.m.-2 a.m., Sun. 3 p.m.-11 p.m. Full bar. **WHY** Because grownups need to be able to drink (and eat) in Hollywood.
WHAT Yeah, the spendy small plates add up fast, but the back patio, anchored by a gorgeous fire pit, is a fantastic place to have a cocktail. Located at the benighted corner of Hollywood and Vine, the restaurant and bar offers a sophisticated alternative to the scene at Katsuya on one hand and the beer-chugging antics at certain bars in the area on the other. The butterscotch pot de crème is a must. **WHO** People who want to be able to hear their companions when they speak, patrons of the Pantages before or after a show (make reservations!). ☼♥

[The Woods] 1533 N. La Brea Ave., Hollywood, 323.876.6612, vintagebargroup.com. Mon.-Fri. 6 p.m.-2 a.m., Sat.-Sun. 8 p.m.-2 a.m. Full bar. **WHY** For a cozier, woodsier Hollywood night.
WHAT Hidden in a La Brea strip mall just above the Sunset Strip, this Hollywood gem is the least obnoxious choice for a drink in the neighborhood. Unpretentious bartenders serve up affordable drinks (happy hour goes until 10!) to a usually low-key crowd, amid cedar-stacked walls and antler chandeliers. Dark, plush booths are ideal for cozy, intimate nights. **WHO** A mix of stylish and frumpy Hollywood dwellers. 🗺️ ♥

[Ye Rustic Inn] 1831 Hillhurst Ave., Los Feliz, 323.662.5757. Mon.-Fri. noon-2 a.m, Sat.-Sun. 9 a.m.-2 a.m. Full bar. **WHY** For reasonably priced drinks and an old-school, divey charm.
WHAT A respectable sports bar that can get crowded, this is a good place to watch a game, especially if you can snag one of the booths. Themed nights, like karaoke on Tuesday and trivia on Sundays, bring out some serious players. The beloved buffalo wings make a great late-night snack. **WHO** The usual Los Feliz hipster crowd and a lot of older regulars. 🗺️ 🏨 🏓

EASTSIDE

[1642 Beer & Wine] 1642 W. Temple St., Echo Park, 213.989.6836. Tues.-Sat. 6 p.m.-2 a.m., Sun. 6 p.m.-midnight. Beer

& wine. **WHY** Come for the live music, which ranges from jazz to bluegrass, and the laid-back bartenders, who make the space feel like an upbeat house party. **WHAT** Hidden inside an unmarked storefront, this romantic and rustic lounge offers a menu of rotating beers and wine in an otherwise craft-booze-barren section of Echo Park. **WHO** Amiable Echo Park and Westlake folks who look like they stepped out of a Mumford & Sons music video. 🎥 ♥

[4100 Bar] 1087 Manzanita St., Silver Lake, 323.666.4460, 4100bar.com. Nightly 6 p.m.-2 a.m. Full bar. **WHY** For a quick introduction to the raucous eastside bar scene or a stop on a Sunset Junction cocktail crawl. Good happy hour, too. **WHAT** One of Silver Lake's early hipster spots is a lively gathering place for couples and groups, with an exotic Moroccan-style dark red interior and generally loud music ranging from '70s hard rock to indie hits. Other than the Dickel Pickleback shot, drinks are standard but decently priced. No food is served, but drinkers can bring in grub from the barbecue that often goes on in the parking lot.
WHO Young imbibers from all over the city looking to check out the Silver Lake scene. 🏯 ♥

[Akbar] 4356 Sunset Blvd., Silver Lake, 323.665.6810, akbarsilverlake.com. Nightly 4 p.m.-2 a.m. Full bar. **WHY** One of Silver Lake's first remodeled dive bars is now one of the area's few remaining gay bars, but in an inclusive, non-WeHo way. **WHAT** Akbar manages to pack a lot into its tiny Middle Eastern–decorated space, including a dance floor. Spacious it's not, but it is a nonstop party of revelers dancing to vintage disco, watching electric ukulele players, and enjoying reasonably priced, straightforward cocktails. "We can tolerate a happy drunk but not a sloppy drunk," reads the bar's mission statement, and we're down with that. **WHO** A cross-section of gay L.A. and a fair amount of straight folks.

[The Association] 110 E. 6th St., Downtown, 213.123.4567, circa93.com/the-association. Mon.-Fri. 6 p.m.-2 a.m., Sat.-Sun. 7 p.m.-2 a.m. Full bar. **WHY** Well-made cocktails in a dark, *Mad Men*–style atmosphere that hints at sinful happenings. **WHAT** A worthy stop on a Downtown bar crawl, the Association makes cocktails that aren't quite as creative as the ones at the Varnish next door, but the sultry space makes up for it with comfy banquette seating, lighting as black as velvet, and weekend DJs. **WHO** Office dwellers enjoy the late-running happy hour after work, while on weekends the crowd is younger and more raucous. ♥

🏯 GROUPS 🎤 KARAOKE ☼ PATIO ♥ ROMANTIC

[Atwater Village Tavern] 3216 Glendale Blvd., Atwater, 323.644.0605, atwatervillagetavern.com. Tues.-Thurs. 11:30 a.m.-midnight, Fri.-Sat. 11:30 a.m.-2 a.m., Sun. 11:30 a.m.-11 p.m. Beer & wine. **WHY** A pub with a real neighborhood feel, as well as a good selection of craft beers and a Mexican-leaning bar food menu. **WHAT** Atwater Village is quickly becoming a trendy neighborhood, and the casually modern Tavern is one of several beer-focused spots to spring up recently. Food from Stop Guac n' Roll includes messy but tasty tacos, burgers, and avocado fries, while 12 taps have a rotating list of mostly SoCal beers from the likes of Golden Road, Stone, and Angel City. A different drink special is offered each day. **WHO** Dog owners who appreciate the small front patio, farmers' market shoppers, eastside locals. ☼

[Baco Mercat] 408 S. Main St., Downtown, 213.687.8808, bacomercat.com. Mon.-Thurs. 11:30 a.m.-2:30 p.m. & 5:30-11 p.m., Fri.-Sat. 11:30 a.m.-3 p.m. & 5:30 p.m.-midnight, Sun. 11:30 a.m.-3 p.m. & 5-10 p.m. Full bar. **WHY** Angelenos know that some of the best bars in the city are actually located inside restaurants; this is one of them. **WHAT** Josef Centeno is the chef behind three of Downtown's best restaurants (Baco Mercat, Bar Amá, and Orsa and Winston), and he puts the same care into crafting his cocktails as he does his signature flatbread sandwich, the baco. Serious eats and a casual atmosphere? It's the perfect duality. Since reservations are so old-school, come early and sidle up at the bar or the patio—but be warned, it's loud as hell inside. **WHO** Chef groupies, loft dwellers, and in-the-know professionals. ♥

[Bar 107] 107 W. 4th St., Downtown, 213.625.7382. Nightly 3 p.m.-2 a.m. Full bar. **WHY** In addition to homeless people, the Historic Core is now populated with well-heeled loft dwellers and the gastropubs that cater to them. This is the antidote. **WHAT** Don't expect craft beers or exotic cocktails. Bar 107 is all about cheap shots of liquor washed down with Rolling Rock, Pabst, or Shock Top. And that's the way it should be. The grungy bar with the red walls is decorated with mannequins topped with freaky, oversize stuffed animal heads. There's a small back room that gets packed and sweaty with dancers when DJs play. **WHO** College students, post-college kids, USC fans, assorted weirdos. ↘ ☞

[Bar Amá] ⍟ 118 W. 4th St., Downtown, 213.687.7000, bar-ama. com. Mon.-Thurs. 11:30 a.m.-2:30 p.m. & 5:30-11 p.m., Fri. 11:30 a.m.-2:30 p.m. & 5:30 p.m.-midnight, Sat. 11:30 a.m.-midnight, Sun.

⍟ ESSENTIALLY L.A.   ↘ DIVE   ☽ QUIET   ☞ VALUE

11:30 a.m.-10 p.m. Full bar. **WHY** Featuring house-made shrubs and artisanal mezcal, Bar Amá's drinks are rustic yet refined and, most importantly, very quaffable. **WHAT** Josef Centeno's Tex-Mex influenced restaurant offers a bar program focused on superb tequila and mezcal cocktails. Feel free to order a flight of tequila, mezcal, or sotol (a little-known Mexican agave spirit) to expand your palate, and don't miss the late-afternoon happy hour every day. **WHO** Tequila fans with discerning tastes and those looking for hip, chef-driven Mexican fare in Downtown. ♥

[Bar Jackalope] Seven Grand, 515 W. 7th St., Downtown, 213.614.0736, sevengrandbars.com. Sun.-Thurs. 8 p.m.-1 a.m. Full bar. **WHY** Bar manager Pedro Shanahan has assembled an impressive 120-bottle selection of scotch, bourbon, and whiskey, from Yamazaki to Pappy Van Winkle. **WHAT** Hidden in the back of Seven Grand, a popular Downtown cocktail bar, this intimate whiskey lounge requires reservations—but don't worry, they're fairly easy to get. Just press the buzzer marked with Japanese characters (Bar Jackalope is inspired by the dark whiskey dens of Tokyo). It's not open on Friday and Saturday, when Seven Grand is busiest. **WHO** Whiskey aficionados and those looking to expand their spirits knowledge more than make the party-bar scene. ♥

[Barbarella] 2609 N. Hyperion Ave., Silver Lake, 323.644.8000, BarbarellaBar.com. Mon.-Wed. 4-11 p.m., Thurs. 4 p.m.-midnight, Fri.-Sat. 4 p.m.-2 a.m., Sun. 10 a.m.-10 p.m. Full bar. **WHY** A dependable spot for groups who want food, beer, and cocktails all in one place. **WHAT** An oddly shaped space that's not entirely sure if it's a sports bar, pinup-girl-theme lounge, or restaurant, Barbarella seals the deal with food and drink specials almost every day, afternoon opening hours, and fruity 10-ounce martinis. Two dozen taps of craft beer, the most in Silver Lake, are also a draw. **WHO** A variety of groups of Silver Lake friends. 📺 🏛

[Bigfoot Lodge] 3172 Los Feliz Blvd., Atwater, 323.662.9227, bigfootlodge.com. Nightly 5 p.m.-2 a.m. Full bar. **WHY** For a kitschy cabin experience right in the city. **WHAT** This large, roomy bar will transport you straight to Mammoth or Lake Tahoe without the long drive. Try their original cocktails like "Bigfoot's Hairy Fire Balls" and "Saza-squatch" if you're not the DD. As of this writing, their notorious bingo night has been reinstated, the second Tuesday of every month. Check their calendar for other fun events. **WHO** Aspiring lumberjacks and their female companions. ↘

[Black Boar] 1630 Colorado Blvd., Eagle Rock, 323.258.8800. Mon.-Fri. 5 p.m.- 2 a.m., Sat.-Sun. 7 p.m.-2 a.m. Full bar. **WHY** Neighboring Highland Park has a zillion bars, but this hunting lodge-style pub is one of the few actually in Eagle Rock. **WHAT** A roaring fireplace with hot cocoa and hot toddies, a handful of craft beers on tap and a foosball table are just a few of the reasons to hang out at the busy Boar. Bring in a pie from nearby Casa Bianca, or grab a drink while waiting for a table at the famous pizza parlor. With a smoking patio and a rocking jukebox filled with British punk tunes, it's the kind of place every neighborhood wishes it had. **WHO** Young semi-hipsters from surrounding hoods.

[The Black Cat] 3909 Sunset Blvd., Silver Lake, 323.661.6369, theblackcatla.com. Mon. 11:30 a.m.-2 a.m., Sat.-Sun. 10 a.m.-2 a.m. Full bar. **WHY** Sophisticated décor and a full menu make this popular Silver Lake bar worth a stop. **WHAT** On the site of the bar that helped usher in the gay rights movement, the Black Cat acknowledges its history with vintage photos but now welcomes a mixed crowd, and crowded it is on weekends. Dishes like mussels, bacon-wrapped dates, and shepherd's pie, along with black walls and eclectic art, evoke a fashionable London pub. With a solid wine list, several good draft beers, and creative crafted cocktails like the Ginger Spice and the Red Hook, all types of drinkers will find their pleasure. **WHO** A more food-focused crowd at brunch and dinner; younger drinkers flood in as the night wears on.

[Broadway Bar] 830 S. Broadway, Downtown, 213.614.9909, broadwaybar.la. Tues.-Fri. 5 p.m.-2 a.m., Sat.-Sun. 8 p.m.-2 a.m. Full bar. **WHY** You want to kick back and relax after catching a show at the Orpheum. **WHAT** The drinks here are nothing special, but the friendly, old-time ambiance sets this place apart. Sit at the bar, where the bartender and regulars will treat you like you've been coming for years, or sit with some friends at one of the lounge benches in the back. With dimmed lights, an ornate ceiling, dark leather seats, and a large circular bar, the Broadway has an upscale vibe that is somehow effortlessly down-to-earth at the same time. **WHO** Bar crawlers, theatergoers, regulars.

[Café Stella] 3932 Sunset Blvd., Silver Lake, 323.666.0265, cafestella.com. Mon.-Sat. 6-11 p.m., Sun. 6-10 p.m. Full bar. **WHY** To experience all the fuss around mixology firsthand. **WHAT** Gruff, lab-coated bartenders serve up seriously delicious cocktails that come pretty close to earning their high price tags at this Sunset Junction hot spot. The enclosed patio and elegant interior are both ideal places to relax on a glamorous occasion and people-watch. Tends to get crowded late. **WHO** The height of Silver Lake society, plus some major babes, sometimes including Jon Hamm. ✪♥

[Caña Rum Bar] 714 W. Olympic Blvd., South Park/Fashion District, 213.745.7090, canarumbar.la. Sat.-Thurs. 8 p.m.-2 a.m., Fri. 6 p.m.-2 a.m. Full bar. **WHY** Some of L.A.'s most original and inspired cocktails in an atmosphere that oozes discreet charm. **WHAT** The mellow ambiance belies the rigorous attention to detail bestowed on every cocktail by Allan Katz and his crew. The location doesn't make it easy to find (you have to walk through the Doheny's parking lot), but once inside you can actually relax and hear yourself talk. Note: It's technically a club requiring a $20 annual membership fee, but they often waive that during happy hour. **WHO** Cocktail aficionados, LA Live refugees who know where to hole up before (or after) a concert, SoDo (south Downtown) hipsters. 👂✪♥

[Casey's Irish Pub] 613 S. Grand Ave., Downtown, 213.629.2353, caseysirishpub.com. Mon. 11:30 a.m.-11 p.m., Tues.-Wed. 11:30 a.m.-midnight, Thurs.-Fri. 11:30 a.m.-2 a.m., Sat. 1 p.m.-2 a.m., Sun. 1-9 p.m. Full bar. **WHY** A cavernous bar-restaurant with one of Downtown's most spacious patios and well-executed pub fare. **WHAT** Casey's is a fine spot for a plate of fish n' chips, a pint on the patio, or a wee dram of Irish whiskey. With wood-paneled walls and an ornate carved bar, the unpretentious pub looks like it could be in olde Dublin, though it opened in the late 1960s. About a dozen beer taps and a wide whiskey selection keep Downtown drinkers happy. **WHO** Sports fans, Downtown workers, college kids. 🏠✪

[Cliff's Edge] 3626 Sunset Blvd., Silver Lake, 323.666.6116, cliffsedgecafe.com. Mon.-Thurs. 6 p.m.-midnight, Fri.-Sat. 6 p.m.-2 a.m. Full bar. **WHY** For the sophisticated but cozy setting, the Thursday oyster happy hour, and the ease of getting the bartender's attention. **WHAT** The restaurant is hidden in a walled garden built around a massive ficus tree, with candles and good food, and the bar is just as elegant and romantic. Found antiques, random nooks, mirrors, and long tables make for leisurely nights sipping fancy margaritas or $3 beers. **WHO** TV directors keeping a low profile and production assistants splurging on a big night out. 👂✪♥

[Club Tee Gee] 3210 Glendale Blvd., Atwater, 323.669.9631.
Mon.-Fri. noon-2 a.m., Sat.-Sun. 10 a.m.-2 a.m. Full bar. **WHY**
Heavy-handed pours and '70s charm. **WHAT** This Atwater gem is a
time capsule of yesteryear that doesn't overthink it. Cozy booths,
friendly bartenders, and a digital jukebox with unlimited options.
Never-crowded spot for a good time if you're in the neighborhood.
Cash only. **WHO** A lower-key crowd lost in the middle ground
between hippie and hipster.

[Cole's] 118 E. 6th St., Downtown, 213.622.4090, colesfrenchdip.
com. Sun.-Wed. 11:30 a.m.-midnight, Thurs.-Sat. 11 a.m.-2 a.m. Full
bar. **WHY** Classic cocktails and sandwiches in an old-timey setting
in the heart of Downtown. And the speakeasy-like Varnish Bar
in the back is one of the coolest watering holes in Los Angeles.
WHAT Vintage L.A. meets the modern cocktail culture at this renovated landmark. It's appropriate that for a tavern that claims to be
the city's oldest public house, the featured (and very well-made)
cocktails are longtime favorites like manhattans and sazeracs. And
the dips—beef, turkey, lamb, or pastrami—and their accompaniments (coleslaw, fries, mac 'n cheese) hit the spot. **WHO** Downtown workers at lunch; an artsier crowd in the evening, especially
during Thursday artwalk.

[Crane's] 810 S. Spring St., Ste. B1, Downtown, 323.787.7966.
Daily 8:30 a.m.-2 a.m. Full bar. **WHY** It's south Downtown's new
neighborhood bar. **WHAT** A truly hidden spot in that it's literally
underground. Near the corner of Eighth Street, you pass through
an unremarkable doorway and walk down a flight of stairs; Peking
Tavern will be on your left, but turn right and you'll be in an old
bank vault that also happens to be one of the most relaxed bars in
the area. You might find a crowd of twenty- and thirtysomethings
dancing and socializing or vociferously rooting for 14-year-old
figure skaters competing in a televised championship. It's that kind
of place. No scene. No attitude. Order a beer and have fun.
WHO Patrons of Terroni who want somewhere more intimate and
less scene-y for an after-dinner drink; Downtown dwellers.

[Drago Centro] 525 S. Flower St., Downtown, 213.228.8998,
dragocentro.com. Mon.-Fri. 11:30 a.m.-2:30 p.m. & 5-10 p.m., Sat.-
Sun. 5-10 p.m. Full bar. **WHY** Who knew that the acclaimed Italian
restaurant also has such a great bar? Plus it has a free shuttle
to and from the Music Center, Staples Center, and the Nokia
Theater—park here and avoid the hassles and fees. **WHAT** Located

🌴 ESSENTIALLY L.A.   ⟍ DIVE   🎵 QUIET   ⑤ VALUE

in a staid office building, chef Celestino Drago's high-end Italian restaurant hides one of the best happy hours Downtown. The large, airy space has a comfortable bar area that extends to the patio. The cocktails are tasty, and the small bites—Kobe sliders with fontina; oysters; pizzas topped with pancetta and a quail egg or pork sausage and squash blossoms—are terrific and surprisingly affordable. **WHO** In-the-know office workers, fans of Italian food. 🏛 ☼ ♥

[The Echo] 🌴 1822 Sunset Blvd., Echo Park, 213.413.8200, attheecho.com. Nightly 8 p.m.-2 a.m. Full bar. **WHY** It's the coolest music bar in L.A. at the moment. People dance, too. **WHAT** Now a compound, the Echo is the upstairs bar part of this music Mecca in Echo Park. (The other part is the Echoplex, which is a bit more of a concert venue, although it's a bar, too.) Some shows have no cover until after 10:30 (like regulars Funky Sole, who get everyone dancing); others might charge $5 to $10. The drinks are on the pricey side for the so-so quality, but you're here to listen and dance and maybe meet like-minded music buffs. Conversation happens on the smoking patio. **WHO** Plaid-wearing, indie-music-loving eastsiders, mostly under 35 except at the free Sunday-afternoon Grand Ole Echo, when down-homey roots music is showcased. ☼

[Edendale] 2838 Rowena Ave., Silver Lake, 323.666.2000, theedendale.com. Mon.-Sat. 5 p.m.-2 a.m., Sun. 11 a.m.-2 a.m. Full bar. **WHY** It doesn't get much better than cocktails on a warm summer night on a historic Silver Lake patio. **WHAT** Two pleasant outdoor areas hung with twinkly lights surround a 1920s firehouse repurposed as a popular gathering spot. Refreshing cocktails include the hibiscus margarita and the G Harwin, with cucumber vodka, apple, lime, and soda; since it's also a restaurant, the wine list is respectable. A photo booth and Sunday brunch add to the festive atmosphere. **WHO** Birthday groups, date-night couples, and often a famous actor or actress. 🎤 🏛 ☼

[The Edison] 🌴 108 W. 2nd St., Downtown, 213.613.0000, edisondowntown.com. Wed.-Fri. 5 p.m.-2 a.m., Sat. 7 p.m.-2 a.m. Full bar. **WHY** To take a glamorous step back in time—and for the double-take you'll experience the first time you spot the Absinthe Fairy. **WHAT** This nostalgic cocktail bar reignites 1920s elegance and romance in an unbelievable multi-level space that was L.A.'s first private power plant. Each night brings new revelries, from live music to aerialists, but it's enough of a show just to wander through the endless nooks and crannies decorated with antiques,

🏛 GROUPS 🎤 KARAOKE ☼ PATIO ♥ ROMANTIC

leather wing chairs, tufted velvet, and old power-plant equipment. Mixologists from all over the country visit here, so the cocktail list changes often, but absinthe is always a crowd favorite, sold by an ethereal winged woman pushing a glowing green cart. To soak up the liquor, try the sweet potato Tesla fries, the grilled cheese with tomato soup, or a couple of Auntie Em's cupcakes. The foolish few who show up in T-shirts or flip flops are turned away by a beautiful blonde wearing seemingly nothing but beads. **WHO** The hippest of the hip (often dressed to the nines) and rockabilly types on Friday and Saturday, and a surprisingly diverse after work crowd on Wednesday and Thursday. 🏠 ♥

[Eighty Two] 707 E. 4th Pl., Little Tokyo/Arts District, 213.626.8200, eightytwo.la. Tues.-Thurs. 6 p.m.-2 a.m., Fri. 5 p.m.-2 a.m., Sat.-Sun. 2 p.m.-2 a.m. Full bar. **WHY** Where else can you play an original Super Mario Bros., Frogger, or Pac-Man arcade game while you drink specialty cocktails? **WHAT** Eighty Two is a "barcade"—the walls are lined with close to 50 classic arcade and pinball games, while a bar and DJ serve up cocktails and beats. The sparse décor and simple wooden furniture make for a classic retro vibe. The tree-filled patio outfitted with heat lamps is a great place to take a break from the games and loud music to enjoy your arcade-theme drink (perhaps the Princess Peach or the Wizard Mode). After working up an appetite from gaming, hit the food truck in the patio, which rotates depending on the day. **WHO** Post-work bros blowing off steam, Nintendo-playing basement dwellers, Simpsons comic-book guys, flannel-wearing, politics-talking USC kids. ✿

[El Cid] 4212 Sunset Blvd., Silver Lake, 323.668.0318, elcidla.com. Mon.-Sat. 6 p.m.-1 a.m., Sun. 11 a.m.-1 a.m. Full bar. **WHY** For a pleasant, never-crowded patio and good margaritas. **WHAT** Down a winding set of steps tucked away from the bustle of Sunset Boulevard above, this Spanish restaurant is known for its patio bar and venue space, and for having a good Sunday brunch. The inside is dark and pleasant enough if your friend's band is playing, but otherwise, skip the cover and enjoy the ample seating outdoors. A great place to try when everywhere else is crowded. **WHO** An unpredictable mix; always a less pretentious than the bars at Sunset Junction. ⬎ 📷 🏠 ✿

[El Compadre] 1449 Sunset Blvd., Echo Park, 213.250.4505, elcompadrerestaurant.com. Daily 11 a.m.-2 a.m. Full bar. **WHY** This old-school Mexican restaurant still flies the guacamole flag near Dodger Stadium. **WHAT** Famous for its flaming margarita, El Compadre is a member of that breed of Mexican restaurant—with mariachis and "careful-this-plate-is-hot" cooking—that is slowly disappearing from the metropolis. Go now before you realize you missed them. **WHO** Families, Dodgers game-goers.

[El Prado] 1805 Sunset Blvd., Echo Park, 213.483.8609, elprado-bar.com. Mon.-Fri. 6 p.m.-2 a.m., Sat.-Sun. 2 p.m.-2 a.m. Beer & wine. **WHY** For the great beer and wine selection and the relaxed, romantic atmosphere. **WHAT** This small, dark wine and beer bar satisfies the snobs while still appealing to a more easygoing crowd. It always has great records playing and the bartenders are friendly. Stop for a quick drink before hopping across the street to a concert at the Echo, or order the cheese plate and settle in for a more leisurely night. **WHO** Upscale drinkers, Echo Park musicians, friends of the bartenders. ☼♥

[The Escondite] 410 Boyd St., Little Tokyo/Arts District, 213.626.1800, theescondite.com. Mon.-Fri. noon-1:30 a.m., Sat.-Sun. 11 a.m.-1:30 a.m. Full bar. **WHY** There's live music most nights, the staff is friendly, the patio has a gorgeous view, and lot parking is ample. What more could you ask for? **WHAT** One of the best-kept secrets in Downtown, this unmarked bar (a neon arrow tips you off) serves local beers, solid classic cocktails, and an outlandishly fun bar menu that includes buffalo-fried mushrooms and a hash-brown-topped burger dubbed the Captain Kangaroo. **WHO** Downtown loft dwellers and other locals relaxing with craft beers and burgers. ☼

[The Falls Lounge] 626 S. Spring St., Downtown, 213.612.0072, thefallslounge.com. Mon.-Fri. 5 p.m.-2 a.m., Sat.-Sun. 1 p.m.-2 a.m. Full bar. **WHY** You're looking for a cheap Downtown happy hour in a cool setting. **WHAT** This comfy, nature-theme bar with walls made from tree trunks and a waterfall flowing under a window behind the bar is a perfect place to meet up with friends Downtown after work. The happy-hour cocktails are six bucks, and with names like the Hunter and the Rustic, many feature such organic ingredients as berries, egg whites, and honey. If you're not in the mood for a cocktail, there's a decent selection of craft beers. Sit at one of the two wraparound leather lounge benches, or take your drink to the small but pleasant patio out front. **WHO** Thirtysomethings meeting friends after work. 🏛 ☼

[Far Bar] 347 E. 1st St., Little Tokyo/Arts District, 213.617.9990, farbarla.com. Mon.–Fri. 11 a.m.–2 a.m., Sat.–Sun. 10 a.m.–2 a.m. Full bar. **WHY** The civilized, light-filled back patio. **WHAT** The main entrance to this Little Tokyo spot reveals a pretty typical Asian fusion restaurant, but go around the back through the alley to a cozy and inviting patio with its own bar. This is the place to stop before or after dinner at one of the many ramen spots nearby; they've got an extensive beer list and many Japanese options, plus their own specialty cocktails. **WHO** Silver Lake dwellers on a Little Tokyo ramen bender. ☼

[Footsie's] 2640 N. Figueroa St., Cypress Park, 323.221.6900. Nightly 5 p.m.-2 a.m. Full bar. **WHY** The stellar jukebox, wood-paneled dive-bar feel, and good no-frills drinks. **WHAT** A relaxed dive bar in the early evening starts lining 'em up after 9 p.m. (especially for the Wednesday 143 night, when a DJ plays '90s R&B, rap, and slow jams), so come early if you want to make the most of the pool table and actually get the bartender's attention. It's more of a PBR and Jack-n-Coke kinda place than a craft-cocktail emporium. Good potato tacos next door if you get hungry.
WHO Dudes with mustaches, girls in plaid shirts, Dodger fans, Gold Line bar-hoppers, Downtown professionals slumming it on their way home to Silver Lake. ＼ ⑤ ☼

[Gallery Bar & Cognac Room] Millenium Biltmore Hotel, 506 S. Grand Ave., Downtown, 213.624.1011, millenniumhotels.com. Nightly 4 p.m.-midnight. Full bar. **WHY** You want a classy and classic after-work cocktail in the heart of Downtown's business district. **WHAT** With its ornate high ceilings, decorative mirrors, and gilded columns, the bar at this grand hotel feels regal but not stuffy. The wine selection is forgettable; the martinis aren't. Neither are the manhattans, and there are several variations of the sophisticated drink to choose from. Jazz livens up the place on Friday and Saturday nights, making it a great date spot. **WHO** Mingle with businessmen in striped shirts, wide-eyed tourists, and professionals who are either making deals or wishing they were. ♪ ♥

[Gold Room] 1558 Sunset Blvd., Echo Park, 213.482.5259. Daily noon-2 a.m. Full bar. **WHY** Free tacos and a cheap PBR-and-tequila-shot deal. **WHAT** On a strip of Sunset Boulevard that seems to have missed the gentrification memo, the Gold Room retains its divey charm, complete with cheap beer and shots, a jukebox, and some friendly but weathered regulars. **WHO** Longtime residents of the neighborhood, plus some newbies. ➘ 🐗

[Golden Gopher] 🎺 417 W. 8th St., Downtown, 213.614.8001,
213nightlife.com/goldengopher. Nightly 5 p.m.-2 a.m. Full bar. **WHY**
A vintage spot with an up-to-date crowd and cocktail selection.
WHAT Hang out on the Gopher's patio tucked between two buildings for a truly urban feel, or buy a bottle to go from one of L.A.'s
only bars with an off-sale license, dating from 1905. A photo
booth, old-school video games, and solid selections of both beer
and whiskey add to the appeal, while the neon sign and gopher
lamps are a nod to the bar's past. **WHO** After-work drinkers at
happy hour, the USC crowd later on. ✺

[The Greyhound Bar & Grill] 5570 N. Figueroa St., Highland
Park, 323.900.0300, the-greyhound.com. Sun.-Thurs. noon-1 a.m., Fri.-
Sat. noon-2 a.m. Full bar. **WHY** An easygoing urban tavern for both
sports fans and cocktail lovers, with a worthy happy hour.
WHAT With the vintage tile floors, wood dividers, and high tin
ceilings, the Greyhound recalls a historic East Coast saloon, even
though it's quite new. There's a wide selection of beers on tap, a
fine wine list, and a surprisingly deep selection of Italian amari
digestive liqueurs. The menu is hearty pub fare. **WHO** Dodger
fans (although some diehards find it too noisy to watch the game
properly) and diverse groups of neighborhood friends.

[The Griffin] 3000 Los Feliz Blvd., Atwater, 323.644.0444. Daily 4
p.m.-2 a.m. Full bar. **WHY** Mix a touch of Harry Potter with a dash
of goth and you get this dark but festive spot. **WHAT** A roaring
fireplace and gothic-looking brick arches give the Griffin the feeling of a medieval drinking hall. A broad whiskey selection is the
focus, though beers and specialty cocktails get some attention, too.
A full menu of booze-friendly food means groups of friends can
hang out here for the night, or wander down the street to several
other Atwater spots. **WHO** A young eastside party crowd. ✺

[The Hermosillo] 5125 York Blvd., Highland Park, 323.739.6459,
thehermosillo.com. Mon.-Thurs. 5 p.m.-2 a.m., Fri.-Sun. noon-2 a.m.
Beer & wine. **WHY** Johnny's is too small and divey but the York is
too big and sceney. **WHAT** The neighborhood of Highland Park
has come up in the world these last few years, and this particular
stretch of York is ground zero for the neighborhood's gentrification. This bar offers a full selection of craft brews and some
decent wines, as well as an unexpectedly tasty array of bites like

pork-belly tacos and grilled cheese sammies. The ring-toss and tabletop shuffleboard games in the back offer some fun. **WHO** Northeast L.A. hipsters. 🏚

[**Honeycut**] 819 S. Flower St., Downtown, 213.688.0888, honey-cutla.com. Nightly 8 p.m.-2 a.m. Full bar. **WHY** Sneak next door to the discotheque to boogie on a lighted dance floor, while sipping draft cocktails from the side bar. **WHAT** This stylish subterranean cocktail den offers a staggering 50 craft cocktails, many on draft, designed by celebrated bartenders Alex Day and David Kaplan. Less time waiting for a hand-muddled cocktail means more time for the dance floor. **WHO** Downtown nightlife lovers in their 20s and 30s who prefer great cocktails to club bottle service.

[**Hop Louie**] 🌴 950 Mei Ling Way, Chinatown, 213.628.4244, hoplouiela.com. Sun.-Thurs. 11 a.m.-midnight, Fri.-Sat. 11 a.m.-1:30 a.m. Full bar. **WHY** Where else can you drink in a pagoda? **WHAT** The Chinese restaurant upstairs doesn't win raves, but it's still worth stopping by the downstairs bar to experience a piece of L.A.'s vanishing Chinatown. Order a simple cocktail or bottled beer, check out the vintage cigarette machine and jukebox, and kick off your own lost weekend, film noir style. **WHO** Downtown artists, business folks feeling artsy, Dodger fans, tourists. ⟋ 💲

[**Hyperion Tavern**] 1941 Hyperion Ave., Silver Lake, 323.665.1941, hyperiontavern.com. Mon. noon–2 a.m., Tues.–Thurs. 10 p.m.–2 a.m., Fri. 9 p.m.–midnight. Beer & wine. **WHY** To drink cheap beer in a poshly decorated law library. **WHAT** This hard-to-find beer bar with sporadic hours and limited seating is full of surprises. Walk in to find two opulent chandeliers and shelves stacked full of actual law books. Thursdays fill up for Sketch Party, when the bartenders bring out butcher paper and drawing supplies and let patrons go to town. With all its restrictions and limited hours, this won't become your neighborhood go-to, but it's a great change of scenery. Cash only. **WHO** Budding artistic types still appreciative of cheap beer.

[**Jay's Bar**] 4321 Sunset Blvd., Silver Lake, 323.666.1898, jaysbar-la.com. Daily 11 a.m.-2 a.m. Full bar. **WHY** A comfortable place to actually sit down on a Friday night for a good drink. **WHAT** The nondescript strip mall exterior hides an elegant, dimly lit gastro-pub that has it all: a top-notch microbrew selection, good specialty cocktails (the Moscow Mule is a house favorite), and great food, whether you're looking for a full dinner or a quick bar snack. Bonus: a good jukebox. **WHO** Young couples on dates, groups of burly hipsters. 🏘 ♥

[Johnny's] 5006 York Blvd., Highland Park, 323.982.0775. Wed.-Mon. 2 p.m.-2 a.m., Tues. 5 p.m.-2 a.m. Full bar. **WHY** A rocking roadhouse in the middle of the city. **WHAT** Less gentrified and more diverse than some of its York Boulevard neighbors, this compact bar has a broad selection of beer, wine, and cocktails. It can get loud with a foosball, darts, and a ping-pong table keeping patrons busy. **WHO** Pierced and leather-clad guys and gals, Occidental students. 🗑

[King Eddy Saloon] 🍸 131 E. 5th St., Downtown, 213.629.2023, kingeddysaloon.com. Nightly 5 p.m.-2 a.m. Full bar. **WHY** Authors John Fante and Charles Bukowski drank at this historically seedy dive bar, which boasts the oldest continuously operating liquor license in L.A. It was recently renovated by the owners of Spring Street Bar, but thankfully, they retained most of the grit. **WHAT** Opt for an Angel City craft beer or a shot of Old Crow whiskey. In other words, keep it simple. **WHO** A sometimes uneasy but always entertaining mix of barflies wandering over from Skid Row, blue-collar DTLA workers, and Arts District loft dwellers. 🎤 🗑

[L&E Oyster Bar] 1637 Silver Lake Blvd., Silver Lake, 323.660.2255, leoysterbar.com. Mon.-Thurs. 5-10 p.m., Fri.-Sat. 5-11 p.m. Beer & wine. **WHY** Take a quick trip to the French seaside at this sophisticated seafood and wine bar. **WHAT** Upstairs, there's a cozy lounge with a romantic window seat for sipping chilled white wine with uber-fresh oysters; downstairs is a bustling bistro with a patio and small bar. Either way, the other fish-focused dishes are as good as the oysters. The well-curated wine list includes dozens of unusual selections from Slovenia and Hungary as well as France, Italy, and the U.S., while beers and ciders are also carefully selected. Not cheap, but neither is flying to Europe. **WHO** Fashionable Silver Lake folk of all ages. ☼ ♥

[La Cita Bar] 336 S. Hill St., Downtown, 213.687.7111, lacitabar. com. Mon.-Fri. 11 a.m.-2 p.m., Sat.-Sun. 10 a.m.-2 a.m. Full bar. **WHY** A spacious, fun, and sometimes rowdy spot to get a beer and get drunk with friends. **WHAT** Vibrant, grubby, relaxed, and loud, the bar is a mix of working-class Mexican guys and drunk hipsters. On Sunday afternoons, the large, mostly covered patio in back is a good spot to have a beer and nurse (or start) a hangover while cumbias play inside. In the evenings, it gets louder as all sorts of music—punk, reggae, hip-hop, and more—blasts the dance floor. **WHO** Folks who want a bucket of Bud Light bottles, people who like to boogie. ↘ 🐘 ☼

[La Cuevita] 5922 N. Figueroa St., Highland Park, 323.255.6871, lacuevitabar.com. Nightly 7 p.m.-2 a.m. Full bar. **WHY** A friendly spot that's easygoing yet sexy. **WHAT** A former goth hangout has grown up and cleaned up, adding a tequila-focused cocktail list but retaining the decorative bat motif and a punk sensibility. Free Taco Tuesdays, a happy hour that stretches to 10 p.m., and two small outdoor areas add to the fun. Reservations are available for groups. **WHO** A multicultural mix of mostly tattooed Highland Park locals. 🐘 ☼ ♥

[Las Perlas] 107 E. 6th St., Downtown, 213.988.8355, 213nightlife.com/lasperlas. Mon.-Fri. 6 p.m.-2 a.m., Sat.-Sun. 8 p.m.-2 a.m. Full bar. **WHY** This festive spot was ahead of the mezcal trend. **WHAT** An excellent tequila selection and Mexican décor that's fun but not cheesy are the highlights at this popular yet low-key bar. Distinctive cocktails like the spicy Poblano Escobar or possibly hallucinogenic Oaxacan Ferry (tequila, absinthe, and Velvet Falernum) are generally delicious, while tequila and mezcal flights are a good way to sample several varieties. The patio overlooking 6th Street is an airy spot in summer. **WHO** Downtown partiers. ☼

[Lazy Ox Canteen] 🌴 241 S. San Pedro St., Little Tokyo/Arts District, 213.626.5299, lazyoxcanteen.com. Sun.-Thurs. 11:30 a.m.-2:30 p.m. & 5-10 p.m., Fri.-Sat. 11:30 a.m.-2:30 p.m. & 5-10:30 p.m. Beer & wine. **WHY** To pretend you're in Barcelona, or the East Village, or maybe Berkeley, if only for an evening, especially if you can snag a sidewalk table. **WHAT** The chef turnover has affected the food at this no-frills, noisy modern pub on the edge of Little Tokyo, but it's consistently remained a good place to get a burger and drink, especially during happy hour (every night but Saturday from 5 to 7), when draft beers and sangrias are half-price, as are some of the small plates. There are some really interesting American small-producer beers on tap, excellent sakes, and good wines from Italy and California. **WHO** A throng of Downtown denizens who appear to lead far more interesting lives than you do. ☼

[The Lexington Bar] 129 E. 3rd St., Little Tokyo/Arts District, 213.291.5723, thelexingtonbar.com. Sun.-Thurs. 3 p.m.-2 a.m., Fri.-Sat. noon-2 a.m. Beer & wine. **WHY** Affordable drinks, daily happy hour, and no TVs, just live entertainment: open mic, karaoke, and bands. **WHAT** The atmosphere here changes throughout the day. Afternoons are casual, centered around cheap beer and wine cocktails and scribbling on the chalkboard walls. At night, it cranks up a notch as friends of the musicians and comics voice their support loudly. **WHO** A young, eclectic crew of drinkers, artists, and raunchy comics. 🪑 📷 🔍

[Library Bar] 630 W. 6th St., Downtown, 213.614.0053, librarybarla.com. Mon.-Fri. 3 p.m.-2 a.m., Sat.-Sun. 7 p.m.-2 a.m. Full bar. **WHY** A convenient literary-themed stop for an after-work drink or weekend rendezvous. **WHAT** Across the street from L.A.'s impressive main library, this bar continues the theme with shelves full of books. Seven craft beers on tap and a selection of unfussy but well-made cocktails complement a gastropub-style menu. It's not a big room, but the patio offers a bit more space. **WHO** A fairly wide age range of office dwellers, Downtown residents, and Historic Core bar crawlers. ☼

[Link N Hops] 3111 N. Glendale Blvd., Atwater, 323.426.9049, linknhops.com. Sun.-Thurs. 11 a.m.-12 a.m., Fri. 11 a.m.-1 a.m. Beer. **WHY** Craft beer, sausage, and fries are ideal partners. **WHAT** More than 20 taps of craft brews are offered at this very casual, sausage-intensive pub next to the equally worthy (and tiny) wine bar 55 Degree Wine. With a kid-friendly menu, TVs for sports fans, and vegan sausages and fish sausages, Link N Hops has the bases covered. The rustic wood walls and furniture have inspired many to call it a good-value alternative to Downtown's Wurstküche. **WHO** Neighborhood families and groups of friends. 📷 ☼

[Little Bear] 1855 Industrial St., Little Tokyo/Arts District, 213.622.8100, littlebearla.com. Mon.-Fri. 11:30 a.m.-2 a.m., Sat.-Sun. 10 a.m.-2 a.m. Full bar. **WHY** So you can pretend you live in Portland or Denver, where every local bar seems to have a selection as good as this. **WHAT** It's all about the beer—and the thick fries crisped in duck fat—at this Arts District pub where the snacks (thick burgers, bread pudding) are almost as impressive as the selection of suds. The taps are heavy on such Belgian beers as Dupont, Leifmans, and Van Steenberge, but they also feature outfits that are closer to home, like the Bruery of Placentia and Saint

Archer of San Diego. **WHO** Fans of good brew, casual socializers who like good food to go with their libations. 🏚

[Little Joy] 1477 Sunset Blvd., Echo Park, 213.935.8276. Nightly 5 p.m.-2 a.m. Full bar. **WHY** No longer a semi-scary dive, it's now a cleaned-up contender in the red-hot Echo Park bar scene. **WHAT** The former cracked-vinyl booths and grotty restrooms have given way to craft brews and specialty cocktails, but Little Joy still retains some of its earlier funky feel. The pool table remains from the dive days, but the music selection has been upgraded to vintage vinyl. A secluded side room can be reserved for parties and groups. **WHO** Dodger fans and indie band types like Strokes drummer Fabrizio Moretti, who named his side project Little Joy after this hangout in his neighborhood. 🏚

[Malo] 4326 Sunset Blvd., Silver Lake, 323.664.1011, malorestaurant.com. Mon.-Thurs. 11 a.m.-11 p.m., Fri. 11 a.m.-2 a.m., Sat. 10 a.m.-2 a.m., Sun. 10 a.m.-11 p.m. Full bar. **WHY** There's plenty of room for any occasion with a bar area, restaurant, and patio, and the tequila selection is primo. **WHAT** Malo is a Silver Lake original, with a punk-inflected jukebox, potent margaritas, and famous ground beef and pickle hard tacos. Organic, skinny, and cucumber margaritas are popular, but it's worth delving deeper into the vast tequila list to sample some lesser-known labels. **WHO** Everyone on the eastside makes it here eventually, from birthday partiers to old friends reuniting. 🏚 ☼

[Más Malo] 515 W. 7th St., Downtown, 213.985.4332, masmalorestaurant.com. Mon.-Thurs. 11 a.m.-11 p.m., Fri.-Sat. 11 a.m. -2 a.m., Sun. 11 a.m.-10 p.m. Full bar. **WHY** A multipurpose, festive Mexican spot with killer tequila selections in Downtown's cocktail gulch. **WHAT** The little sister of Silver Lake's longtime Malo has a similar menu but a much more impressive setting, with lofty frescoed ceilings, wood paneled walls, and a 1970s flashback lounge in the basement. A private tequila bar in the former jewelry store's vault is a swank place for intimate events. While the updated Mexican fare is sometimes uneven, the tequila-centric cocktails always go down perfectly, and it's a fine place to get educated in the more than 240 tequila and 30 mescals on offer. Be warned: It's loud. **WHO** Office workers at happy hour, spillovers from Seven Grand and Bottega Louie.

[Melody Lounge] 939 N. Hill St., Chinatown, 213.625.2823.
Mon.-Fri. 5 p.m.-2 a.m., Sat.-Sun. 2 p.m.-2 a.m. Beer & wine.
WHY A craft beer Mecca hides behind a funky old sign at this
Chinatown treasure. **WHAT** From the outside, Melody Lounge
appears to be a karaoke bar that has seen better days. But once
inside, a blackboard crammed with hard-to-find brews, a turntable
playing the blues, and a flotilla of festive lanterns signal that it's
now a flagship for the swinging new multicultural Chinatown.
WHO Artsy beer drinkers and Dodger fans who don't mind that
there's no food or cocktails.

[Mo-Chica] 🌴 514 W. 7th St., Downtown, 213.622.3744,
mo-chica.com. Sun.-Thurs. 11:30 a.m.-10 p.m., Fri.-Sat. 11:30 a.m.-11
p.m. Full bar. **WHY** After work or before a Downtown bar tour, the
festive cocktails at this swinging Peruvian spot will get the night
started right. **WHAT** More of a restaurant than a bar, there's a
refreshing selection of drinks like a guava pisco sour, jalapeño-in-
fused watermelon margarita, or pineapple-mezcal Oaxacalifornia
Love to go with such exotic dishes as alpaca stew. **WHO** Downtown workers, refugees from crowded nearby Bottega Louie.

[Mohawk Bend] 🌴 2141 Sunset Blvd., Echo Park, 213.483.2337,
mohawk.la. Mon.-Thurs. 11:30 a.m.-midnight, Fri. 11:30 a.m.-2 a.m.,
Sat. 9:30 a.m.-2 a.m., Sun. 9:30 a.m.-midnight. Full bar. **WHY** In a
10,000-square-foot space that held an historic theater, Mohawk
Bend boasts an enviable selection of craft beers and one of the
nicer patios in this part of town. **WHAT** A full-service restaurant
that's great for drinking, too. Ask the knowledgeable servers for
beer recommendations to help narrow it down from the whopping
72 taps, or try a thoughtfully crafted and cheekily named cocktail
from the seasonally rotating menu. **WHO** Beer freaks, vegans,
burger lovers, and hungry neighborhood residents, many of whom
sport jaunty headwear and artsy tats. ✪

[Monty Bar] 1222 W. 7th St., Westlake, 213.228.6000, montybar.
com. Sat.-Wed. 8 p.m.-2 a.m., Thurs.-Fri. 5 p.m.-2 a.m. Full bar.
WHY Cheap shots and cans of craft beer are plentiful, but the
bartenders know how make a proper gimlet, too. **WHAT** Housed
in what was formerly a seedy pool hall, this grand saloon was re-
stored to its gritty glory by Downtown bar guru Cedd Moses. Stop
by for the good happy hour on Thursdays and Fridays from 5 to 9,
or comelater on many nights for DJ-fueled fun. **WHO** A surprising

blend of young professionals and artsy types, along with salty
Westlake locals. ⟍ 🖅

[The Morrison] 3179 Los Feliz Blvd., Atwater, 323.667.1839,
themorrisonla.com. Sun.-Thurs. noon-11 p.m., Fri.-Sat. noon-1 a.m.
Full bar. **WHY** For burgers and beers after golfing or horseback riding, or try an Atwater bike-and-beer crawl from here to the area's
other pubs. **WHAT** The Morrison has a vaguely Scottish theme, but
it's more of a sports bar that also works well for groups. The menu
sticks to variations on burgers, with a solid selection of beers on
tap from both the U.S. and the U.K. and a deep whiskey list.
WHO Regular folks from Glendale, Atwater, and Frogtown. 🏯

[The Oinkster] 2005 Colorado Blvd., Eagle Rock, 323.255.OINK
(6465), theoinkster.com. Sun.-Thurs. 11 a.m.-10 p.m., Fri.-Sat. 11
a.m.-11 p.m. Beer & wine. **WHY** For a rotating selection of quality
beers and the best ube shake anywhere. **WHAT** This order-at-the-
counter gourmet fast-food joint stocks a small but tasty selection
of suds from such local breweries as Eagle Rock, Craftsman, and
Mission, and the regulars who snag patio seating often hang out
for a second round after their pulled-pork sandwiches have been
gobbled up. Even better than the beers are the milkshakes—they're
all good, but the showstopper is the one made with Filipino purple
yam (ube), coconut ice cream, and milk. It's a lavender-hued cup
of awesomeness. **WHO** Oxy students and tastefully tattooed Eagle
Rock parents with their adorably outfitted kids. 🖅 ✿

[Pattern Bar] 100 W. 9th St., South Park/Fashion District,
213.627.7774, patternbar.com. Mon.-Thurs. noon-midnight, Fri.-Sat.
noon-2 a.m. Full bar. **WHY** An oasis of civilized drinking in the
midst of the frenetic garment district. **WHAT** White-tile walls inter-
spersed with fashion-themed props like antique sewing machines
give this airy corner bar a sophisticated New York feel. Cocktails
are divided into Pret à Porter and more elaborate Haute Couture
selections, alongside a small but well-curated selection of bottled
beers and wine. Large booths and a menu of cheese, charcuterie,
and snacks make it a convenient spot for groups to watch the
Downtown action. **WHO** Fashion students from FIDM, garmentos,
artists. 🏯

[Peking Tavern] 806 S. Spring St., South Park/Fashion District, 213.988.8308, pekingtavern.com. Mon.-Wed. 5 p.m.-midnight,
Thurs.-Sat. 5 p.m.-1:30 a.m., Sun. 5-11 p.m. Full bar. **WHY** Because

it is, quite literally, an underground restaurant and bar. **WHAT** Go through an unprepossessing door on Spring Street, walk downstairs, and veer left. (Veer right and you'll be in Crane's, another nifty south Downtown bar.) If you want the sort of regionally specific, precisely executed Chinese cuisine you'll find all over the San Gabriel Valley, you're in the wrong place. If, however, you want credible pot stickers and scallion pancakes to go with a brew or a light, fizzy cocktail as you relax after work and watch the game on one of the overhead TVs, this is your spot. **WHO** Nearby office workers, Downtown residents, diners who don't want to drive out to the 626 but want Chinese food that's a little more authentic than what they'll get at their neighborhood restaurant.

[Perch] 🌴 448 S. Hill St., Downtown, 213.802.1770, perchla.com. Mon.-Wed. 4 p.m.-1 a.m., Thurs.-Fri. 4 p.m.-2 a.m., Sat. 11 a.m.-2 a.m., Sun. 11 a.m.-1 a.m. Full bar. **WHY** Because you need a rooftop bar Downtown that isn't overpriced and played out (like the Standard) or impossible to get into (like the Ace). **WHAT** This rooftop bar and restaurant boasts wraparound patios with gorgeous views of Pershing Square on one side and Bunker Hill on the other. The décor is art deco, the food is French (coq au vin, onion soup), and the vibe is mellow—but you should dress upscale casual, and come early if you don't want to deal with crowds. **WHO** People trying to impress a date, a business contact, or an out-of-town relative, and well-off Downtown hipsters and business types. ✿♥

[Public School 612] 612 S. Flower St., Downtown, 213.623.1172, publicschool612.com. Nightly 4 p.m.-midnight. Full bar. **WHY** Quality suds and happy hour in the Financial District. **WHAT** There are 20 craft drafts, with ten fixed (from such California standouts as North Coast, Green Flash, and El Segundo) and 10 rotating options, including a couple of ultra-smooth "nitros." Weekday afternoons (from 4 to 7 p.m.) feature $4 beer specials, $5 well drinks, and $10 half-liter wine carafes. **WHO** Bankers, brokers, and other members of the Downtown workforce.

[Red Lion Tavern] 🌴 2366 Glendale Blvd., Silver Lake, 323.662.5337, redliontavern.net. Daily 11 a.m.-2 a.m. Full bar. **WHY** Because it feels like Oktoberfest every day of the year. **WHAT** This 50-year-old landmark specializes in German sausages and liters of German beer from breweries like Spaten and Hofbräu. The Alpine-village decor is delightfully kitschy—even the waitresses wear traditional Bavarian getups. **WHO** Silver Lake residents craving the biergarten experience and a heaping plate of schnitzel. 🛍 🏛 ☼

[Redwood Bar & Grill] 316 W. 2nd St., Downtown, 213.680.2600, theredwoodbar.com. Daily 11 a.m.-2 a.m. Full bar. **WHY** Solid pub grub, stiff drinks, and good tunes. **WHAT** Ink-stained L.A. Times staffers used to hang out here when it was a true dive bar, but the pirate-theme update retains a certain divey feel. Fish 'n chips, crunchy coleslaw and hefty burgers go down well with ale or cocktails, which in turn are well suited to the often-worthwhile live music that happens most nights. **WHO** Downtown office workers during the day; music-loving younger folk at night.

[Rivera] 🌴 1050 S. Flower St., South Park/Fashion District, 213.749.7460, riverarestaurant.com. Mon.-Fri. 11:30 a.m.-2 p.m. & 5:30-10 p.m., Sat.-Sun. 5:30-10 p.m. Full bar. **WHY** This area of Downtown near L.A. Live can seem corporate, but the bespoke cocktails at this nuevo Latino restaurant are one of a kind. **WHAT** One of the first spots to get on board with modern mixology has gone through a few menu concepts, but the creative cocktails with Latin touches (like hard-to-find damiana liqueur) remain a high point. Ever had a cocktail garnished with crushed grasshoppers or beef jerky? Sounds strange, but they're usually delicious. The array of rare tequilas is also impressive. **WHO** Business heavyweights, concertgoers, Lakers season-ticket holders.

[The Roost] 3100 Los Feliz Blvd., Atwater, 323.664.7272, roostcocktails.com. Daily noon-2 a.m. Full bar. **WHY** One of the area's few remaining dives, with quirky décor and customers to match. **WHAT** Regulars might grumble over a makeover that brought in a full menu and got rid of the free (stale) popcorn, but it was probably high time to freshen up the poultry-themed spot for basic drinks that still boast the "stiffest pours in town." **WHO** Grizzled old-timers, rockabilly locals, slumming scenesters. 🠖 🛍

[Seven Grand] 515 W. 7th St., Downtown, 213.614.0737, sevengrandbars.com. Mon.-Wed. 5 p.m.-2 a.m., Thurs.-Fri. 4 p.m.-2 a.m., Sat.-Sun. 7 p.m.-2 a.m. Full bar. **WHY** The best whiskey selection in town. **WHAT** Known for its premium whiskey selection, this place delivers with inventive whiskey cocktails and rare bottles from master distilleries, fun to try on the rocks. Whether you can handle your dark liquor or not, the Prohibition-era vibe, pool tables, and warm, dark décor make it a fun place to check out after dinner Downtown. Expect crowds and slow service on the weekends. **WHO** A testosterone-heavy crowd. ♥

[The Short Stop] 1455 Sunset Blvd., Echo Park, 213.482.4942. Mon.-Fri. 5 p.m.-2 a.m., Sat.-Sun. 2 p.m.-2 a.m. Full bar. **WHY** It's less trendy than it once was, but there's always something going on at this historic bar. **WHAT** A longtime hangout for cops from the Rampart Division retained some of its police memorabilia when it became one of the first bars in the area to be gentrified. With a photo booth, vintage video games and pool table in one room and a DJ and dance floor in another, there's no excuse for boredom. Drink selections are fairly standard but include several craft beers, a few signature cocktails, and $2 PBRs before Dodger games. **WHO** Dodger fans, Echo Park bar crawlers.

[Smog Cutter] 864 N. Virgil Ave., Silver Lake, 323.660.4626. Daily 2 p.m.-2 a.m. Full bar. **WHY** A memorable dive bar experience and karaoke with no shame. **WHAT** The only real place to drink along this not-yet-gentrified strip of East Hollywood, it's a quick walk from Silver Lake. Enjoy the cheap drinks, be nice to the many regulars, and belt out an old tune without worrying about impressing the crowd. Note that the songbook hasn't been updated since 2002. Cash only. **WHO** Old-timers at the bar and rowdy revelers over from Silver Lake. 🦎 🎤 🔑

[Sonny's Hideaway] 5137 York Blvd., Highland Park, 323.255.2000, sonnyshideaway.com. Tues.-Sun. 5 p.m.-midnight. Full bar. **WHY** Easily the best place in Highland Park, if not most of Northeast L.A., to find prepared and intriguing cocktails. **WHAT** Austin bartender J. Kelly O'Hare and his team revive and riff on boozy beverages like bourbon fig punch and pot-still rum with amaro. The dark leather booths and dim lighting fit the mood just right. **WHO** Young and hip Highland Park locals classing it up for the evening. ♥

[The Standard] 🌴 550 S. Flower St., Downtown, 213.892.8080, standardhotels.com/downtown-la. Daily noon-1:30 a.m. Full bar. **WHY** A killer Downtown view and a rocking scene with DJs most nights. **WHAT** Relax in a waterbed pod near the tiny pool or snack on pretzels in the whimsical biergarten atop the modernistic Standard Hotel. If it's too cold to party on the roof, try the bars in the ping-pong club on the second floor. Cover charge some nights. **WHO** Young revelers.

[Taix 321 Lounge] 🌴 1911 Sunset Blvd., Echo Park, 213.484.1265, taixfrench.com. Mon.-Tues. 11:30 a.m.-1 a.m., Wed.-Sat. 11:30 a.m.-1 a.m., Sun. noon-10 p.m. Full bar. **WHY** One of L.A.'s most historic restaurants harbors a comfy lounge with non-stodgy live music. **WHAT** The dining rooms of this L.A. institution are getting a bit frayed, so stick to the lounge, where onion soup and escargots are served alongside a decent selection of beers and cocktails. Live bands, often of the alt-country variety, play semi-acoustic sets several nights a week. It's worth noting that while the food is only nominally French, Taix offers a deep wine list with some venerable vintages, sometimes at bargain prices. **WHO** Young Echo Park music and history lovers mingle with customers who've been eating and drinking at Taix for 50, 60, or 70 years. 💲 🏛

[Tam O'Shanter] 🌴 2980 Los Feliz Blvd., Atwater, 323.664.0228, tamoshanter.com. Mon.-Fri. 11 a.m.-11 p.m., Sat.-Sun. 10:30 a.m.-midnight. Full bar. **WHY** A Hollywood set designer's vision of a Scottish inn with a cozy pub area. **WHAT** The cavernous 90-year-old restaurant is full of multigenerational celebrations, but the more intimate pub area is a snug place for an Irish coffee near the fireplace. Live music on weekends and a trivia night keep the pub lively, while a dozen beers on tap emphasize American craft brews over U.K. varieties. Hand-carved meat sandwiches are available in the Ale and Sandwich Bar. **WHO** The pub area skews younger than the restaurant, but it's still a wide mix of drinkers.

[Thirsty Crow] 2939 Sunset Blvd., Silver Lake, 323.661.6007, thirstycrowbar.com. Mon.-Fri. 5 p.m.-2 a.m., Sat.-Sun. 2 p.m.-2 a.m. Full bar. **WHY** A compact whiskey-focused saloon that draws a quintessentially Silver Lake clientele. **WHAT** It's not large, but the dim lighting, round bar, and antiques-laden decor are the perfect match for the neighborhood, with #WhiskeyWednesday specials, live music on some nights, and competent cocktails. Good happy hour. **WHO** The bearded, the suspendered, the tattooed.

[Tiki Ti] 🌴 4427 Sunset Blvd., Silver Lake, 323.669.9381, tiki-ti.com. Wed.-Sat. 4 p.m.-2 a.m. Full bar. **WHY** Seats are scarce, but the flamboyant Polynesian knickknacks and knockout cocktails make this unique destination worth it. It's also one of the few bars that still allows smoking inside. **WHAT** The most iconic tiki bar in Los Angeles can trace its roots directly back to Trader Vic's, often credited for launching the national tiki movement in the 1940s. The family of bartenders running the show sling specialties like the Ray's Mistake and the Navy Grog with a backdrop of glowing volcanoes and bamboo behind them. Cash only. **WHO** Seasoned regulars and Silver Lake bar-hoppers who know the value of a properly made mai tai. 🍸 📷

[Upstairs Bar at the Ace Hotel] 933 S. Broadway, South Park/Fashion District, 213.235.9660, acehotel.com/losangeles. Daily 11 a.m.-2 a.m. Full bar. **WHY** The view. **WHAT** The issue with this pricey rooftop bar at Downtown's ultra-hot Ace Hotel is getting in. Hotel guests can waltz right in; in theory, it's pretty easy for any reasonably dressed person to get in before 8 on weeknights and before 2 p.m. on weekends. But YMMV—sometimes there's a long line, sometimes doormen seem to turn people away just because, and sometimes the whole place is taken over for a private party. If you want to make the scene at L.A.'s of-the-moment bar, try calling first to see if you can get put on the list. Or just have your agent pull strings. **WHO** Hotel guests, Downtown business hipsters, gorgeous young Asian women.

[The Varnish] 🌴 Cole's, 118 E. 6th St., Downtown, 213.622.9999, thevarnishbar.com. Nightly 7 p.m.-2 a.m. Full bar. **WHY** The pioneer in what has become a speakeasy fad in L.A., with a discreetly marked door at the back of Cole's and exquisitely crafted cocktails. **WHAT** 1920s-style barmen, a jazz soundtrack, and fresh fruit juices make the Varnish old-school—yet it's up to date on the latest in mixology. **WHO** The Downtown bar-crawling crowd is youngish, but high-end cocktails keep out drinkers looking for cheap well drinks and a loud party scene. 🎧

[Verdugo] 3408 Verdugo Rd., Glassell Park, 323.257.3408, verdugobar.com. Mon.-Fri. 6 p.m.-2 a.m., Sat.-Sun. 3 p.m.-2 a.m. Full bar. **WHY** Well-selected beers from small breweries in a location that's a bit hard to find, but worth the search. **WHAT** Choose from two rooms and a beer garden with picnic tables for sampling rare Belgian and California craft brews at this hidden hot spot. There's a full bar, wine, and special cask-beer nights, but no food—ah, but you can find plenty of taco trucks and street vendors nearby. **WHO** Craft-brew geeks from Eagle Rock, Highland Park, Silver Lake, and environs. 📷 🏠 ☼

[Villain's Tavern] 1356 Palmetto St., Little Tokyo/Arts District, 213.637.4153, villainstavern.com. Tues.-Fri. 5:30 p.m.-2 a.m., Sat.-Sun. 3 p.m.-2 a.m. Full bar. **WHY** Live music and the perfect Arts District hideaway. **WHAT** There's a lot to love about Villains: Some come for the food, some for the smoking patio, many for the great bluegrassy bands performing outside most nights, not to mention the deliciously crafted cocktails served in, of course. mason jars. **WHO** Everyone wants to pass as cats. ☼

[Wendell] 656 S. Main St., Downtown, 213.622.7200. Sun.-Wed. 8 p.m.-2 a.m., Thurs.-Sat. 4 p.m.-2 a.m. Full bar. **WHY** A small and lively bar in the heart of Downtown's most happening area. **WHAT** Along with a full selection of quality booze, this tiny bar offers a surprising quantity of great beers from across the country. Skilled bartenders whip up tasty cocktails with speed and precision, or they'll serve you a 12% Speedway Stout for just $7, an absolute steal. **WHO** A well-dressed, younger crowd hailing from the neighboring lofts. 🏚 ☼

[Wolf & Crane] 366 E. 2nd St., Little Tokyo/Arts District, 213.935.8249, wolfandcranebar.com. Mon.-Fri. 5 p.m.-2 a.m., Sat.-Sun. 3 p.m.-2 a.m. Full bar. **WHY** If you want to inject a jolt of stylish nightlife into your evening after a sushi or ramen dinner nearby. **WHAT** Little Tokyo's hip anime-tinged bar is all clean lines and polished wood, with room for dancing or lounging and a long list of quaffable highball cocktails and smooth Japanese whiskeys. DJs hold court most nights. **WHO** Weekend crowds tend to be young, Asian, and looking to party, but the happy-hour crowd is pleasantly sedate.

[Wurstküche] 800 E. 3rd St., Little Tokyo/Arts District, 213.687.4444, wurstkuche.com. Daily 11 a.m.-1:30 a.m. Beer & wine. **WHY** A relaxed beer-garden vibe, good European drafts, and great sausages. **WHAT** This industrial-hip beer garden at 3rd and Traction keeps it simple: You got your beer, your sausage, and your fries. What more could you possibly need? With your Belgian or German draft beer or cool bottled soda, have an order of crisp Belgian fries, and by all means try a sausage, too. The vegetarian ones are as good as vegetarian sausages can be, but the brats are better; adventurous sorts try the rattlesnake-rabbit-jalapeño. **WHO** By day, a youngish crowd of creative types; by night, an even younger crowd of Downtown bar-hoppers.

[The York] 🌴 5018 York Blvd., Highland Park, 323.255.9675, theyorkonyork.com. Daily 10:30 a.m.-2 a.m. Full bar. **WHY** Local microbrews, good wine by the glass, and tasty, affordable modern pub chow. Try the quick-fried garbanzo beans, the soups, the shrimp bruschetta, and the fish 'n chips. **WHAT** The pub in this high-ceilinged old brick building was one of the harbingers of what would happen to Highland Park, where home prices are shooting up and fedora-clad white kids stroll the boulevard in search of Stone IPAs. But we still love the York as much as ever. Order a drink and a bowl of homemade soup or a Cuban pulled-pork sandwich from the bartender, and someone will deliver the goods to your table. We wish it was as uncrowded as in the early days, but we're happy for the its success. **WHO** A nice mix of both newcomers and longtime residents of Highland Park and south Eagle Rock, along with slummers from Pasadena and Los Feliz.

[Yxta Cocina Mexicana] 601 S. Central Ave., Downtown, 213.596.5579, yxta.net. Mon.-Wed. 11:30 a.m.-9 p.m., Thurs.-Fri. 11:30 a.m.-10 p.m., Sat. 5-10 p.m. Full bar. **WHY** More than 60 kinds of tequila and the best margaritas Downtown. Plus great parking, almost unheard around here. **WHAT** Yxta Cocina sits in no man's land, not quite part of Downtown's Historic Core or the Arts District, which is probably why it doesn't stay open late. But the restaurant, owned by Jesse Gomez (who also owns El Arco Iris in Highland Park and two Mercados), makes great margaritas. During the daily happy hour, they're only $6 along with tasty small plates like potato tacos and shrimp taquitos. Go exotic and get the Jamaica margarita, made with hibiscus-infused tequila, or splash out and spend an extra couple bucks on the Cadillac margarita—it's so strong we can't remember what's in it, but it's worth it.
WHO Tequila connoisseurs, Arts District lofties. 🏛

SAN GABRIEL VALLEY

[1886 Bar] 🌴 The Raymond, 1250 S. Fair Oaks Ave., Pasadena, 626.441.3136, theraymond.com. Sun.-Wed. 5-10 p.m., Thurs.-Sat. 5 p.m.-2 a.m. Full bar. **WHY** Downtown-style cocktail chic in a formerly frumpy Pasadena landmark restaurant. **WHAT** It was a stroke of genius for the owners of the Raymond, a pricey restaurant in a circa-1886 cottage, to turn space over to cocktail guru Aidan Demarest (of Edison and Seven Grand fame). The drinks are terrific, the cozy interior has a real speakeasy feel, and the candlelit patio is pure romance. Fancy bar food (get the onion rings) and good but not-too-loud music. It's not cheap, so come early for happy hour if you're frugal. **WHO** Who knew Pasadena could attract such hipsters? And that said hipsters would be willing to share a bar with gray-haired Caltech professors and well-groomed Pasadena moms? ☼ ♥

[**38 Degrees Alehouse**] 100 W. Main St., Alhambra, 626.282.2038, 38degreesalhambra.com. Mon. 11:30 a.m.-midnight, Tues.-Thurs. 11:30 a.m.-1:30 a.m., Fri.-Sat. 11:30 a.m.-2 a.m., Sun. 11:30 a.m.-12:30 a.m. Beer & wine. **WHY** An excellent selection of craft beers in a somewhat unexpected location. **WHAT** 38 Degrees caters to its suburban neighborhood with sports-bar trappings and lots of TVs—but with 36 taps, the beer selection is unparalleled in the area. Try a flight to experience the full range of flavors that lean heavily on California brews but also tour such hops Meccas as Oregon, Colorado, Delaware, and Belgium. The menu has all the burgers and onion rings of the usual pub but goes a little more gastro with such dishes as a boar banh mi, jambalaya and, for dessert, a stout mousse. **WHO** Beer enthusiasts who turn out for tap takeovers from favorite brewers, sports fans. 🏟

[**Al's Cocktails**] 413 W. Las Tunas Dr., San Gabriel, 626.281.8638. Daily 7 a.m.-2 a.m. Full bar. **WHY** Some bars are just kind of divey, but Al's is the real thing. **WHAT** From the neon sign out front, to the friendly bartenders and cheap drinks inside, all the way to the man at the end of the bar who's been there since it opened at 7 a.m., this is an old-fashioned community watering hole. Cash only. **WHO** Day drinkers who enjoy an afternoon at the bar and twenty-somethings looking for a cheap night out with friends. 🔧 💲

[**Altadena Ale & Wine House**] 2329 Fair Oaks Ave., Altadena, 626.794.4577, altadenaalehouse.com. Mon.-Fri. 5 p.m.-2 a.m., Sat.-Sun. 3 p.m.-2 a.m. Beer & wine. **WHY** A proper locals' pub, where conversation is valued as much as the temperature of the Guinness. **WHAT** It was a risk for the owners to open this flea-market-furnished pub on North Fair Oaks in a "transitional" part of Altadena, but their risk has been rewarded with a loyal clientele, who come to enjoy the surprisingly deep selection of international beers (English, Irish, Belgian, American) and French wines, as well as a few terrific Champagnes and ciders. If you're lucky, a talented team of taco-makers will have set up shop out by the back door to balance out the alcohol with some nourishment. **WHO** JPL scientists, construction workers, artists—a typical Altadena mix. 💲

[Barney's Beanery] 99 E. Colorado Blvd., Old Pasadena, 626.405.9777, barneysbeanery.com. Daily 10 a.m.-2 a.m. Full bar. **WHY** Three levels of cheap drinks, karaoke, billiards, foosball, and reveling college students. **WHAT** It's hard to describe Barney's as a singular establishment, because it really seems like three. On the main level there's a massive bar, colorful vinyl booths, abundant flat-screens, and a converted double-decker bus; in the basement, amateur vocalists belt out '80s rock anthems; and upstairs is Q's pool hall. Even with all this space, be warned that it gets really crowded on weekends. **WHO** Raucous PCC and Caltech kids, pool sharks, karaoke enthusiasts. 🐾🏸🔧

[The Blind Donkey] 53 E. Union St., Old Pasadena, 626.792.1833, theblinddonkey.com. Mon.-Fri. 4 p.m.-2 a.m., Sat.-Sun. 1 p.m.-2 a.m. Full bar. **WHY** The best whiskey bar in the SGV also serves solid beers and inventive cocktails. **WHAT** The whiskey selection here is unparalleled for miles in any direction, featuring some of the best bottles from the U.S., Ireland, and, of course, Scotland. If bourbon and single-malts aren't your thing, the eight rotating taps always feature quality suds, and it has great Belgian bottles, too. The bartenders are friendly and approachable—don t hesitate to ask questions or get advice. **WHO** Aficionados of fine bourbon, rye, whiskey, and scotch. 🍸

[The Colorado Bar] 2640 E. Colorado Blvd., East Pasadena, 626.449.3485. Daily noon-1:30 a.m. Full bar. **WHY** Stiff, cheap drinks, pool tables, a surprising amount of quality brews, friendly bartenders, and an eclectic jukebox make this East Pasadena's go-to dive bar. **WHAT** A true neighborhood watering hole, this venerable Pasadena bar is a friendly place where people become regulars quickly. Check out the jukebox, full of nostalgia—the bartender might even sponsor a few songs if he likes your musical taste. **WHO** A crowd as diverse as the music selection: weathered war vets, quasi-philosophers from PCC, and blue-collar workers of all ages. 🔧 🐾🏸

[Congregation Ale House] 300 S. Raymond Ave., Pasadena, 626.403.2337, congregationalehouse.com. Mon.-Thurs. 11:30 a.m.-1 a.m., Fri. 11:30 a.m.-2 a.m., Sat. 11 a.m.-2 a.m., Sun. 11 a.m.-midnight. Beer & wine. **WHY** A mellow hangout with excellent tap beer, a great front patio, and tasty sausages. **WHAT** The pub this part of Pasadena had been waiting for, Congregation has a goofy church-of-beer theme, complete with waitresses in Catholic school uniforms. Its popularity has made parking a challenge, but it's worth walking a block or two to sit with a few friends on a patio table to enjoy a Belgian ale and a duck sausage on a bun. **WHO** Art Center and Caltech grad students, tech startup folks, beer lovers of all ages. 🍷 🎎 ☼

[Dog Haus Biergarten] 93 E. Green St., Old Pasadena, 626.683.0808, doghaus.com. Sun.-Thurs. 11 a.m.-midnight, Fri.-Sat. 11 a.m.-2 a.m. Full bar. **WHY** For the build-your-own Bloody Mary bar, $10 beer/shot creations, fancy hot dogs, and "Sunday Funday" (all day happy hour on Sundays). **WHAT** While there's always a solid draft list, don t let the name fool you—this beer garden also has a full bar, and well drinks are just $4 during happy hour. There are equally good deals on select drafts. Settle in at a communal table with an Old Town Dog and an ale and you'll make some new friends in no time flat. **WHO** A hip, younger crowd with an affinity for the affordable. 💵 🎎 ☼

[The Flintridge Proper] 464 Foothill Blvd., La Cañada, 818.790.4888, theproper.com. Mon.-Thurs. 11:30 a.m.-midnight, Fri. 11:30 a.m.-1 a.m., Sat. 8:30 a.m.-1 a.m., Sun. 8:30 a.m.-10 p.m. Full bar. **WHY** Well-made cocktails, an excellent daily happy hour, and a clubby setting that makes you forget you're in a strip mall. **WHAT** The Proper is an upscale but informal hangout for La Cañada's lawyers, bankers, and real estate brokers. The food isn't as good as we'd like, but the bar makes a proper cocktail, and if you're a gin drinker, you'll be in heaven—it boasts the largest gin selection in L.A. **WHO** Prosperous La Cañadans who are fine with paying $15 for a burger and $12 for a cocktail (which is actually not bad, given cocktail prices these days).

[Freddie's 35er] 12 E. Colorado Blvd., Old Pasadena, 626.356.9315, 35erbar.com. Mon.-Thurs. 3 p.m.-2 a.m., Fri. 12:30 p.m.-2 a.m., Sat.-Sun. 10 a.m.-2 a.m. Full bar. **WHY** Affordable booze and monthly $3 beer specials make this a good stop on an Old Town bar hop. **WHAT** Part sports, part dive bar, Freddie's is bigger than it looks from the front. The main level is dotted with TVs, while the basement is a dark lounge and dance area. No cover and reasonable drinks draw the younger clientele; spinning DJs in the basement add to the appeal. **WHO** Twenty- and thirtysomethings crawling around Colorado Boulevard's many watering holes; grizzled sports fans swilling cheap domestic beer. 🥃 💵 🎎 ☼

[The Glendale Tap] 4227 San Fernando Rd., Glendale, 818.241.4227. Mon.-Thurs. 5 p.m.-2 a.m., Fri.-Sun. 1 p.m.-2 a.m. Beer & cider. **WHY** A hidden gem for beer lovers with pool tables and and a rocking jukebox. **WHAT** Beer and cider are the only drinks at this mellow spot between Atwater and Glendale, but oh, what a selection, with 52 taps ranging from Smog City's Saber Tooth Squirrel to Stone Espresso Imperial Russian stout. Bartenders are happy to dole out tastes, while peanuts, pretzels, and pasties help wash down the suds in this bar decorated with car memorabilia. **WHO** Committed hopheads and refugees from the crowded bars of Silver Lake. 🍺

[Griffin's of Kinsale] 1007 Mission St., South Pasadena, 626.799.0926, griffinsofkinsale.com. Mon.-Tues. 3:30 p.m.-1 a.m., Wed.-Fri. 3:30 p.m.-2 a.m., Sat. noon-2 a.m., Sun. noon-midnight. Full bar. **WHY** Actual nightlife in South Pas! **WHAT** A proper Irish pub a short walk from the South Pas Metro station, Griffin's is a real neighborhood place, where the guy who owns the toy store up the street might play a set with a friend on a Thursday night. The acoustics aren't great (it gets loud) and furnishings are sparse, but the Guinness, pub grub, and conviviality make up for any shortcomings. **WHO** Guinness fans, Irish-music buffs, families, and barflies.

[Jay-Dee Café] 1843 W. Main St., Alhambra, 626.281.6887. Daily 6 a.m.-2 a.m. Full bar. **WHY** Because after you've finished your Fosselman's milkshake across the street, you need an adult libation. **WHAT** Despite its name, this is no café. This is a dive bar, maybe the only one in Alhambra, and it comes complete with a jukebox, a dart board, and a pool table. Outside, it's an unremarkable gray-brown building. Inside, there's a giant stuffed moose head, sports paraphernalia, and photos from patrons. There are maybe three beers on tap, but you don't come here for artisanal suds. You plunk yourself on a bar stool, order a Corona, and do this day after day until you become a regular. **WHO** Anyone who likes friendly conversation, cheap beer, and pretending they're in a saloon in the Midwest. 🍺

[King's Row] 20 E. Colorado Blvd., Old Pasadena, 626.793.3010, kingsrowpub.com. Mon.-Thurs. 10:30 a.m.-1 a.m., Fri.- Sat. 10:30 a.m.-2 a.m., Sun. 11 a.m.-2 a.m. Full bar. **WHY** Beer is serious business at Old Pasadena's original gastropub. **WHAT** It seems like new gastropubs pop up every week, jumping on the craft-beer bandwagon, but too many forget to focus on the "pub" part of the equation. Not so at King's Row, where GM James Willis also acts as resident Cicerone and professional beer buyer. Expect superb bottles and drafts from small breweries, as well as highly acclaimed Belgian ales. **WHO** Ale aficionados from all over the SGV. 🎏 ☼

[Lucky Baldwins] 17 S. Raymond Ave., Old Pasadena, 626.795.0652, luckybaldwins.com. Daily 8:30 a.m.-1:30 a.m. Beer & wine. **WHY** For 63 beers on tap, including some wonderful Belgians, along with such reliable pub standards as pasties and a tasty chicken curry. **WHAT** Co-owner David Farnsworth is originally from the north of England, and with partner Peggy Simonian he's created an authentically English pub in a brick-walled Old Town space, with nooks, crannies, and a lovely patio on the pedestrian alley in back. Aficionados come from far away for such annual events as the Belgian beer festival in February and Oktoberfest, when German beers are front and center. **WHO** Caltech students, professors, and others who prefer earnest conversation over a good pint to a raucous bar scene. 🍸 🗺 ☼

[Lucky Baldwins Delirium Pub & Café] 21 Kersting Court, Sierra Madre, 626.355.1140, luckybaldwins.com. Daily 8:30 a.m.-1:30 a.m. Beer & wine. **WHY** For 46 beers on tap, with great choices from Ireland, England, and Belgium, and solid English fare, including a good chicken curry. **WHAT** A pleasantly old-school pub (pressed tin ceilings, polished wooden floors, walled patio) that perfectly suits its old-fashioned setting in Sierra Madre's village center. In the back is a tiny but richly rewarding package shop with a few British foodstuffs and hard-to-get beers. **WHO** Patagonia-clad locals taking a break from restoring their Craftsman cottages and hiking the Mt. Wilson Trail. 🍸 🗺 ☼

[Neat] 1114 N. Pacific Ave., Glendale, 818.241.4542, neatbarglendale.com. Mon.-Wed. 4:30 p.m.-12:30 a.m., Thurs.-Fri. 4:30 p.m.-2 a.m., Sat. 7 p.m.-2 a.m., Sun. 7 p.m.-midnight. Full bar. **WHY** Hip but not pretentious, with a dark, clubby feel, a fireplace, and a great half-price happy hour weekdays from 4:30 to 6:30. **WHAT** The gimmick in this small, cozy bar is that drinks are served neat. When it first opened, whiskeys were the specialty; that's given way somewhat to craft cocktails served in two glasses, one with the booze, the other with the mix of juices/bitters/whatever. You can still get a good whiskey neat, listen to great music that's not too loud, and discuss Richard Linklater films and the state of the Pixies' music with a couple of friends. **WHO** Who knew Glendale had so many dudes with fedoras and skinny pants? ♥

[Old Towne Pub] 66 N. Fair Oaks Ave., Old Pasadena, 626.577.6583, theoldtownepub.com. Nightly 4 p.m.-2 a.m. Full bar. **WHY** For live music and an open-air beer garden in a hidden Old Town alley. **WHAT** It feels like you re a wizard bringing friends here for the first time, as it really is hidden (walk north from Colorado up Fair Oaks on the east side of the street and look for a green gate near Holly). Inside you'll find rock and punk bands on a minuscule stage, reasonably priced drinks, and a smoke-filled back porch. It's also a little cleaner than most dives, although the bathrooms can be suspect. **WHO** The cool kids and those aspiring to be cool. ⟍ 📷 🏚 ☼

[Otis Bar at La Grande Orange] 260 S. Raymond Ave., Old Pasadena, 626.356.4444, lagrandeorangecafe.com. Mon.-Thurs. 11 a.m.-10 p.m., Fri. 11 a.m.-11 p.m., Sat. 10 a.m.-11 p.m., Sun. 9 a.m.-9 p.m. Full bar. **WHY** Classy bar and lounge with direct access to the Gold Line's Del Mar Station. **WHAT** The Metro system in L.A. is the safest way to bar hop between neighborhoods, and Otis might be the closest to any stop we know of. Less than a minute's walk from the platform, and you ll be planted in big, cushy seats sipping a hand-crafted cocktail. The Misfit (a grapefruit-basil gimlet) or Sara's Aperol Spritz are both winners. **WHO** Affluent, well-dressed businessmen and women. ♥

[Slaters 50/50] 61 N. Raymond Ave., Old Pasadena, 626.765.9700, slaters5050.com. Sun.-Thurs. 11 a.m.-11 p.m., Fri.-Sat. 11 a.m.-midnight. Full bar. **WHY** Offering 100 taps of quality beer from all over the country and world, Slaters served more than 1,000 different draught beers in 2013. **WHAT** With plenty of flat screens and an immense beer selection, Slaters is the perfect spot to grab a pint and watch the game. This is especially true during their happy hour, when a rotating selection of 10 (mostly craft) beers are offered for only $3.50, a steal for L.A. **WHO** Suds and sports fans from around the Southland. 📷 🏚

[T. Boyle's Tavern] 37 N. Catalina Ave., Pasadena, 626.578.0957, tboylestavern.com. Mon.-Fri. 3 p.m.-2 a.m., Sat.-Sun. 11 a.m.-2 a.m. Beer & wine. **WHY** A solid selection of draft beer, as well as free darts, pool, and shuffleboard; Action Trivia nights on

Sundays and Tuesdays are fun. **WHAT** Located down a small alley (Rhodes Alley) parallel to Colorado Boulevard, this low-key brick pub is semi-hidden, which might suggest a speakeasy. But inside the single heavy door, it's revealed to be more a roomy sports bar than anything else, with more than ten TVs, copious amounts of beer, and smack-talking sports buffs. The weeknight happy hour brings $1 tacos and discounts on all the tap beers. **WHO** L.A. sports fans, PCC and Caltech students, and that one guy who never loses at pool. ⌇ 🏦 🏛

[**The Tap Room**] 🌴 Langham Huntington Hotel, 1401 S. Oak Knoll Ave., Pasadena, 626.568.3900, pasadena.langhamhotels.com. Mon.-Thurs. 2 p.m.-1 a.m., Fri.-Sat. noon-2 a.m., Sun. noon-midnight. Full bar. **WHY** When you need to celebrate or seduce. **WHAT** Our favorite eastside place to celebrate a big occasion, the Langham's bar is a thing of beauty, from the old-money, living room–style interior to the fabulous heated terrace overlooking the hotel grounds. The cocktails and the bar chow (lobster corn dogs, Kobe beef sliders) are as superb as the bill is high. But it's less expensive, and lots more fun, to eat and drink here than at the hotel's ambitious dining room. **WHO** New-era prepsters from the best Pasadena families. 🦻 🏛 ✿ ♥

EAST VALLEY

[**Black Market Liquor Bar**] 11915 Ventura Blvd., Studio City, 818.446.2533, blackmarketliquorbar.com. Nightly 5 p.m.-2 a.m. Full bar. **WHY** Another restaurant that's worth coming to just for the cocktails. **WHAT** The place doesn't have much signage, but once you find it, it's like you've stepped into basement of a stylish modern castle. The drink menu, developed by bartenders Pablo Moix and Steve Livigni, changes weekly, which means the cocktails are playful, seasonally inspired, and sometimes quite strong. And they go great with the house-made dill potato chips. **WHO** Residents of the Valley who want to drink like they're in Los Feliz. ♥

[**Blue Dog Beer Tavern**] 4524 Saugus Ave., Sherman Oaks, 818.990.2583, bluedogbeertavern.com. Mon.-Fri. 11:30 a.m.-11 p.m., Sat.-Sun. 11 a.m.-11 p.m. Beer & wine. **WHY** A relaxed neighborhood bar with an uncommonly good beer selection and premium burgers. **WHAT** If you've ever wished your favorite craft beer bar served decent food, you're finally home. The burgers are large and messy, made with high-quality stuff, and they're a buck or two cheaper than they'd be at most self-proclaimed gastropubs. Can't decide between a pilsner and a Belgian strong ale? Choose a flight of four beers from any of their eight taps. Another three dozen bottles and cans round out the impressive beer menu. Any place that has Unibroue's Fin du Monde on tap knows a thing or two about beer. **WHO** Beer fiends, burger hounds, cubicle dwellers splurging on lunch, thirty- and fortysomethings relaxing and chatting, and younger folks whooping it up and flirting. ☼

[**District Pub NoHo**] 5249 Lankershim Blvd., North Hollywood, 818.732.7319, districtpubnoho.com. Sun.-Thurs. 11 a.m.-midnight, Fri.-Sat. 11 a.m.-2 a.m. Beer & wine. **WHY** A generous selection of craft beer (discounted at the daily 2 to 7 p.m. happy hour), as well as fantastic gourmet sausages and burgers. **WHAT** In the heart of NoHo's Arts District, this trendy gastropub gives a nod to its old Hollywood roots with mounted black-and-white photos and round-the-clock showings of Turner Classics. Grab a quick drink at the bar to enjoy on the outdoor patio or have a seat inside and try the bratwurst—or be adventurous and go for the alligator. **WHO** Art Institute students, beer enthusiasts, Arts District wanderers. ☼

[**El Bar**] 3256 Cahuenga Blvd. W., Universal City, 323.851.5111, vintagebargroup.com/el-bar.php. Mon.-Fri. 5 p.m.-2 a.m., Sat.-Sun. 8 p.m.-2 a.m. Full bar. **WHY** Tasty $3 margaritas at happy hour (weeknights 5 to 9), comfy seating for small groups, and a good strip-mall location in a neighborhood that needed a chill bar. **WHAT** This member of the Vintage Bar Group avoids the corporate-chain-bar feel, thanks to its easygoing atmosphere, sofa seating areas, and dim red lighting. The theme is ostensibly Spanish/Mexican, although that's not particularly evident in the drink menu, other than the good tequila list. The DJ keeps the music at conversation-allowing levels, at least before 9 p.m. **WHO** Hollywood Hills thirtysomethings and an after-work crowd from the many nearby studios, production companies, and network offices. 🏠 ♥

[**The Federal Bar**] 5303 Lankershim Blvd., North Hollywood, 818.980.2555, thefederalbar.com. Mon.-Sat. 11:30 a.m.-2 a.m., Sun. 10 a.m.-2 a.m. Full bar. **WHY** Great crowd, tunes, drinks, and brews, although the food could use a little improvement. **WHAT** Music venue operator Knitting Factory Entertainment runs this gastropub in an old bank building, which has upscale pub fare and plenty of microbrews and wines to wash it all down. Burgers

are a good bet, particularly the Greco lamb burger with feta and tzatziki. Live music in the upstairs lounge many nights.
WHO NoHo hipsters and studio workers kicking back.

[The Good Nite] 10721 Burbank Blvd., North Hollywood, 818.850.3485, thegoodnite.com. Nightly 9 p.m.-2 a.m. Full bar. **WHY** You've set your heart on singing karaoke, even if it is a Monday. Or a Tuesday. Or a Wednesday. **WHAT** The Good Nite provides entertainment every night of the week: In addition to the nightly karaoke, there's a comedy open mic every Monday, frequent DJ appearances, and themed events that typically have drink discounts. If you're looking for a place to sing, party, or dance on a stripper pole, it's a good bet. Check the online calendar before you head over. **WHO** Youngsters looking to blow off steam. 🎤 🔧

[Laurel Tavern] 🌴 11938 Ventura Blvd., Studio City, 818.506.0777, laureltavern.net. Daily noon-2 a.m. Full bar. **WHY** Great drinking and a well-edited lineup of scrumptious bar food, including skewered chunks of pork belly so succulent they'll make you weak in the knees. **WHAT** The Valley's coolest gastropub is a long, streamlined room with exposed brick walls and French doors opening onto the busy boulevard. Some of the nicest barkeeps in town make sure patrons are well lubricated with tasty $12 craft cocktails, an ambitious California-centric draft-beer list, and terrific wines by the glass (almost all $10 or less) or bottle. To eat are excellent burgers, a top-notch house salad; and a generous bowl of steamed P.E.I. mussels. **WHO** Industry folk unwinding after a long day behind the cameras and neighbors who have adopted this as their local.

[The Local Peasant] 14058 Ventura Blvd., Sherman Oaks, 818.501.0234, thelocalpeasant.com. Mon.-Fri. 4 p.m.-2 a.m., Sat.-Sun. 11 a.m.-2 a.m. Full bar. **WHY** Terrific small-plates fare and upscale nibbles to go with cocktails, wine, and microbrews. **WHAT** The peasants of Sherman Oaks and environs quickly made themselves at home here, where well-made cocktails, a lengthy list of craft beers, and hand-picked bottlings from nearby wineries help fuel the buzz. We can't resist the crisp potato chips sprayed with malt vinegar, or the deviled eggs with bacon, or the grilled peach salad with fennel. Be prepared: When the Peasant gets busy (most nights), the noise level is excruciating. **WHO** Locals relaxing after a day at the office or on the set, and gastropub pilgrims making the rounds.

🌴 ESSENTIALLY L.A.   ➘ DIVE   🍸 QUIET   💲 VALUE

[NoBAR] 10622 Magnolia Blvd., North Hollywood, 818.753.0545, vintagebargroup.com/no-bar.php. Mon.-Thurs. 7 p.m.-2 a.m., Fri. 6 p.m.-2 a.m., Sat.-Sun. 8 p.m.-2 a.m. Full bar. **WHY** For an inviting NoHo hangout and a very generous happy hour: every night until 10 it has two-for-one cocktails, $5 wines, and $2 PBRs. **WHAT** This faux dive bar is part of the Vintage group that owns several other similar places, and we have to give them credit for doing it right. Interesting jukebox, good pool table, exceptionally nice bartenders, and a great, late happy hour. **WHO** Good-looking but not too fratty twenty- and thirtysomethings; friends meeting for a drink and a chat after work. 🍸 🏠

[Oil Can Harry's] 11502 Ventura Blvd., Studio City, 818.760.9749, oilcanharrysla.com. Mon. & Wed. 3:30-7:30 p.m., Thurs. 3:30 p.m.-12:30 a.m., Fri. 3:30 p.m.-2 a.m., Sat. 8 p.m.-2 a.m., Sun. 11:30 a.m.-9 p.m. Full bar. **WHY** For excellent karaoke upstairs on Fridays and Saturdays, country line dancing on Thursdays, and the hugely popular retro disco dancing on Saturdays. **WHAT** One of L.A.'s most convivial and straights-friendly gay bars, Oil Can Harry's is just plain fun. It's technically a gay cowboy bar that's partial to country music, but all types come here. The smallish dance floor is always full, and the $1 jello shots fuel the upstairs karaoke, which is one of the best in town. Cash only. **WHO** Gay men and the straight women and men who love them. 🎤

[Pineapple Hill Saloon & Grill] 4454 Van Nuys Blvd., Sherman Oaks, 818.789.0679, pineapplesaloon.com. Daily 11:30 a.m.-2 a.m. Full bar. **WHY** For a no-frills, conversation-oriented bar in the heart of the Valley. **WHAT** It's not a sports bar, but there's always a game or match on; it's not a theme bar, but Wednesday is '80s night, when regulars crank up the big hair; it's not a skanky dive bar, but it's not a craft-cocktail joint either. Pineapple Hill is just a good Val place to get a drink and catch up with a friend or make a new one. The food is best avoided. **WHO** Valley grownups, some of whom have been hoisting here for a decade or two. 🍸 🍸

[The Red Door] 🍸 10057 Riverside Dr., Toluca Lake, 818.277.3884. Sun.-Fri. 5 p.m.-2 a.m., Sat. 8 p.m.-2 a.m. Full bar. **WHY** A chill, chic watering hole in Toluca Lake with a speakeasy vibe and decent upscale bar food. **WHAT** Enter from the alley in back, look for the red door, and head in to the best studio bar in the Valley. The music's good and not so loud that conversation is impossible (at least before 10), the lights are dim, the cocktails are well made, and the vibe is relaxed. Come early if you want to snag one of the comfy, low-slung couches. **WHO** TV directors, grips, day players, DPs, editors—in short, an everyday studio crowd. ♥

[Sardo's] 🌴 259 N. Pass Ave., Burbank, 818.846.8126, sardosbar. com. Mon.-Sat. 10 a.m.-2 a.m., Sun. 9:30 a.m.-2 a.m. Full bar. **WHY** Because you've always wondered if porn stars can sing. **WHAT** Tuesday is porn-star karaoke night (really—it's called PSK for short) and Friday is family night (really). Only in Burbank! The rest of the week brings comedy and music open mic (Mondays), professional comedy (Wednesdays), trivia (Thursdays), and huge TVs if you're looking to catch the game; karaoke happens every night. The food isn't great, but the cheap drinks and numerous events make Sardo's a fun and popular place. No cover but an enforced two-drink minimum. **WHO** Experienced karaoke singers, lively groups of twentysomethings, lots of regulars. 🍸 🎎 🔭

[Tiki No] 4657 Lankershim Blvd., North Hollywood, 818.766.0116. Nightly 5 p.m.-2 a.m. Full bar. **WHY** Enjoy serious, well-made cocktails without the pretensions: the bar uses fresh-squeezed juices, traditional Caribbean rums, and a fantastic selection of tiki mugs. **WHAT** This modern tiki bar, complete with lit torches outside, received a menu ramped up by the guys behind the Roger Room. Try a frozen piña colada or the concoction called Chief Lapu Lapu. **WHO** A rather young, fun-loving Studio City crowd looking for a casual hangout. 🍸

[Tonga Hut] 🌴 12808 Victory Blvd., North Hollywood, 818.769.0708, tongahut.com. Nightly 4 p.m.-2 a.m. Full bar. **WHY** If you try all 80 tiki drinks in one year, you'll gain a plaque on the "Wall of Drooling Bastards." **WHAT** This North Hollywood gem claims the title of oldest tiki bar in Los Angeles. With thatched booths, a miniature waterfall, and a jukebox filled with surf rock, the room is as much fun as the drinks. **WHO** Nostalgic Valleyites looking for offbeat cocktails and a taste of retro L.A.

[Tony's Darts Away] 🌴 1710 W. Magnolia Blvd., Burbank, 818.253.1710, tonysda.com. Mon.-Thurs. noon-2 a.m., Fri. 11 a.m.-2 a.m., Sat. 10 a.m.-2 a.m., Sun. 10 a.m.-1 a.m. Beer & wine. **WHY** Because darts, vegan sausages, and quality beer go well together. Even in Burbank. **WHAT** A neighborhood pub with more than 40 draft beers, Tony's has a no-bottle policy—all beers, wines, and sodas are served on draft. The multi-animal/no-animal sausage menu comes with the de rigueur selection of über toppings, and a nice chili comes "sin carne" for vegetarians. A few good salads, sweet potato fries, and house-made potato chips round out the menu. Oh, and did we mention darts? **WHO** Eco-beer geeks and studio refugees who don't feel the need to be seen in Hollywood or Downtown. 🐨

WEST VALLEY

[Ireland's 32] 13721 Burbank Blvd., Van Nuys, 818.785.4031, irelands32.com. Mon.-Fri. noon-1:30 a.m., Sat.-Sun. 10 a.m.-1:30 a.m. Full bar. **WHY** A friendly Irish pub in the heart of the Valley, with the right sort of beer (Guinness, Harp, Smithwick's), good live music, and karaoke. **WHAT** More a dive bar than a charming Irish pub, this is still an Irish bar through and through. The draft beer is good, the bands are fun (sometimes country, sometimes soul, sometimes Irish), and the Tuesday and Sunday karaoke nights are terrific. The weeknight happy hour (until 8 p.m.) is a bargain. **WHO** A friendly mix, from twentysomethings here to see a band or sing karaoke to red-faced, middle-aged guys honoring their Irish heritage by drinking too much. 📶 🐨 🀄 🔑

[Pickwick's Pub] 21010 Ventura Blvd., Woodland Hills, 818.340.9673, pickwickpub.com. Sun.-Wed. 11 a.m.-midnight, Thurs.-Sat. 11 a.m.-1:30 a.m. Full bar. **WHY** Fourteen draft beers (stouts, lagers, ales, and ciders) at modest prices, live music, and a fun trivia night. **WHAT** A proper English pub with a proper English barkeep, often-good bands, and acceptable pub grub. The pretty, open-layout room is equally comfortable for dining or just getting together for drinks. Note that in football season, it's a Packers hangout. **WHO** Friendly and loyal West Valley regulars, mostly young, including some very good darts players. 🎵 🐨

WESTSIDE: CENTRAL

[Akasha] 🌴 9543 Culver Blvd., Culver City, 310.845.1700, akasharestaurant.com. Mon.-Thurs. 8 a.m.-9:30 p.m., Fri. 8 a.m.-10:30 p.m., Sat. 9 a.m.-10:30 p.m., Sun 10:30 a.m.-9 p.m. Full bar. **WHY** Because you want a farm-to-table restaurant where the cocktails are as good as the food. **WHAT** Located on a prime corner of Culver City's restaurant row, chef Akasha Richmond's market-driven restaurant is stylish, not pretentious, sustainable without being bland, and grown-up but not stuffy. The libations generally involve organic liquors mixed with fresh fruit syrups and veggie purées, which you can sip at a streetside table while watching stylish locals stroll by. As a bonus, the wine list is pretty damn good. **WHO** Westside foodies, Sony employees, a devout cadre of neighborhood residents, and fans of sustainable fare.

[Alibi Room] 12236 Washington Blvd., Culver City, 310.390.9300, alibiroomla.com. Mon.-Sat. 5:30 p.m.-2 a.m. Beer & wine. **WHY** To eat Kogi's tacos and other good things without having to stand in line at the truck—plus you can have a Duvel Golden Ale or Los Carlos Malbec with your kim chee–sesame quesadilla. **WHAT** We loved this chill neighborhood pub before Kogi took over the kitchen, and now we love it more, although now too many other people do, too. Come early if you want to snag some of the comfy, low-slung seating, and go wild sampling the Korean tacos, Korean spiced fries, and tofu and citrus salad. To drink are good-value wines by the glass, bottled beers, and a handful of hip draft brews.
WHO Twentysomething studio toilers meeting after work, with some middle-aged Culver City locals for good measure. ⑤

[The Arsenal] 12012 W. Pico Blvd., West L.A., 310.575.5511, arsenalbar.com. Tues.-Fri. 5 p.m.-2 a.m., Sat. 6 p.m.-2 a.m. Full bar. **WHY** You're on the westside, where interesting watering holes aren't abundant, but even if they were, you'd still choose to come here. **WHAT** In addition to boasting an awesome neon sign, the bar displays an impressive array of old-timey guns and weaponry on its walls. (It is called the Arsenal, after all.) It's dark and divided into two main areas, the mellow bar and restaurant side and the loud, clubby side. After being spruced up a few years ago, it's less of a dive than it once was, but beer and basic cocktails (G&T, rum and Coke) are still your best bets. That advice is true for the food: Stick to the burgers and poutine fries. **WHO** Longtime westsiders and twentysomethings who want a place to party without going to a club. ⌟

[Backstage Bar & Grill] 10400 Culver Blvd., Culver City, 310.839.3892, backstageculvercity.com. Daily 11 a.m.-2 a.m. Full bar. **WHY** The drinks here are already cheap, but the daily happy hour (yup, weekends too) from 4 to 8 makes it easy to become a regular here. **WHAT** Here's a place that wears its dive-bar status as a badge of honor. Except for the competition among karaoke divas, there's nothing stylish and no scene here—and that's why pretty much everyone in the area ends up at the Backstage sooner or later.

WHO *American Idol* wannabes, Sony employees who don't have expense accounts, cool kids, scuzzballs, cubicle drones set free after another day of servitude. ⚲ 🎤 🏚 🔑

[The Bar & Lounge] 🍸 Hotel Bel-Air, 701 Stone Canyon Rd., Bel-Air, 310.472.1211, dorcestercollection.com. Mon.-Thurs. 2:30 p.m.-midnight, Fri.-Sat. 2:30 p.m.-2 a.m., Sun. 11 a.m.-midnight. Full bar. **WHY** For a small-batch bourbon or a meticulously crafted cocktail served in Baccarat, in a setting of serene luxury.
WHAT To celebrate a big anniversary or your company's acquisition for eight figures, hoist a few in the bar in one of the country's finest hotels. Spago's Lee Hefter created the cocktails, as well as the bar menu (a perfect club sandwich for $19). Settle into a modern club chair by the fireplace, listen to the low-key live music, and revel in the 1% life. **WHO** The genuinely wealthy and the trying-to-be-wealthy. 🍸 ♥

[The Bar at the Culver Hotel] 9400 Culver Blvd., Culver City, 310.558.9400, culverhotel.com. Mon.-Thurs. 7 a.m.-11 p.m., Fri.-Sat. 7 a.m.-2 a.m., Sun. 7 a.m.-10 p.m. Full bar. **WHY** Drink where the Munchkins once stayed. **WHAT** A National Historic Landmark, this beautiful triangular structure, opened in 1924 and once owned by Charlie Chaplin (who reportedly lost it to John Wayne in a poker game), is most famous as the residence for members of the Wizard of Oz cast during the film's 1938 production. The hotel has two bars: In the lobby, you can sink into an armchair as you gaze at the gorgeous gilded decor and listen to jazz in the evenings. Upstairs, at the small speakeasy-style Velvet Lounge (only open Thursday to Saturday after 8 p.m.), sip a perfect manhattan and pretend it's still the Jazz Age. **WHO** Flappers, bootleggers, history buffs. ♥

[Bigfoot West] 10939 Venice Blvd., Palms, 310.287.2200, bigfootwest.com. Nightly 5 p.m.-2 a.m. Full bar. **WHY** Because you want to get your buzz on in a bar with a touch of rustic style *and* an impressive selection of bourbon, scotch, rye, and beer.
WHAT The westside compatriot of the Bigfoot Lodge in Atwater features the same sort of woodsy décor as the original with a little less of its tragic hipsterdom. The craft beer selection is thoughtful, and the cocktails are top-notch—standards like sazeracs and manhattans, but the bartenders will also mix you an old fashioned with bacon-infused simple syrup or a margarita with fresh sage.
WHO The young and loud; anyone who appreciates a daily happy hour that starts at 5 and goes until 9; the occasional Sasquatch. ✿

🏚 GROUPS 🎤 KARAOKE ✿ PATIO ♥ ROMANTIC

[Blind Barber] 10797 Washington Blvd., Culver City, 310.841.6679, blindbarber.com. Mon.-Tues. noon-midnight, Wed.-Sat. noon-2 a.m., Sun. noon-6 p.m. Full bar. **WHY** If the owners of Urban Outfitters started a bar, this would be it. **WHAT** The schtick here is that to enter the speakeasy-ish bar, located behind a Best Buy on one of Culver City's most unassuming stretches, you have to go through a door at the back of the barbershop, which isn't just for show; it offers legitimate shaves and haircuts. Once you're in (consider making reservations on busy weekend evenings), sip cocktails with lots of ingredients in the long, dark bar.
WHO Bearded hipsters, millennials with money.

[Boardwalk 11] 🎤10433 National Blvd., Palms, 310.837.5245, boardwalk11.com. Nightly 5 p.m.-2 a.m. **WHY** One of L.A.'s best karaoke bars. It even has happy hour karaoke at 6 p.m. Tuesday through Friday. **WHAT** This is on-stage karaoke, run by (skilled) DJs, with a library of more than 50,000 songs, and a good bar to keep signers lubricated. If you really want to sing, come early to beat the crowds; after 9, there's either a two-drink minimum or a $10 cover. **WHO** A really diverse mix of people who get a kick out of karaoke, from young folks who recent graduated with a theater degree to older folks who've come here for years. 🎤

[Caulfield's Bar & Dining Room] Thompson Hotel, 9360 Wilshire Blvd., Beverly Hills, 310.388.6860, caulfieldsbeverlyhills.com. Daily 7 a.m.-11 p.m. Full bar. **WHY** Beverly Hills has so few decent bar that you have to take what you can get. **WHAT** Everything at Caulfield's, located in the base of the Thompson Hotel, is slightly overpriced considering what you get, but the ambiance is classy and romantic with a touch of throwback charm (the Depression-era mural in the restaurant is a knockout). Squint and you might think you're in a New York bistro. The rooftop pool and bar area is really the way to go; stick to basic cocktails, and as you sip your martini you can gaze down at Beverly Hills spread out below you. **WHO** Thompson Hotel guests, wealthy businessmen with their mistresses, people afraid of driving east of La Cienega. ♥

[City Tavern] 9739 Culver Blvd., Culver City, 310.838.9739, city-tavernculvercity.com. Mon.-Wed. 11:30 a.m.-10 p.m., Thurs.-Sat. 11:30 a.m.-11 p.m., Sun. 11:30 a.m.-9 p.m. Beer & wine. **WHY** Beer, beer, and more beer. **WHAT** Imagine Santa Monica's Library Ale House crossed with that pinnacle of burgers and brews, Father's Office, and you'll get a sense of this large and airy spot. The nearly two dozen taps feature all sorts of interesting offerings, some from local breweries, some from abroad, and there are other beers in bottles and cans. The bartenders are happy to pour you a taste, but if you still can't commit you can, for around $4, get a small glass of anything on tap. The food is simple and solid—burgers, fish and chips—and the best place to enjoy it is on the large patio. **WHO** Patrons of the nearby Kirk Douglas Theatre popping in before or after a show, beer connoisseurs. 🏛 ☼

[Cozy Inn] 11155 Washington Pl., Culver City, 310.838.3826. Daily 6 a.m.-2 a.m. Full bar. **WHY** Not a dive but not a gastropub or craft-anything place—just a regular, friendly neighborhood bar in a good Culver City location. And if you need a Corona at 6:30 a.m., they'll take care of you. **WHAT** Sick of $15 cocktails made from organic bitters sourced from the Amazon rain forest? Come to the Cozy Inn, order a shot or a bottle of Heineken, talk to your friends, and play a game of pool, darts, or shuffleboard. **WHO** Regulars challenging each other to shuffleboard games. 🎤 🏛 ☼

[Craftbar] 10100 Constellation Blvd., Century City, 310.279.4180, craftrestaurantsinc.com. Mon.-Fri. 11:30 a.m.-2:30 p.m. & 6-10 p.m., Sat. 6-10 p.m. Full bar. **WHY** A slightly more affordable version of Tom Colicchio's terrific (and adjacent) Craft restaurant, brother to the New York original. **WHAT** Everything on the menu in the front lounge and patio at Craft is $6 to $19 and just as interesting: baby beets with gorgonzola, flatbread with fontina and wild mushrooms, veal-ricotta meatballs. Wine and drink prices are breathtaking. **WHO** Junior ICM agents reveling in their potential while their bosses seal the deal over $59 Washugyu steaks inside. 🍸 ☼ ♥

[Father's Office] 3229 Helms Ave., Culver City, 310.736.2224, fathersoffice.com. Mon.-Thurs. 5 p.m.-1 a.m., Fri.-Sat. noon-2 a.m., Sun. noon-midnight. Full bar. **WHY** The justly famed medium-rare burger topped with caramelized onions, smoked applewood bacon and blue cheese is worth the wait, the price and the fat grams. Only you can decide if it's worth the hype. **WHAT** The square footage is greatly improved from the Santa Monica original, with lots of patio seating, and the frenzy from its early days of popularity has abated, so it's easier now to enjoy one of Sang Yoon's famous burgers, some sweet potato fries, and a small-producer tap beer or two. No substitutions on the famous burger and no kids (21 and over only). **WHO** Youngish men who take their beer and burgers very seriously. ☼

Bars & Cocktail Lounges

[The Mandrake] 2692 S. La Cienega Blvd., Culver City, 310.837.3297, mandrakebar.com. Sun.-Mon. 6 p.m.-midnight, Tues.-Thurs. 5 p.m.-midnight, Fri.-Sat. 5 p.m.-1 a.m. Full bar. **WHY** With movie nights and guest DJs, this cool-kid bar feels like something out of Silver Lake or Echo Park, without being overblown. **WHAT** A low-key speakeasy that manages to forgo the pretension, the Mandrake makes such good classic cocktails as French 75s and daiquiris—which are consumed in equal amounts with PBRs and whiskey shots. **WHO** Hayden Tract artists and Culver City twentysomethings looking to cut loose. ⚓ 📷 ☼

[Nic's Beverly Hills] 453 N. Cañon Dr., Beverly Hills, 310.550.5707, nicsbeverlyhills.com. Mon.-Wed. 4 p.m.-midnight, Thurs.-Sat. 4 p.m.-2 a.m. Full bar. **WHY** Dress-up fun in the heart of Beverly Hills, with a piano bar, often-good jazz, and a walk-in vodka freezer that brings out the Russian in everyone. **WHAT** Larry Nicola was well ahead of the cocktail craze that's swept L.A.—he decamped from Silver Lake some years ago to open this swank (and only slightly tongue-in-cheek) Beverly Hills boîte. Come for a martini, come for a meal, come for some jazz— but note that the scene gets louder and more intense after 9 p.m. on weekends. **WHO** Suave youngsters and hip middle-agesters who value a well-made cocktail, a proper platter of oysters, and a good piano player. Some are famous, but Larry keeps 'em on the down-low. 🏛 ☼ ♥

[Oldfield's Liquor Room] 10899 Venice Blvd., Palms, 310.842.8066, oldfieldsliquorroom.com. Nightly 5 p.m.-2 a.m. Full bar. **WHY** A serious cocktail bar that still manages to be both approachable and comfortable. **WHAT** Oldfield's is a rare find among the current crop of retro-modern bars—a subdued, stylized place that foregoes overwrought affectation for an actual sense of homey history. Drinks like the Blonde Comet (bourbon, peach brandy, Angostura bitters, and fresh grapefruit and lemon) go down impossibly easy, which make it all the better to unwind in the bar's perfectly dim bistro-meets-speakeasy setting. **WHO** Westside cocktailians and neighborhood drinkers out for a date. ♥

[Picca] 🌴 9575 W. Pico Blvd., West L.A., 310.277.0133, piccaperu.com. Nightly 6-11 p.m. Full bar. **WHY** Uncommonly good cocktails, with or without the memorable modern Peruvian food. **WHAT** Chef Ricardo Zarate has gotten plenty of attention for his creative Peruvian dishes, but the cocktails by local mixology hero

Julian Cox are equally worthwhile. The platonic ideal of a pisco sour is always on the menu, but other imaginative seasonal drinks range from the Dante Belpepper with mezcal, red bell pepper, and carrot habañero air to the Sherry Manilow, with cinnamon and pomegranate. Snack on ceviches or skewers at the cozy upstairs room or the bar facing the kitchen. **WHO** 20th Century Fox executives, cocktail connoisseurs, Peruvian ex-pats. 🍸

[**Public School 310**] 9411 Culver Blvd., Culver City, 310.558.0414, publicschool310.com. Daily 11:30 a.m.-midnight. Full bar. **WHY** For an impressive selection of rotating craft beers along the main drag in Culver City. **WHAT** Thankfully, the schoolyard schtick isn't taken too far (no uniforms), and the composition-book menus and notepad drink lists are fun. Summer afternoons are perfect for sitting on the outside patio during "recess" (i.e. happy hour) and people-watching. **WHO** A stylish crowd of millennial professionals, and the hipper members of their mom 'n dad's generation, too. 🏛 ☼

[**Rush Street**] 9546 W. Washington Blvd., Culver City, 310.837.9546, rushstreetculvercity.com. Mon.-Wed. 11:30 a.m.-11:30 p.m., Thurs.-Fri. 11:30 a.m.-1:30 a.m., Sun. 10:30 a.m.-11:30 p.m. Full bar. **WHY** Food that's much better than it has to be, given that it's a tribute to Chicago's Rush Street, a strip known for its bar scene, not fine dining. Order the truffle asiago fries while you peruse the menu. Good happy hour, too. **WHAT** In an enormous, barn-like room in the heart of Culver City, Rush Street serves snazzy cocktails and an eclectic array of dishes, from terrific sandwiches and salads at lunch to an even more varied assortment at dinner: lobster and shrimp egg rolls, falafel sliders, a spinach, shiitake and gorgonzola pizzam one of the best tortilla soups we've ever eaten. So this is a place to eat while you drink. Just note that the crowds can be considerable. **WHO** Sony Studios foodies and lots of sideburned dudes in hats and gals in teeny dresses. 🍸

[**Seventy 7**] 3843 Main St., Culver City, 310.559.7707, seventy-7lounge.com. Nightly 5 p.m.-2 a.m. Full bar. **WHY** Lounge around, pretend you're in a speakeasy, and get to know your neighbors. **WHAT** You'll have to walk down an alley behind Culver City's strip of popular taverns and restaurants to find this place. Once you do, it's intimate and Victorian in theme. Or would that be Parisian? Hard to know. Sure, the drinks usually have too many ingredients and the music can be comedically loud, but that doesn't

mean you can't have a good time. The atmosphere is festive.
WHO Youngsters who don't know (or care) how craft cocktails
should taste.

[Tattle Tale Room] 5401 Sepulveda Blvd., Culver City,
310.390.2489, tattletaleroom.com. Daily 6 a.m.-2 a.m. Full bar.
WHY So you can hear—or sing—that caterwauling rendition of
your favorite Coldplay song. **WHAT** There are pool tables and TV
screens, but Tattle Tale, with its fantastic red and blue striped exterior, is all about the karaoke. And the regulars who perch themselves on the red leatherette bar stools. If you've ever wondered
where you can find the mythical neighborhood bar where everyone
really will know your name, look no further. Start coming in daily
and you'll meet a fantastic cross-section of the city. **WHO** Everyone from 78-year-old retirees to 22-year-old bros. 🌴 📷 🔍

[Ten Pound] Montage Hotel, 225 N. Cañon Dr., Beverly Hills,
310.860.5808, montagehotels.com/beverlyhills. Tues.-Sat. 5 p.m.-mid-
night. Full bar. **WHY** It's about as close as a public bar can get to
being a private club. **WHAT** Just above Scarpetta in the Montage
Hotel complex, you'll find one of L.A.'s most discreet bars. It specializes in a single brand of liquor, Macallan Scotch, and you can
get a dram that's been aged for 64 years. The bar is all dark wood,
buttery leather, and Lalique crystal, and if you want your Macallan
on the rocks, you'll get an ice sphere made of water imported from
the Scottish highlands. The lights are low; so is the volume. You
won't need to lean in to hear your date, but you might want to.
WHO People with money and power, people who want to feel like
they have money and power, readers of *Cigar Aficionado*. 🔇 ♥

[The Wellesbourne] 10929 W. Pico Blvd., West L.A.,
310.474.0102, thewellesbourne.com. Mon.-Sat. 5 p.m.-2 a.m. Full bar.
WHY If you want to relax with a proper negroni by the fireside,
while still feeling like you're part of the scenester crowd. **WHAT** A
hidden cocktail gem near Westwood, this dim, book-filled, parlour
house themed bar can produce a dynamite sazerac, even if the
more rowdy patrons seem to prefer a Jack and Coke. **WHO** UCLA
grad students cutting loose and date night couples drinking before
a movie.

[Westside Tavern] Westside Pavilion, 10850 W. Pico Blvd.,
Rancho Park, 310.470.1539, westsidetavernla.com. Sun.-Thurs. 11
a.m.-10 p.m., Fri.-Sat. 11 a.m.-11 p.m. Full bar. **WHY** For a post-mov-

ie drink and nosh that doesn't involve a food court or corporate chain. **WHAT** This mall pub is better than it needs to be, with a great craft beer list, a first-rate burger, and inventive but not too silly cocktails, from a solid pisco sour to a tequila concoction with pressed basil, agave, lime, grapefruit, and jalapeño bitters. **WHO** Friends and families sporting Nordstrom shopping bags. 🏕

[X-Bar] Hyatt Regency Century Plaza, 2025 Ave. of the Stars, Century City, 310.228.1234, xbarla.com. Mon.-Fri. 4 p.m.-2 a.m., Sat. 6 p.m.-2 a.m. Full bar. **WHY** Because mall shopping requires constant refueling with mocha-espresso martinis and chile-lime crab cakes. **WHAT** Cocktails with cheesy names like the astrology-inspired Leo and Scorpio (which arrive tableside in the appropriate birthstone color) are actually pretty good, if overpriced and on the sweet side. Garlic fries with chipotle aioli will come to the rescue to temper the sweetness. A pleasant spot for a Century City drinks-and-hors d'oeuvres rendezvous. **WHO** Shoppers and CAA agents who have discovered this gorgeous open-air outdoor patio, as well as out-of-towners convinced that all L.A. bars are required to have the same slick designer with a penchant for white-on-white. ☼ ♥

WEST OF THE 405

[Abuelita's] 🌴 137 S. Topanga Canyon Blvd., Topanga, 310.455.8788, abuelitastopanga.com. Mon.-Thurs. 4 p.m.-midnight, Fri.-Sun. 11:30 a.m.-midnight. Full bar. **WHY** You're in Topanga Canyon; where else are you going to go? **WHAT** The comfort food at this Mexican restaurant is unremarkable, but the margaritas are strong, and the spacious wood patio is the perfect place to drink them. It's a charming rustic haven with overgrown foliage, the sound of crickets (and the occasional coyote), and a rivulet of water within earshot. **WHO** Aging hippies, creative recluses, local families, and other residents of the canyon community who don't want to drive down the hill. ☼

[Bar Food] 12217 Wilshire Blvd., Brentwood, 310.820.3274, barfoodla.com. Mon. 11:30 a.m.-11 p.m., Tues.-Thurs. 11:30 a.m.-midnight, Fri. 11:30 a.m.-1 a.m., Sat. 11 a.m.-1 a.m., Sun. 11 a.m.-11 p.m. Full bar. **WHY** A solid happy hour and an exceptional whiskey selection. **WHAT** One thing's for sure, it's not cheap, but this is Brentwood, so what would you expect? A mitigating factor is the daily happy hour, when beer specials are $4, wine and wells are $6, and select cocktails are $7. The whiskey and scotch list is most

impressive, ranging from old standbys to rare offerings, like Yamazaki's 18-year-old single-malt. **WHO** Well-off, trendy drinkers
from west of the 405. 🏯

[Bar Toscana] 11633 San Vicente Blvd., Brentwood,
310.826.0028, bartoscana.com. Mon.-Sat. 11:30 a.m.-3 p.m. & 5:30-
11 p.m., Sun. 5-10 p.m. Full bar. **WHY** Because people need somewhere to drink in Brentwood. **WHAT** Situated next to longstanding
Italian restaurant Toscana, this swank, nominally Italian bar goes
heavy on the Amaro, Cynar, Campari, and Fernet. The cocktails
are a few bucks more expensive than they deserve to be, but the
décor is pretty and clever. Suitable for a happy-hour cocktail, especially if you have an expense account. **WHO** Well-off folks who
live or work within a two-mile radius, including women who carry
handbags that cost more than a normal person's rent. ♥

[Barkowski] 2819 Pico Blvd., Santa Monica, 310.998.0069,
barkowski.com. Daily 5 p.m.-2 a.m. Beer & wine. **WHY** If you can tune
out the obnoxious concept, you can enjoy a craft beer and a game
of bumper pool. **WHAT** Why anyone would open a Disneyfied watering hole (in Santa Monica, no less!) inspired by L.A.'s poet of
the dive bar, Charles Bukowski, is baffling; after all, he's the first
guy who'd be turfed out of an establishment like this. Nevertheless if you want to sip a craft beer (the selection here is good) or a
soju cocktail (the owners are pursuing a full liquor license) under
pictures of the man and quotes from his works, here's your spot.
If you want a slightly more authentic dose of Bukowski, hit one of
the places in which he actually drank, like the King Eddy on the
edge of Downtown's Skid Row, although even that place has been
gussied up. Cash only. **WHO** College kids, post-college kids —
mostly, people who don't know anything about Bukowski. ⟍

[Brewsters Beererie] Four Points Sheraton Hotel, 9750 Airport
Blvd., Westchester, 310.645.4600, fourpointslax.com/brewsters-bar-
near-lax. Daily 11 a.m.-1:30 a.m. Full bar. **WHY** For an airport hotel
bar, it doesn't get much better than this beer selection. There's
a full bar, but everyone drinks beer, so we're labeling this place
a tap room. **WHAT** Craft-brew-loving travelers should make an
immediate stop at Four Points, even if it's just for a layover pint.
Sharing the comfortable lounge area with hotel guests, locals
enjoy Wednesday-night beer tastings and special beer events every
third Friday. The 16 rotating taps feature top California breweries, and the huge bottle list includes such European standouts

as Mikkeller, Drie Fonteinen, and Schneider. **WHO** LAX travelers fed up with overpriced swill and westside beer lovers who actually make a pilgrimage here. 🏘

[Brü Haus] 11831 Wilshire Blvd., Brentwood, 310.473.2337, bruhauspub.com. Sun.-Wed. 11 a.m.-midnight, Thurs.-Sat. 11:30 a.m.-2 a.m. Beer & wine. **WHY** Some 30 taps and an abundance of bottles from some of the best breweries in the U.S., Germany, and Belgium. **WHAT** This modern pub makes it easy to expand your knowledge of quality beer by sampling from a flavor profile you already enjoy:yeast, malt, hop, or fruit. Found between two bars on Wilshire that cater almost exclusively to UCLA students, Brü Haus seems a little classier than its neighbors, so expect to pay a bit of a premium for the variety and quality. **WHO** Well-dressed millennial professionals. ☼

[The Bungalow] 🌴 Fairmont Hotel, 101 Wilshire Blvd., Santa Monica, 310.899.8530, thebungalowsm.com. Mon.-Fri. 5 p.m.- 2 a.m., Sat. 2 p.m.-2 a.m., Sun. 2 p.m.-10 p.m. Full bar. **WHY** For luxe beachside lounging and celeb spotting, plus very good tequila cocktails. **WHAT** Attached to the Fairmont Hotel, this multi-roomed lounge attracts a relaxation-seeking crowd from far and wide, and has fireplaces, ping-pong and pool tables, couches, intimate booths, and indoor and outdoor spaces to wander. It feels like a house party at your wealthy Malibu friend's pad—except for the long line to get in on weekends. **WHO** Young Hollywood suits, tourists, and on weekend nights, a more nightclub crowd. ♥

[Busby's West] 3110 Santa Monica Blvd., Santa Monica, 310.828.4567, busbysla.com. Mon.-Fri. 11 a.m.-2 a.m., Sat.-Sun. 9 a.m.-2 a.m. Full bar. **WHY** Enough flat-screen and projection TVs to broadcast every sporting event on cable, and probably satellite, too. **WHAT** While enjoying the immensely popular happy hour (where $4 will get you a draft beer, well drink, or glass of house wine), fans can also play foosball, pool, air hockey, and arcade basketball. Seating is ample, so bring the whole group; however, when an L.A. team is playing, it gets really crowded. **WHO** West-side sports fanatics rocking their favorite team's jersey. 📺 🏘 ☼

[Cabo Cantina] 11829 Wilshire Blvd., Brentwood, 310.312.5840, cabocantina.com. Sun.-Thurs. 11:30 a.m.-midnight, Fri.-Sat. 11:30 a.m.-1 a.m. Full bar. **WHY** The Mexican schtick is taken to the ex-treme, but the generous happy hour will surely get you in a south-of-the-border mood. **WHAT** Stick to the cheap stuff and this is of the best values on the westside, offering a daily happy hour from 4 to 8 and 10 to midnight, where most drinks are two for one. Don t be upsold on the giant fishbowl margaritas, which look enticing but are discounted drinks, which is conveniently not mentioned. Big sporting events and weekends tend to be packed. **WHO** UCLA students and young westsiders looking to fiesta. 🗺️ 🥾

[Cameo Bar] Viceroy Hotel, 1819 Ocean Ave., Santa Monica, 310.260.7500, viceroyhotelsandresorts.com. Daily 11 a.m.-12:30 a.m. Full bar. **WHY** For a chic hotel bar experience near the beach, complete with lounge and poolside drinking. **WHAT** Plastered in whites, brights, and chandeliers, Cameo feels a little Miami. Order a cocktail—preferably a martini—at the main bar before heading outside toward the poolside cabanas to mingle and people-watch. **WHO** Dressed-up, middle-aged professionals making new friends and dropping glances. ☼ ♥

[Chez Jay] 🌴 1657 Ocean Ave., Santa Monica, 310.395.1741, chezjays.com. Mon. 2 p.m.-midnight, Tues.-Fri. 11:30 a.m.-2 a.m., Sat.-Sun. 9 a.m.-2 a.m. Full bar. **WHY** Because every other bar in Santa Monica abounds with tourists, hammered college students, and artisanal cocktails. **WHAT** Can a dive bar with its floor covered in sawdust and peanut shells really charge *$14* for a martini? Welcome to Chez Jay. Opened in 1959 and located half a block from the Santa Monica Pier, its unassuming facade (look for the captain's wheel) reveals a friendly hideaway where old-school steaks and shrimp cocktails populate the menu. This is the bar that time (almost) forgot. Development has threatened its existence in recent years, but Chez Jay has so far fought off the ravages of gentrification. **WHO** Santa Monica residents who know how miraculous it is that a neighborhood bar this friendly and authentic manages to exist so close to the seaside city's tourist traps. 🥄 🎐

[Copa D'Oro] 217 Broadway, Santa Monica, 310.576.3030, copadoro.com. Mon.-Wed. 5:30 p.m.-midnight, Thurs.-Sat. 5:30 p.m-2 a.m. Full bar. **WHY** For cocktails you won't find at the corner bar—really good ones. **WHAT** Cocktail guru Vincenzo Marianella's Promenade-adjacent lounge feels like a cozy Manhattan bar, thanks to its weathered brick walls, French-mod leather wingbacks, well-coiffed bartenders, and big-city prices. If you want to spend $13 for a gin and tonic here, that's your business, but the smart money's on such modern concoctions as the Pancho Villa (tequila, sweet vermouth, Aperol, peach bitters) and classics as the Algonquin (rye, dry vermouth, pineapple juice). Add very good paninis and shareable dips, and you've got a well-balanced meal, at least in some circles. **WHO** The young and the restless.

[The Daily Pint] 2310 Pico Blvd., Santa Monica, 310.450.7631, thedailypint.net. Mon.-Fri. 2 p.m.-2 a.m., Sat.-Sun. 11 a.m.-2 a.m. Full bar. **WHY** At least two cask-conditioned "real" ale firkins always on tap and what has to be the largest Scotch collection in California. **WHAT** This dark, tattered bar hardly looks like much—until you open the menu and discover hundreds of interesting beers and whiskeys. The cask ales, typically from San Diego breweries, vary weekly, and the fantastic house-made potato chips go down just as easy. **WHO** Regulars who look as tired as the barstools, home brewers after a club meeting, and college students pretending that they always spring for good beer.

[Father's Office] 🌴 1018 Montana Ave., Santa Monica, 310.736.2224, fathersoffice.com. Mon.-Thurs. 5 p.m.-1 a.m., Fri.-Sat. noon-2 a.m., Sun. noon-midnight. Beer & wine. **WHY** A chance to decide for yourself whether this is the best burger in America. **WHAT** When Sang Yoon, formerly chef at Michael's, said goodbye to haute cuisine to open a pub, he set about creating a world-class hamburger. It's a rare, dry-aged beef patty topped with Maytag blue cheese, smoked applewood bacon and caramelized onions—and don't even think about asking for substitutions. The dark, shotgun bar has only a few bistro tables, and even with the larger branch in Culver City, the line's often out the door. The ever-changing selection of seasonal boutique beers is worth waiting for, but the over-21 rule is strictly enforced, so leave the kids at home. **WHO** Beer and burger aficionados.

[Finn McCool's] 2700 Main St., Santa Monica, 310.452.1734, finnmccoolsirishpub.com. Mon.-Fri. noon-2 a.m., Sat.-Sun. 10 a.m.-2 a.m. Full bar. **WHY** For a fantastic old carved wooden bar from Ireland, Guinness on tap, good Irish appetizers (try the mini Yorkshire puddings), and, on Sunday afternoon, musicians playing Irish tunes around an old wooden table, just like in Galway. **WHAT** The bar gets boisterous late on weekend nights, but at other times this handsome, high-ceilinged pub from L.A.'s best-known Irish chef, Gerri Gilliland, is a surprisingly sweet spot. We'd advise passing on the dinner entrées in favor of the much better appetizers, snacks, and desserts. They move a lot of Guinness

here, and the deft bartenders are fun to watch. **WHO** Families for
weekend lunches; mates meeting for a few pints and a meal in the
evening.

[**Freddy Small's Bar and Kitchen**] 11520 W. Pico Blvd.,
West L.A., 310.479.3000, freddysmalls.com. Mon.-Thurs. 5:30 p.m.-
1 a.m., Fri. 5:30 p.m.-2 a.m., Sat. 6 p.m.-2 a.m. Full bar.
WHY Because Plan Check on Sawtelle is packed. **WHAT** Just a
little bit south of Sawtelle's Little Osaka neighborhood, this nifty
little tavern is dark, loud, casually chic, and filled with millennials
chowing down on small plates and guzzling intriguing cocktails.
The menu items can be overly fussy and definitely spendy, but the
fried brussels sprouts are a crowd-pleaser. **WHO** A devoted crowd
of regulars who come here for after-work drinks or to party on
weekend evenings.

[**The Gaslite**] 2030 Wilshire Blvd., Santa Monica, 310.829.2382,
thegaslite.com. Mon.-Fri. 2 p.m.-2 a.m., Sat.-Sun. 9 a.m.-2 a.m. Full
bar. **WHY** Fun karaoke in Santa Monica. **WHAT** Regulars forgive
the Gaslite for being a dive bar without dive-bar prices, because
the nightly karaoke is so good, and the bartenders are nice folks.
Drinks are cheaper before 9 p.m., and you're less likely to encoun-
ter a line then, so come a little early, especially if you really want
to sing. **WHO** A diverse mix, from drunk older guys to packs of
sorority sisters. 🎾 🎤

[**Harvelle's Blues Club**] 🌴 1432 4th St., Santa Monica,
310.395.1676, harvelles.com. Nightly 8 p.m.-2 a.m. Full bar.
WHY The best blues bar on the westside also features an outstanding burlesque show. **WHAT** Talented blues and jazz performers
pack this small venue, which serves reasonably priced cocktails,
wine, and beers. The Toledo burlesque show on Sundays is high
energy and fronted by one of the most talented performers in Hollywood. Get there early—the show's popularity generally means
a long line. **WHO** Jazz and blues fans who enjoy a well-made
cocktail. ♥

[**Library Alehouse**] 2911 Main St., Santa Monica,
310.314.4855, libraryalehouse.com. Mon.-Fri. 11:30 a.m.-midnight,
Sat.-Sun. 11 a.m.-midnight. Beer & wine. **WHY** For dozens of beers
on tap, mainly Californian, Belgian, and German brews, which
you can try in four-ounce, five-shot sample flights. **WHAT** This
aptly named bar has a polished professor vibe with better-than-av-

erage bar food: chipotle shrimp quesadillas, a solid build-your-own beef, turkey, veggie, or salmon burger, and salmon fish 'n chips. The outdoor patio is quite appealing, but you'll get better service if you can snag a seat at the bar. **WHO** Beer-loving regulars at the bar and Santa Monica families on the outdoor patio. 🍷 ☼

[Liquid Kitty] 11780 W. Pico Blvd., West L.A., 310.473.3707, liquidkitty.com. Mon.-Fri. 5 p.m.-2 a.m., Sat.-Sun. 8 p.m.-2 a.m. Full bar. **WHY** A dark and sexy place to have a martini while old burlesque flicks are projected on the wall and punk tunes blast your eardrums. **WHAT** Liquid Kitty has the perfect combo: drinks that are strong AND cheap. Not as cheap-as-a-dive-bar cheap but much better tasting. The namesake cocktail is a Ketel One martini served with an unfiltered cigarette—and it comes in medium or large, because this bar is serious about getting you sozzled. Even before you pour any alcohol down your gullet, people might think you're tipsy since it's so easy to trip in the dim lighting. Nicotine addicts will appreciate the indoor smoking patio. Bonus: The winking-neon martini-glass sign is fabulous. **WHO** Drinkers who like their cocktails served strong and without any bullshit pretension. ♥

[The Living Room] 🌴 Shutters on the Beach, 1 Pico Blvd., Santa Monica, 310.458.0030, shuttersonthebeach.com. Sun.-Thurs 11:30 a.m.-12:30 a.m., Fri.-Sat. 11:30 a.m.-1 a.m. Full bar. **WHY** The California dream. **WHAT** The upper lobby of this fabulous oceanfront hotel holds one of our favorite hotel bars in L.A., where the sofas are inviting, the French rosés are crisp, and the ocean view is enchanting. Sunday and Monday bring jazz piano, Tuesday is Spanish night, and weekends host a jazz duo. Order a smoked-salmon flatbread or some Humboldt Fog cheese to go with your drink, and you'll want for nothing. **WHO** Suave, prosperous people whose linen shirts and sheaths complement their tans. 🎵 ♥

[Lost & Found] 11700 National Blvd., West L.A., 310.397.7772. Daily 6 a.m.-2 a.m. Full bar. **WHY** Cheap booze + local weirdos = everything a dive bar should be. **WHAT** A sign claims that happy hour lasts all day. It's probably meant as a joke, but the drinks are so cheap we're inclined to believe it. Through the swinging doors there are fraying brown vinyl seats, a pool table, a jukebox, and plenty of regulars who, like the decor, may have been here since the '80s. Cash only. **WHO** Hardcore drinkers of every age, stripe, and size, as well as locals who (hopefully) live within walking distance. 🍸 🎱

[Mom's Bar] 12238 Santa Monica Blvd., West L.A., 310.820.6667, momsbar.com. Mon.-Thurs. 4 p.m.-2 a.m., Fri.-Sat. 11 a.m.-2 a.m. Full bar. **WHY** Here's a place that actually lives up to its motto: "Cheap Drinks, Good People." **WHAT** The big space has a little bit of everything: ping-pong tourneys on Tuesday nights, karaoke on Wednesdays, six TV screens tuned to sporting events, gregarious regulars, a back room, a smoking patio, and a daily happy hour from 4 to 8 p.m., during which all the drinks and domestic beers are $1 off—and they're not expensive to begin with. Mom would be proud. **WHO** UCLA students, recent UCLA grads, middle-aged drinkers, and pretty much everyone else. ⟋ 🗺 🏛 🔑

[O'Brien's Irish Pub] 2941 Main St., Santa Monica, 310.396.4725, obriensonmain.com. Daily noon-2 a.m. Full bar. **WHY** Food that's a notch above the pub norm, including the generous slices of Scottish smoked salmon on wheat toast with capers, green onions, and horseradish, or the banger sandwich, a crusty baguette filled with sausage and grilled onions. **WHAT** This comfortable Irish pub, with its plank floors, brick walls, and flat-screen TVs, is popular for its better-than-average food, lunch specials, and sports, sports, sports. Skylights and windows keep football afternoons from having that *Lost Weekend* feeling. Sunday afternoons bring live music on the front patio. **WHO** Lively, sometimes rowdy Ocean Park locals, sports fans, and young singles. ☿

[On the Waterfront Café] 205 Ocean Front Walk, Venice, 310.392.0322, waterfrontcafe.com. Mon.-Fri. 11 a.m.-11 p.m., Sat.-Sun. 9:30 a.m.-11 p.m. Beer & wine. **WHY** Good German brats, fat pretzels, and German beer on tap, including a hefeweizen that goes down very well on a sunny beach afternoon while the boardwalk parade flows by. **WHAT** A refreshing break from the generic sidewalk cafés that line the Venice boardwalk, this place is a German beer garden with decent food and convivial picnic-table seating. Fun for a weekend lunch or weekday sunset happy-hour beer-and-brat. **WHO** An amusing mix of scruffy local regulars and tourists, all of whom seem happy all the time; sometimes after a few Erdingers on tap they can get *really* happy. 🎵 🗺 ☿

[Plan Check Sawtelle] 1800 Sawtelle Blvd., West L.A., 310.288.6500, plancheck.com. Sun.-Wed. 11:30 a.m.-10 p.m., Thurs. 11:30 a.m.-11 p.m., Fri.-Sat. 11:30 a.m.-midnight. Full bar. **WHY** If you think that a burger topped with ketchup leather should pair with an equally wacky beverage. **WHAT** The flagship of Ernesto

Uchimura's burger hangout features local craft beer and off-the-wall drinks created by cocktail chef Matthew Biancaniello, including ones made with strawberry-infused gin and balsamic, or aloe liqueur and truffle salt. Snaps for the great happy hour, with $3 to $5 snacks and good drink deals. Great list of Japanese whiskeys, too. ☼

[Roosterfish] 🌴 1302 Abbot Kinney Blvd., Venice, 310.392.2123. Daily 11 a.m.-2 a.m. Full bar. **WHY** Even trendy Abbot Kinney needs a down-home watering hole. **WHAT** The longstanding gay watering hole is known for cheap drinks, a limited beer selection, and service that can be, uh… sporadic. Sometimes, you get a friendly bartender. Oftentimes, you don't. Cash only. **WHO** Young gay guys, older gay guys, neighborhood residents, refugees from First Fridays. ⚑

[San Francisco Saloon] 11501 W. Pico Blvd., West L.A., 310.478.0152, sfsaloon.com. Daily 11:30 a.m.-1 a.m. Full bar. **WHY** You're a San Francisco sports fan craving an Anchor Steam and a sourdough patty melt. **WHAT** This old-timey West L.A. favorite is the must-go destination for Bay Area expats, as well as a reliable spot for a burger and beer. **WHO** 49ers, Giants, or Warriors fans who love to drink while cheering on their teams.

[Scopa] 2905 Washington Blvd., Venice, 310.821.1100, scopaitalianroots.com. Nightly 5 p.m.-2 a.m. Full bar. **WHY** The Bullocks Wilshire cocktail—made with bourbon, rum, and Cynar—is already a modern classic in the L.A. drink scene. **WHAT** Pull up a stool at the long, L-shaped bar and watch Steven Livigni and Pablo Moix mix elegant cocktails from an artfully curated, illuminated wall of spirits behind the counter. You can move on to dinner in this brick-walled Italian-American restaurant or stay happy keeping your barstool warm. **WHO** Venice couples in their 30s looking for an evening of refinement. ♥

[Steingarten] 10543 W. Pico Blvd., West L.A., 310.441.0441, steingartenla.com. Mon. 5-11 p.m., Tues.-Wed. noon-11 p.m., Thurs. noon-midnight, Fri.-Sat. noon-1 a.m., Sun. 11 a.m.-11 p.m. Full bar. **WHY** Your friendly neighborhood German beer hall, now with a stellar list of brews and an array of snazzy sausages. **WHAT** Every neighborhood should have a place like this. Large, friendly, and unpretentious, it's equally comfortable for highbrow beer geeks and families with young children. In warm weather, the patio is the perfect spot for a warm pretzel, a cone of crisp fries, and a spicy Hungarian sausage (or maybe a platter of bock, brat, and duck-and-bacon wurst), all of which should be accompanied by a rare Trappist ale or hearty imperial stout. **WHO** Craft beer addicts, westsiders desperate for a good happy hour, neighborhood families, Fox execs, and cubicle workers sneaking a lunchtime beer. ☼

[Stout Burgers & Beers] 111 Santa Monica Blvd., Santa Monica, 310.260.8679, stoutburgersandbeers.com. Sun.-Thurs. 11:30 a.m.-midnight, Fri.-Sat. 11:30 a.m.-2 a.m. Beer & wine. **WHY** Thirty mostly California-sourced beers on tap that taste even better when you're ogling the Pacific Ocean. **WHAT** The popular Hollywood beer bar's most recent offshoot, just a few doors down from Ocean Avenue. Grab a table on the patio, order a brew, and enjoy the breeze. **WHO** Third Street shoppers and beachgoers. ☼

[Suite 700] 🌴 Shangri-la Hotel, 1301 Ocean Ave., Santa Monica, 310.394.2791, shangrila-hotel.com. Sun.-Wed. 4 p.m.-midnight, Thurs.-Sat. 4 p.m.-2 a.m. Full bar. **WHY** Classic cocktails in goblets and vintage ship's-deck views of palm trees and the Pacific. **WHAT** This streamline moderne boutique hotel was redone to within an inch of its 1939 glamour, yet it retains its quiet, hideaway feel. The cocktail menu reflects the era—old fashioneds, Singapore slings—while the food is contemporary and local: goat cheese–stuffed dates with smoked almond pesto, grilled flatbreads topped with ingredients from the farmers' market, right outside the door. Take advantage of the weeknight happy hour in one of four chic spaces, including the rooftop patio that really does feel like a ship's deck. Come early to beat the crowds if you want the rooftop view. **WHO** Men in jeans, women in stilettos, and anyone with a yen to be Nick or Nora Charles. ☼♥

[Tasting Kitchen] 1633 Abbot Kinney Blvd., Venice, 310.392.6644, thetastingkitchen.com. Mon.-Thurs. 6:30-11:30 p.m., Sat.-Sun. 10:30 a.m.-2:30 p.m. & 6-11:30 p.m. Full bar. **WHY** Because you're waiting to get a table at the restaurant. **WHAT** It's one of the best restaurants in the city, and chef Casey Lane's market-driven inventiveness extends to the cocktails. The libations menu changes frequently and is full of herbs and fresh fruit juices. The place gets packed in the evenings and it's loud, so if you want a quiet place this isn't it. But if you want to drink amid super stylish, beachy locals, this is your joint. **WHO** Venice hipsters, foodies.

🌴 ESSENTIALLY L.A.　🥢 DIVE　🍸 QUIET　💲 VALUE

[The Tripel] 333 Culver Blvd., Playa del Rey, 310.821.0333, thet-ripel.com. Mon.-Thurs. 5 p.m.-close, Fri. noon-close, Sat.-Sun. 10:30 a.m.-close. Beer & wine. **WHY** Its gourmet burgers are famous in the South Bay, and the refined drink menu is a refreshing change-up from the dive bars along Jefferson Boulevard. **WHAT** This dark and stylish gastropub is located just steps from the beach. It combines chef-driven comfort food with a great list of exotic and local beers, plus a few wines by the glass. Finding seating in the minuscule space can be tough, so go early if you plan to dine in. **WHO** LMU kids who prefer Belgian ales over Bud Light, and Playa del Rey residents looking for a night on the town.

[Venice Ale House] 🌴 2 Rose Ave., Venice, 310.314.8253, venicealehouse.com. Daily 10 a.m.-10 p.m. Beer & wine. **WHY** The best place to drink on the Venice boardwalk. **WHAT** The board-walk's bars may be known for overpriced mediocrity, but this place holds to a higher standard. It has an unequaled craft-beer selection and a terrific roster of quality California wines. If the weather's good, call ahead to reserve a seat on the patio, where the people-watching is legendary. **WHO** A solid mix of regulars, weekend beachgoers, and tourists looking for good beer. ☼

[Waterloo & City] 12517 W. Washington Blvd., Mar Vista, 310.391.4222, waterlooandcity.com. Sun.-Mon. 5-11 p.m., Tues.-Thurs. 5 p.m.-midnight, Fri.-Sat. 5 p.m.-1 a.m. Full bar. **WHY** Tasty cocktails, a comfortable bar, a menu with something for every-one, and an extensive happy hour menu from 5 to 7 on Tuesdays through Saturdays. **WHAT** The name is a tribute to owner/chef Brendan Collins's home country, England, but his cooking is not English—his training is French, and his experience includes a long stint at Mélisse. Now, in the 1960s building that long housed the Crest family restaurant, he's created a relaxed pub, where you can nurse a beer at the bar, sample from the good list of $12 cocktails and share a crisp-crusted pizza with a friend, or have a full-fledged dinner or weekend brunch. Good food, creative drinks, reasonable prices, and free parking have made it a hit. **WHO** An amusing mix, from young hipsters at the communal table, to middle-aged businesspeople checking each other out, to senior couples having a date night. ☼

[West 4th and Jane] 1432 4th St., Santa Monica, 310.395.6765, west4thjane.com. Mon.-Thurs. 5 p.m.-2 a.m., Fri.-Sat. noon-2 a.m., Sun. noon-midnight. Beer & wine. **WHY** For the outstanding beer selection, particularly notable on the touristy Third Street Promenade. **WHAT** With 18 draft options, ranging from light and refreshing to hop-forward and full-bodied, this quaint pub is a worthy destination near the beach. There's also a fine daily happy hour, where most brews and sangria cost $5 and several wines are $7. **WHO** Promenaders and friends playing tabletop Connect Four. 🐚

[Ye Olde King's Head] 🌴 116 Santa Monica Blvd., Santa Monica, 310.451.1402, yeoldekingshead.com. Mon.-Fri. 9 a.m.-2 a.m., Sat.-Sun. 8 a.m.-2 a.m. Full bar. **WHY** Fresh beer, tasty English pub fare, and a gregarious and interesting crowd. **WHAT** L.A.'s best-known pub has grown over the decades, now boasting two pub rooms and a dining room stretching between the Promenade and the shore. It's touristy as hell, but it's saved by the quality of food and the 20-some beers on tap. Try the sausage rolls, vegetable samosa, fish 'n chips, or shepherd's pie. **WHO** College students and tourists (including visitors from England) in the busier pub side, quieter conversationalists in the "snug," and fish-'n-chips-eating families in the dining room.

SOUTH BAY TO SOUTH L.A.

[Auld Dubliner] 71 S. Pine Ave., Long Beach, 562.437.8300, aulddubliner.com. Mon.-Fri. 11 a.m.-2 a.m., Sat.-Sun. 8 a.m.-2 a.m. Full bar. **WHY** Spirit-lifting traditional Irish music on Sunday afternoons, fun bands (from the party-ska Untouchables to easygoing folk-rock) most nights at 10 p.m., and good beer and pub grub. **WHAT** It's a small chain, and it's situated in an impossibly corporate-looking site near a bunch of chain stores and the Convention Center, but the Auld Dubliner feels lived in and comfortable, it has a fine lineup of draft beers (Guinness, Harp, Newcastle, Smithwick's), a growing roster of craft beers (Stone Delicious IPA, Duchess de Borgogne, Eel River Raven's Eye), and the Irish food is solid. **WHO** Downtown Long Beach suits for happy hour, a livelier crowd later for the live music. 🎭

[Bottle Room] 6741 Greenleaf Ave., Whittier, 562.696.8000, thebottleroombar.com. Mon.-Fri. 3 p.m.-midnight, Sat. noon-midnight, Sun. noon-10 p.m. Beer & wine. **WHY** A smart selection of beer and wine and a very good burger. **WHAT** The Bottle Room is a gastropub in the truest sense, a casual place where classics are tweaked and craft beers and small-batch wines flow. The restaurant's signature burger follows the Father's Office mold with sweet onion relish, arugula, and blue and Swiss cheeses. In the right season, there might be a nice heirloom tomato salad with barbecued prawns or baby beets topped with crumbles of feta and golden raisins. There are strong flatbreads and sandwiches, too, but ultimately it all falls back on the burger. **WHO** Whittier locals just off work and neighbors in for a leisurely drink.

[Congregation Ale House] 201 E. Broadway Ave., Long Beach, 562.432.2337, congregationalehouse.com. Mon.-Thurs. 11:30 a.m.-1 a.m., Fri. 11:30 a.m.-2 a.m., Sat. 11 a.m.-2 a.m., Sun. 11 a.m.-midnight. Full bar. **WHY** Lively suds and modern pub grub. **WHAT** Congregation may take its religious shtick too far—stained glass windows, Catholic school uniforms, Monday "mass"—but it's one of Long Beach's essential beer bars, with a commendable list of Belgian and craft brews. The menu presents done-up pub classics like a pork and goat cheese sausage sandwich, grilled rib-eye burger, and a fresh pretzel with Chimay cheese. Just leave room for more beer. **WHO** Beer-swillers from all over Long Beach. 🏠 ☼

[The Federal Bar] 102 Pine Ave., Long Beach, 562.435.2000, lb.thefederalbar.com. Mon.-Fri. 11:30 a.m.- midnight, Sat.-Sun. 10:30 a.m.-midnight. Full bar. **WHY** Serious cocktails in a gorgeous art deco bank building. **WHAT** A welcome addition to party-hard Pine Avenue that eschews the club scene for classy (but certainly not stuffy) sophistication. The gastropub features a sizable bar that can concoct very good classics (try the Gold Rush) as well as timely twists on old favorites. There's a respectable beer and wine list, too. **WHO** Cocktail aficionados and revelers looking for a slightly quieter night out.

[Hudson House] 514 N. Pacific Coast Hwy., Redondo Beach, 310.798.9183, hudsonhousebar.com. Mon.-Thurs. 5 p.m.-1 a.m., Fri.-Sat. 3 p.m.-1 a.m., Sun 3 p.m.-midnight. Full bar. **WHY** A casual bar and gastropub with culinary ambition and attractive prices. **WHAT** With a handful of local beers (think Strand and Smog City), plus more than 50 bottles, Hudson House is definitely a beer lover's hangout. But the gastropub also shakes up some commendable cocktails with house-made syrups and bitters. The place even goes so far as embark on its own barrel aging. **WHO** Neighborhood folks stopping by for a relaxed beer and a nosh. 🍸

[Joe Jost's] 🍸 2803 E. Anaheim St., Long Beach, 562.439.5446, joejosts.com. Mon.-Sat. 10 a.m.-11 p.m., Sun. 10 a.m.-8 p.m. Full bar.

WHY A Long Beach rite of passage that serves the coldest beer in town. **WHAT** Joe Jost's is a local landmark, a neighborhood pub that happens to attract dedicated drinkers from all over the city and beyond. There's nothing here other than ice-cold beer, a few pool tables, and good company—and that's more than enough. The bar is a virtual time capsule (it was founded in 1924) and full of pubby memorabilia. Save room for a pickled egg or two. **WHO** Graying baby boomers, pool enthusiasts, twentysomethings thirsty for a huge schooner. 🕱 🕱

[**Manhattan Beach Post**] 1142 Manhattan Ave., Manhattan Beach, 310.545.5405, eatmbpost.com. Mon.-Thurs. 5 p.m.-10 p.m., Fri. 11:30 a.m.-10:30 p.m., Sat. 10 a.m.-10:30 p.m., Sun. 10 a.m.-10 p.m. Full bar. **WHY** David LeFevre's lauded gastropub is just as much fun as a bar as it is a restaurant. **WHAT** A globe-hopping menu matched by an equally worldly wine list that travels from South Africa to Italy and beyond. Selections are smart and playful. Cocktails are inventive and pair good craft spirits (like Templeton rye) with loads of ingredients plucked from (or at least inspired by) the farmers' market. **WHO** Bronzed South Bay locals and foodies looking for a good drink. 🕱

[**Nelson's**] 🕱 Terranea Resort, 100 Terranea Way, Palos Verdes, 310.265.2836, terranea.com. Sun.-Thurs. 11 a.m.-10 p.m., Fri.-Sat. 11 a.m.-11 p.m. Full bar. **WHY** Solid pub fare and a good bar with reasonable prices, given the oh-wow oceanfront setting. **WHAT** You can hardly do better at sunset than to score an outdoor picnic table, with or without your dog, at this casual café-bar on what appears to be the westernmost tip of the United States. Named for the fictional Mike Nelson of *Sea Hunt* fame (it was filmed on the coves below), Nelson's is an unpretentious place in a fancy resort, with a respectable clam chowder, a lush pulled-pork sandwich, a great kids' menu, and a swell bar. Inside are TVs for sports and windows for views; outside are teak tables, fire pits, and more ocean than you can imagine. **WHO** Hotel guests and a lot of PV locals, who come here to meet friends, watch a game, or treat their kids. 🕱 ✿

[**Observation Bar**] 🕱 1126 Queens Hwy., Long Beach, 562.499.1740, queenmary.com. Sun.-Thurs. 11:30 a.m.-midnight, Fri.-Sat. 11:30 a.m.-2 a.m. Full bar. **WHY** An art deco classic with an unrivaled ocean and coastline view. **WHAT** Climb aboard the historic Queen Mary and you'll take a step back in time. The Observation

Bar is the famous ship's well-preserved watering hole, a gorgeous space with an equally beautiful view of downtown Long Beach. Classic, handcrafted cocktails abound—try an Old Fashioned or Pimm's Cup. **WHO** Multiple generations of Long Beach drinkers and a few inevitable tourists. 🏯 ♥

[The Pike] 1836 E. 4th St., Long Beach, 562.437.4453, pikelongbeach.com. Mon.-Fri. 11 a.m.-1:30 a.m., Sat.-Sun. 9 a.m.-2 a.m. Full bar. **WHY** A glass of Long Beach nostalgia and a side of rock 'n roll. **WHAT** Themed around the lost icons of Long Beach—namely the long-gone Pike amusement park—the bar is a mainstay on Retro Row. There are basic cocktails, but beer (mostly of the microbrew variety) is the drink of choice. Squeeze in on weekends to hear DJs spinning everything from Lee Hazelwood to Os Mutantes. **WHO** A well-inked crowd looking to party and ex-punkers hoping to spot owner and Social D drummer Chris Reece. 📷 🏯

[The Prospector] 2400 E. 7th St., Long Beach, 562.438.3839, prospectorlongbeach.com. Mon.-Fri. 11 a.m.-2 a.m., Sat.-Sun. 8 a.m.-2 a.m. Full bar. **WHY** A homey, Western dive with cheap drinks and no attitude. **WHAT** Styled like a saloon straight out of the 1970s, the Prospector has hosted some of Long Beach's most legendary karaoke nights. It's also one of the best places to catch local live music. But beyond that, it's the kind of place where old regulars can peacefully share space with eager newcomers. **WHO** Longtime regulars, CSULB grads, and live-music lovers. 🎤 📷 🏯 🌐 🔧

[Purple Orchid] 221 Richmond St., El Segundo, 310.322.5829. Mon.-Fri. 3:30 p.m.-2 a.m., Sat.-Sun. 2 p.m.-2 a.m. Full bar. **WHY** The tropical ambiance and strong cocktails (like the Blue Hawaiian and the Funky Monkey) are as restorative as an island getaway. **WHAT** This "exotic" lounge near LAX is one of the last bastions of tiki culture on the westside, serving flaming scorpion bowls with comically large straws. **WHO** Aloha-shirt-wearing South Bay suburbanites and local college kids drinking cheap beer and kitschy tiki cocktails. 🎤 🏯

[The Red Leprechaun] 4000 E. Anaheim St., Long Beach, 562.343.5560, redleprechaun.com. Tues.-Fri. 11 a.m.-10 p.m., Sat. 9 a.m.-10 p.m., Sun. 9 a.m.-5 p.m. Beer & wine. **WHY** A civilized Irish pub with a deft, modern touch. **WHAT** The Red Leprechaun looks like a classic Irish-American pub, sure, but the bar and restaurant forgoes most of the overwrought iconography that plagues so many bars. Instead, it offers a refined take on the pub experience, with local trippels and milk stouts alongside pints of Guinness and suave takes on such Irish classics as shepherd's pie. **WHO** Low-key pub hounds and small groups out for a comparatively quiet couple of drinks. 🏠

[Simmzy's] 229 Manhattan Beach Blvd., Manhattan Beach, 310.546.1201, simmzys.com. Mon.-Thurs. 11 a.m.-11 p.m., Fri. 11 a.m.-midnight, Sat. 10 a.m.-midnight, Sun. 10 a.m.-11 p.m. Beer & wine. **WHY** An open-air beach bar in Manhattan Beach with good food and drink. **WHAT** Not much more than a single room opening onto a street patio, this tiny gastropub has two dozen really good rotating tap beers, gobs of wine by the glass, and an Angus burger with sweet smoked onions, cheddar, and garlic aioli that rocks. Don't skip the fries. **WHO** Bikini-clad locals who've never heard of "No shoes, no shirt, no service"—yet somehow don't look out of place. ☼

[The Stache] 941 E. 4th St., Long Beach, 562.506.2529, thestachebar.com. Daily 2 p.m.-2 a.m. Full bar. **WHY** Serious cocktails with a no-frills attitude. **WHAT** The Stache, like so many things Long Beach, is a working man's cocktail bar. There are no dim Edison bulbs or $16 drinks—just a casual collection of city dwellers who all appreciate a finely made $8 drink. The classic Moscow Mule is in fine form here, with house-made ginger beer, fresh mint and organic vodka served in a chilly copper mug. **WHO** Any and all who want to split the difference between upscale bar and neighborhood dive. 🔪 💲

[The Stave] 170 The Promenade North, Long Beach, 562.612.4750, thestavebar.com. Daily noon-2 a.m. Full bar. **WHY** A little bit of downtown L.A. in downtown Long Beach. **WHAT** The Stave could stand in for any number of classic downtown cocktail bars, a low-key doppelganger outfitted with polished subway tiles, rich woods, and a stamped ceiling. But the bar is more than just looks—the Stave ushered in a new wave of whiskey appreciation in Long Beach. With more than 100 types of whiskey, bourbon, and scotch, it's no wonder the place is a beacon for the suit-and-tie crowd. **WHO** Nine-to-fivers unwinding after work and whiskey enthusiasts. ☼

[Tony's on the Pier] 🌴 210 Fisherman's Wharf, Redondo Beach, 310.374.1442, oldtonys.com. Daily 11:30 a.m.-2 a.m. Full bar. **WHY** A time capsule of Southern California tikidom. **WHAT** Tony's seems trawled straight from the sea, with all kinds of maritime knick-knacks adorning the place. But there's no irony here—the bar and restaurant is refreshingly earnest, perfectly proud of the fact that it hasn't changed in some 50 years. Drinks are brightly colored and potent. Order a mai tai and you get to take home the souvenir glass, too. **WHO** Older locals sporting Hawaiian shirts and South Bay bar crawlers taking in the sunset. 🛶 🏚

[V Room] 918 E. 4th St., Long Beach, 562.437.4396. Daily 6 a.m.-2 a.m. Full bar. **WHY** One of Long Beach's quintessential dives. **WHAT** The V Room is everything you want out of a dive bar: dim lighting, a pool table, and CCR on the jukebox. Beer and cocktail choices are standard, but you don't come here expecting much else. Enjoy the conversation with the regulars and kick back a couple with Long Beach's hip, young urbanites. Cash only. **WHO** Grizzled regulars by day and tattooed thirtysomethings by night. 🛶 🎤

[The Whale and Ale] 327 W. 7th St., Long Beach, 310.832.0363, whaleandale.com. Mon.-Tues., Thurs. 11:30 a.m.-3 p.m. & 5-9 p.m., Wed. 11:30 a.m.-3 p.m. & 4-9 p.m., Fri. 11:30 a.m.-3 p.m. & 5 p.m.-midnight, Sat. 1-10 p.m., Sun. 1-9 p.m. Full bar. **WHY** A classic and classy pub in the heart of the harbor. **WHAT** The fish and chips are reason enough to visit the Whale and Ale, but the British-style pub is also one of San Pedro's finer drinking establishments. En-robed in oak, the bar serves some beers from San Pedro Brewing Company as well as the likes of Goose Island. There's Guinness, of course, but a cold glass of Boddingtons might be more in keeping with the Southern California harbor-town setting. **WHO** An older crowd looking for the best of both worlds: a filling dinner and a festive bar.

Wine Bars

Every neighborhood deserves a friendly wine bar, and while not every L.A. neighborhood has one, there are plenty of good ones. The focus in this chapter is on truly wine-centric places, from bars to retailers with an inviting tasting room. You'll find plenty more good vino in the Bars + Cocktail Lounges chapter, as well as in Breweries + Tap Rooms.

Wine Bars

GROUPS KARAOKE PATIO ROMANTIC

CENTRAL CITY

[3Twenty Wine Lounge] 320 S. La Brea Ave., Fairfax District, 323.932.9500, 320southwine.com. Sun.-Thurs. 6-10 p.m., Fri.-Sat. 5:30-11 p.m. Full bar. **WHY** Your friendly neighborhood sipping spot located at 3rd and La Brea, an area that's underserved when it comes to watering holes. **WHAT** Low-key but polished, this wine bar has a welcoming atmosphere and some 40 bottles "on tap" via Enomatic machines, which allow you to try small pours before you settle on a selection. Another two dozen bottles are available by the glass. The list is heavy on overpriced, middle-of-the-road Italian reds, which like the food (diver scallops, brussels sprouts, bruschetta) isn't terribly memorable, but owner Edgar Poureshagh is. He's incredibly friendly and more than happy to offer suggestions for food and vino pairings or share his knowledge about wine in general. **WHO** Couples on dates, groups of friends hanging out after work, and anyone who enjoys a glass of wine in a refined spot without a lot of fuss. ♥

[A.O.C.] 🌴 8700 W. 3rd St., Beverly/Third, 323.859.9859, aocwinebar.com. Mon. 11:30 a.m.-10 p.m., Tues.-Fri. 11:30 a.m.-11:30 p.m., Sat. 10 a.m.-11 p.m., Sun. 10 a.m.-10 p.m. **WHY** A happy buzz fueled by excellent wines by the glass and perfectly ripe cheeses—and staff members who know more than just their name. The daily 5 to 7 p.m. happy hour is a great deal, given that this is an upscale place. **WHAT** Suzanne Goin and Caroline Styne's wine bar and small-plates restaurant continues to set the L.A. standard. It's not cheap, but the quality is high, from the international collection of wines, to the crafted cocktails, to the superb menu of Cal-Mediterranean fare. Try to score a table on the patio (for one thing, it's quieter), and don't skip dessert—all the better to linger with a glass of Muscat. **WHO** D girls, agents, and food-and-wine lovers traveling from the Palisades and Pasadena. ☼

[Bar Covell] 🌴 4628 Hollywood Blvd., Los Feliz, 323.660.4400, barcovell.com. Sun.-Thurs. 5 p.m.-midnight, Fri.-Sat. 5 p.m.-2 a.m. **WHY** The owners, alums of nearby Café Stella and Silver Lake Wine, know exactly what the neighborhood wants: zero pretension and decent value. It's just too bad that the patio is usually filled with smokers. **WHAT** This Los Feliz wine and beer bar has a rustic-industrial feel, with a weathered wood bar and comfy bar stools. A carefully curated wine list offers some 40 well-priced varieties at a time, as well as an excellent list of craft beers. A light menu includes cheese and charcuterie plates and light bites from Heirloom LA. **WHO** Los Feliz locals more interested in conversation and a good glass of wine than making a scene. ☼ ♥

[Cube Café] 615 N. La Brea Ave., Melrose, 323.939.1148, cubemarketplace.com. Nightly 5-11:30 p.m. **WHY** For the amazing cheeses, the brick-oven pizzas, and the in-the-know staff, eager to pair the perfect Barbera with your braised bacon and peach pizza. Oh, and for the spiffy upscale market. **WHAT** This intimate neighborhood café, cheese bar, and marketplace serves a pricey Italian-driven menu rich with farmers' market produce, house-made pastas, killer fried chicken, an evolving selection of more than 85 varieties of cheese, and salumi from Salumi Salame, the Fatted Calf, and Pio Tosini, to name a few. Our only complaint: very expensive wines. **WHO** Attractive, youthful Hollywood people, including a pop starlet or two. Don't be afraid to sit at the bar and mingle with the knowledgeable bartender and cheese guru. 🔈 ☼

[The Know Where Bar] 5634 Hollywood Blvd., Hollywood, 323.871.4108, theknowwherebar.com. Sat.-Tues. 8 p.m.-2 a.m., Wed.-Fri. 5:30 p.m.-2 a.m. **WHY** An artsier option for beer and wine. **WHAT** This posh hole-in-the-wall serves beer and wine only, including some unexpected but worth-a-try beer cocktails. Velvet couches and a streamline moderne design add a welcome sophisticated option to the neighborhood, ideal for a leisurely post-dinner glass of wine. **WHO** A post-art opening crowd. ♥

[Little Spain] Farmers Market, 6333 W. 3rd St. #120, Fairfax District, 323.634.0633, littlespainla.com. Mon.-Thurs. 9 a.m.-9 p.m., Fri.-Sat. 9 a.m.-10 p.m., Sun. 9 a.m.-8 p.m. **WHY** Tapas, sangria, and paella make a lively addition to the Original Farmers Market. **WHAT** At a long wine bar and a few tables, Farmers Market visitors sip reasonably priced Spanish wines, and larger groups linger over pitchers of fruity sangria. Tapas include *pa amb tomaquet* (tomato-smeared toast with charcuterie, cheese, or vegetables), fried calamari, chicken and ham croquetas, and addictive mini chorizo sausages. Five types of paella make a heartier meal, and beers and food products round out the Iberian bounty. **WHO** Tourists from all over the world, and workers from CBS and the Writers Guild. ☼

[Monsieur Marcel] Farmers Market, 6333 W. 3rd St., Fairfax District, 323.939.7792, mrmarcel.com. Mon.-Sat. 9 a.m.-9 p.m., Sun. 9 a.m.-7 p.m. **WHY** Outdoor French-wine sipping in the heart of the historic Farmers Market at Fairfax and Third. **WHAT** Before every neighborhood had its own wine bar, there was Monsieur Marcel, a casually classy oasis where you could sip a glass of rose or perhaps a cab franc while slicing into steak frites and feeling très chic. Its location makes it a prime perch for people-watching, and the adjacent market is a great place to pick up brie de meaux and other fancy foodstuffs. **WHO** Casual wine drinkers, refugees from the Grove, fans of midday happy hour. ☼

[Rascal] 801 S. La Brea Ave., Mid-Wilshire, 323.933.3229, rascalla.com. Mon.-Sat. 5-11 p.m., Sun. 5-10 p.m **WHY** A sweet neighborhood wine bar that's a little off the beaten path. **WHAT** This unassuming yet charming beer and wine bar has a full menu with creative dishes that add up to more than just bar snacks. Though there are only six beers on tap, a creative selection of beer and wine cocktails, not to mention several good wines for just $7 to $9 a glass, should keep any drinker happy. **WHO** Office workers and apartment dwellers from Wilshire's Miracle Mile corridor. 🗟

[Vintage Enoteca] 7554 W. Sunset Blvd., Hollywood, 323.512.5278, vintageenoteca.com. Mon.-Fri. noon-midnight, Sat.-Sun. 11 a.m.-midnight. **WHY** For the excellent weekday happy hour (5 to 7 p.m.) and the easygoing atmosphere. **WHAT** A real find in Hollywood, Vintage matches a good, fairly priced list of small-producer wines (plus some good ciders and beers) with a menu of well-executed wine-bar standards: salumi, deviled eggs, meatballs, warm farro salad, flatbreads, and sliders. Monday is grilled cheese night. **WHO** Pre-Pantages and pre-Bowl folks and refugees from the Hollywood nightclub scene. ☼♥

EASTSIDE

[55 Degree Wine] 🌴 3111 Glendale Blvd., Atwater, 323.662.5556, 55degreewine.com. Sun.-Thurs. 5:30-10 p.m., Fri.-Sat. 5:30-11 p.m. **WHY** The brick-walled, candlelit basement tasting room has become perhaps the coolest spot in Atwater every night. **WHAT** This eastern outpost of Santa Monica's Wine Expo is an oenophile hot spot in newly hip Atwater. The specialty is small-producer Italian wines at low prices, and more recently they've added some terrific beer tastings. Upstairs is the shop, and downstairs is the atmospheric tasting room. To accompany your drinking are cheeses and hummus, and you can also order pizzas

Wine Bars

from neighboring Crispy Crust. **WHO** Young wine buffs from Atwater, Highland Park, and Silver Lake. 🛍 ♥

[Bacaro] 🌴 2308 S. Union Ave., USC, 213.748.7205, bacarola. com. Mon.-Wed. 5-10 p.m., Thurs.-Sat. 5-11 p.m., Sun. 10:30 a.m.- 2:30 p.m. & 5-10 p.m. **WHY** Because you're bored with most wine-bar offerings and tired of paying through the nose for a glass of wine or a craft beer. Come on Sunday evening for terrific $17 wine and cheese flights, or Monday nights for half off all wine by the glass. **WHAT** On a funky block between Pico-Union and USC is a tiny haven for wine (and beer) lovers, where the wines of the day are artfully written on the blackboard walls. The kitchen turns out Venetian-style *cichetti* (small bites), including a caprese salad, grilled pizzas, and such heartier dishes as oven-roasted bone marrow; almost all the dishes are a mere $8. Bacaro is one of those spots you wish would open within walking distance of your house, a place where enthusiasm for esoteric Italian bottlings is matched by a menu of unfussy, simply delicious snacks. **WHO** Oenophiles from USC and West Adams with more taste than dough. 🍸 🛍

[Barbrix] 🌴 2442 Hyperion Ave., Silver Lake, 323.662.2442, barbrix.com. Mon.-Fri. 6 p.m.-1:30 a.m., Sat.-Sun. 11 a.m.-3 p.m. & 6 p.m.-1 a.m. **WHY** A bohemian-chic indoor/outdoor wine bar with spot-on Mediterranean-inspired small plates. **WHAT** Interesting, well-priced wines from California to Croatia are the centerpiece of this house-turned-festive wine bar. The food's just as good, from cheese and charcuterie samplers to flavorful farmers' market vegetable salads and meaty plates of Lindy & Grundy bratwurst and sirloin burgers. If you hope to hold a conversation, reserve a table on the quieter off-the-street patio—inside, it's lively but deafening. The happy hour is only available at the bar, which is a bummer. **WHO** The hippest people in Silver Lake, which is saying something. ✿ ♥

[BottleRock] 1050 S. Flower St., South Park/Fashion District, 213.747.1100, bottlerockla.com. Mon.-Sat. 11:30 a.m.-1 a.m., Sun. 4:30-11 p.m. **WHY** To taste oddball whites, rare reds, and exotic microbrews, especially during the 4:30 to 7 "rush hour," when the deals are very good. **WHAT** On the ground floor of the Metropolitan Lofts building, in starkly modern rooms lined with hundreds of intriguing bottles, this branch of the Culver City original is one of Downtown's most intelligent wine-and-food destinations. It's gotten a little more sports-bar-like, which is unfortunate, but

Wine Bars

🏛 GROUPS 🎤 KARAOKE ✿ PATIO ♥ ROMANTIC

hopefully management will leave that scene to nearby L.A. Live. The 900-plus wines and beers are all available for retail sale, a boon for nearby loft dwellers. **WHO** Pre-concert/game folks trying to avoid L.A. Live until the last possible minute.

[Colorado Wine Co.] 🍷 2305 Colorado Blvd., Eagle Rock, 323.478.1985, cowineco.com. Tues.-Thurs. 4-9 p.m., Fri. 4-11 p.m., Sat. 1-11 p.m., Sun. 1-9 p.m. **WHY** Friday flight night, a great value at $15 for a five-wine flight with cheese, and easygoing tasting-room fun every night but Monday, and weekend afternoons, too. **WHAT** The slogan here is "Wine for everyone," and that's refreshingly evident in the tastings, which feature generous pours at fair prices. Swell wine-friendly food trucks (Grilled Cheese, Louks Greek) pull up regularly. **WHO** Attractive, friendly people in an attractive, friendly space in the hip heart of Eagle Rock. 🗃

[Eastside Luv] 1835 E. 1st St., Boyle Heights, 323.262.7442, eastsideluv.com. Wed.-Sun. 8 p.m.-2 a.m. **WHY** Never a dull moment here, thanks to local punk bands, mariachi performances, and themed karaoke nights. **WHAT** This lively Chicano-inspired dive may call itself a wine bar (no hard alcohol), but most regulars opt for a spicy Michelada instead. There's also sangria, wines from Spain and Baja California, and, to honor the elders, Boone's Farm. **WHO** Chipsters (so-called Chicano hipsters) and old-school Boyle Heights artists. 🖎 🔍

[Mignon] 128 E. 6th St., Downtown, 213.489.0131, mignonla.com. Sun.-Thurs. 6 p.m.-midnight, Fri.-Sat. 6 p.m.-1 a.m. **WHY** A wee, charming spot with interesting and affordable wines and French-style snacks—just the place to transition from the work day to the evening. **WHAT** The smart folks behind one of our favorite wine bars, Bacaro, run this 600-square-foot spot in the heart of Downtown. Where Bacaro's focus is Italian, here it's French, with unusual, affordable European wines by the glass and a few great beers, too. To eat are quality cheeses, charcuterie, escargots, pâté, and a fine French-style ham-and-brie sandwich. Seats are few, so quit work early to snag a barstool. **WHO** Downtowners who'd rather talk to their companions and have a good glass of wine than make a bar scene. 🗃 ✿

[Pour Haus Wine Bar] 1820 Industrial St., Little Tokyo/Arts District, 213.327.0304, pourhauswinebar.com. Mon.-Thurs. noon-10 p.m., Fri. noon-midnight, Sat. 3 p.m.-midnight, Sun. 11 a.m.-10 p.m.

🍷 ESSENTIALLY L.A.   🖎 DIVE   🌙 QUIET   🗃 VALUE

WHY Sitting on the leafy cement patio, it's easy to pretend you're in San Francisco. **WHAT** The Arts District is one of downtown's hippest neighborhoods, full of lofts and crafty local businesses. This intimate, carefully curated wine bar caters to that scene with knowledgeable staffers who are happy to talk about the finer points of Lambrusco but won't make you feel silly for asking what it is. It's relaxed and conducive to conversation, making it a great spot to linger on a lazy weekend afternoon or unwind after work. **WHO** Value-seeking Downtowners who come for the daily happy hour with its $5 flatbreads and oxtail tacos. ☼

[Silver Lake Wine] 🌴 2395 Glendale Blvd., Silver Lake, 323.662.9024, silverlakewine.com. Mon. & Thurs. 5-9 p.m., Sun. 3-5 p.m.; store hours are more extensive. **WHY** Informed yet unpretentious tastings three days a week. **WHAT** The wine-loving scene to make is the Thursday (5 to 9 p.m.) flight tasting, at $12 a three-taste flight, with an extra bonus of the Let's Be Frank hot dog truck parked out front. Sunday brings a more serious tasting ($20, reservations required), and Monday evening is a casual night of tasting wines and cheeses. **WHO** Devoted regulars who buy all their wine here.

SAN GABRIEL VALLEY

[Bodega Wine Bar] Paseo Colorado, 260 E Colorado Blvd., Pasadena, 626.793.4300, bodegawinebar.com. Nightly 5 p.m.-1 a.m. **WHY** A sleek, dimly lit wine bar full of solid bottles, affordable glasses, and charismatic bartenders. **WHAT** A well-rounded selection of wine (as well as soju and beer) served in a modern setting, Bodega has a different vibe than most other Old Town Pasadena establishments. It is located off the drag in the Paseo Colorado, which classes up the place a bit. This isn t to say it's uppity or outlandishly expensive—Wednesdays feature $20 bottles of both reds and whites, ideal for small groups. **WHO** A young, hip-for-Pasadena crowd escaping the tweens and families at the nearby ArcLight and Islands. 🏛 ☼ ♥

[Everson Royce] 🌴 155 N. Raymond Ave., Old Pasadena, 626.765.9334, eversonroyce.com. Sun.-Mon. 10 a.m.-8 p.m., Tues.-Thurs. 10 a.m.-9 p.m., Fri.-Sat. 10 a.m.-10 p.m. **WHY** Friday-night tastings with the Let's Be Frank truck parked out front for sustenance. **WHAT** The nice folks from Silver Lake Wine are behind this brick-walled Old Pasadena wine bar, which you'll find after walking through the (excellent) retail shop. When the store is open, the bar is open, and you can try any of eight regularly changing wines by the glass at more than fair prices. Official tastings are Tuesday and Friday evenings and Saturday afternoons. **WHO** Friendly, low-key wine buffs. 🍷 🈂️

[Monopole Wine] 21 S. El Molino Ave., Pasadena, 626.577.9463, monopolewine.com. Thurs.-Sat. 11 a.m.-10 p.m., Sun. noon-6 p.m. **WHY** A nice place to sip wine in the increasingly vibrant Playhouse District. **WHAT** A charming tasting room behind a charming retail store in a charming neighborhood in charming Pasadena, Monopole is best known for its blind tastings, which are great fun. Prices are fair, and you can get a good plate of cheese and bread to accompany the vino. **WHO** Date-nighters, theatergoers, and students of wine.

[POP Champagne & Dessert Bar] 33 E. Union St., Old Pasadena, 626.795.1295, popchampagnebar.com. Sun. & Tues.-Thurs. 5 p.m.-11 p.m., Fri.-Sat. 5 p.m.-midnight; closing times may vary. **WHY** For the decadence of Champagne and chocolate soufflé, plus a solid happy hour every day from 5 to 7 p.m. **WHAT** Crystal chandeliers, brick walls, and hardwood floors set the stage for a place where people come to celebrate. Besides French Champagnes and rich desserts, there are California wines, craft beers, and lots of small plates to go with the drinks: mussels, pork-belly skewers, olives, and prosciutto-wrapped shrimp. It's packed on weekends, so reserve. **WHO** Girls' night out posses. ♥

[Vertical Wine Bistro] 🌴 70 N. Raymond Ave., Old Pasadena, 626.795.3999, verticalwinebistro.com. Sun. & Tues.-Thurs. 5-10 p.m., Fri.-Sat. 5-11 p.m. Full bar. **WHY** A sophisticated spot with a terrific happy hour, a remarkable wine list, and comfortable seating. **WHAT** Dark woods and dark leather lend an air of New York–style elegance to this second-floor bar and restaurant, making it the most civilized place to drink in Old Pasadena. There's a full bar, but wine is the focus, with more than 30 poured by the glass and hundreds by the bottle. The bar menu (caramelized-onion flatbreads, moules frites, shishito peppers) is very good. **WHO** Well-dressed Pasadenans of all ages. 🍷 ♥

[Wine Detective] The Commons, 146 S. Lake Ave. #109, Pasadena, 626.792.9936, winedetective.com. Sun.-Thurs. 3-11 p.m., Fri. 3 p.m.-midnight, Sat. 1 p.m.-midnight. **WHY** A comfortable place to sit, sip, nosh, and talk, with two lounge-y seating areas, a wooden communal table, and room to stand and chat around the gleaming tasting machines. **WHAT** Part retail store, part wine bar, and part high-tech tasting center, this quiet spot was created by two wine-loving couples who invested in Enomatic machines, which make tasting a fun game. Pours can be as small as one ounce and as large as you like, and prices are in the $2 to $5 an ounce range. To eat are cheeses, charcuterie, flatbreads, and *pintxos*, small, open-face Basque sandwiches. The happy hour (4 to 7 p.m. daily) brings $5 house wines and a few discounted dishes. **WHO** Friends meeting after work to taste and talk. 🍷

EAST VALLEY

[Luna Vine Wine Bar] 3206 W. Magnolia Blvd., Burbank, 818.561.4305, lunavinewinebar.com. Sun.-Tues. 4-11 p.m., Fri.-Sat. 4 p.m.-midnight. **WHY** Amazing zucchini fritters (basically zucchini doughnuts) and the perfect, crisp Languedoc Picpoul to go with them. **WHAT** At prime time (6:30 to 8:30) every barstool and table in this friendly, narrow storefront is full, and for good reason. The wine by the glass list is creative and fairly priced, and the small-plates food is fantastic. Don't miss the lamb meatballs, zucchini fritters, stuffed piquillo peppers, and assortment of goat cheeses. Thursday is grilled cheese night, and it's a good one. **WHO** An after-work crowd of neighbors and studio folks.

[Spin the Bottle Wine Studio] 10139 1/2 Riverside Dr., Toluca Lake, 818.509.7813, spinthebottlewines.com. Tues.-Wed. noon-8 p.m., Thurs. noon-9 p.m., Fri.-Sat. noon-10 p.m., Sun. noon-5 p.m. **WHY** An unpretentious wine bar and retail store that's a perfect fit for small-town, pedestrian-friendly Toluca Lake. **WHAT** Run by a couple of earnest, friendly wine-loving guys, Spin the Bottle is a simple place with a small bar, a couple of seating areas inside and out, and a lot of unusual, delicious, small-producer wines. The food is just snacks, so plan on stopping here before or after dinner. **WHO** Chill studio folks, Toluca Lake homeowners, young couples who'd rather sip a glass of Pinot Noir than hit a bar scene. 🍷 ☼

WEST VALLEY

[Blue Table] 28912 Roadside Dr., Agoura Hills, 818.597.2583, bluetable.net. Mon.-Sat. noon-10 p.m., Sun. noon-7 p.m. **WHY** A chic, new wine bar in a part of town that really needed one. **WHAT** The West Valley is now that much more appealing thanks to the new wine and cheese bar attached to the Blue Table gourmet deli and market. Owner Gina Marcione, she of the impressive height and dazzling smile, honors her Italian heritage in the collection, but there are wines from everywhere, with an impressive library of cheeses to accompany them. **WHO** Suburban homeowners escaping the kids for a glass of wine or two. 🍷 ☼

WESTSIDE: CENTRAL

[BottleRock] 3847 Main St., Culver City, 310.836.9463, bottlerockculvercity.com. Sun.-Mon. 4-10 p.m., Tues.-Thurs. 4-11 p.m., Fri.-Sat. 4 p.m.-1 a.m. **WHY** Comfy couches, an iPad menu of many wines, and good bar snacks (roasted Marcona almonds, prosciutto-wrapped dates, tuna tartare), plus (surprisingly, for a wine bar) a terrific beer menu. **WHAT** This hybrid wine bar/wine shop sits on the cusp of trendy, but fortunately it stays just this side of cozy. A good stop for a pick-me-up and a snack, and the $5 happy hour (4 to 7 p.m. daily) is terrific. **WHO** Folks waiting for their reservation at the Wallace and post-movie sippers.

[Ugo] 3865 Cardiff Ave., Culver City, 310.204.1222, cafeugo.com. Sun.-Thurs. 5:30-11 p.m., Fri.-Sat. 5:30 p.m.-1 a.m. **WHY** Every neighborhood needs a wine bar. **WHAT** Part of the Italian café next door, this wine bar is one of those Enomatic-machine places. Pop a prepaid card into one of them and get a one-ounce pour so you can taste your vino before you commit, or keep sampling all night long. The focus is on Italian reds, but there are also a few whites and a handful of wines from Chile, Argentina, and even California. Plus, you can order calamari and other snacks from the restaurant. **WHO** New couples out on dates, longtime couples picking up takeout, and people shaking off the workday with a glass of wine. ☼

WEST OF THE 405

[Bar Pintxo] 109 Santa Monica Blvd., Santa Monica, 310.458.2012, barpintxo.com. Sun.-Wed. noon-10 p.m., Thurs. noon-11 p.m., Fri.-Sat. noon-midnight. **WHY** Spanish wines and California-inspired tapas, including jamón serrano and outstanding

sautéed calamari, served until midnight on weekends. **WHAT** This
New York shotgun-style bar has tapas lined up behind a counter
up front, a sidewalk "counter" and a half dozen bar tables in back
for a delicious—though pricey—snack and glass of good Spanish
vino. Visit between noon and 6 every day to get albondigas or
croquetas for $6 and a glass of cava for just $4. **WHO** Fans of
chef/owner Joe Miller who don't want the commitment of a full
meal at Joe's; couples out for a glass of wine and a light bite after
a movie in an area dominated by louder pubs and bars. ☼

[Bodega Wine Bar] 814 Broadway, Santa Monica, 310.394.3504,
bodegawinebar.com. Nightly 5 p.m.-1:30 a.m. **WHY** It's a perfect
spot for a good-deal happy hour or post-movie glass of wine
and nosh—fairly priced, unpretentious, and well located in the
heart of Santa Monica. Wednesday is $20 bottle night. **WHAT**
A well-rounded selection of wine (as well as soju and beer), a
comfortable modern setting, and modest prices make this place
worth knowing about. It's more about conversation and lubrication
than wine fussiness, which is exactly what the regulars like about
it. And because it's a little hidden, it's easier to find a seat than at
the other Paseo hot spots. **WHO** A good-looking, youngish crowd
escaping the teenagers on the Promenade. 🏠

[Malibu Wines] 🍷 31740 Mullholland Hwy., Malibu,
818.865.0605, malibuwines.com. Daily 11 a.m.-7 p.m. (later on summer weekends). **WHY** A little bit of Sonoma in the Santa Monica
Mountains. **WHAT** Bring a picnic lunch to this hillside vineyard
and stone tasting room, buy a bottle of good local wine (two labels, Semler and Saddlerock), and stake out one of the rustic tables
to live just a little of the California dream. **WHO** Wine day-trippers
and some Malibu locals. 🔊 ☼♥

[Primitivo Wine Bistro] 1025 Abbot Kinney Blvd., Venice,
310.396.5353, primitivowinebistro.com. Mon.-Fri. noon-2:30 p.m. &
5:30 p.m.-midnight, Sat.-Sun. 11 a.m.-3 p.m. & 5:30 p.m.-midnight.
WHY For wine-friendly and delicious tapas (olives with smoked
almonds, patatas bravas, sausages with pretzel bread) and $5 wine
during happy hour. **WHAT** Is it a set design or tapas bar? You be
the judge. But first you'll have to land one of the small wooden
tables in the high-ceilinged space that's filled with columns, old
stained-glass church windows, and acres of linen drapes. The by-
the-glass collection of wines is extensive, if rather costly.
WHO Lots of beautiful Venice folk. ☼♥

🏠 GROUPS   🎤 KARAOKE   ☼ PATIO   ♥ ROMANTIC

[Venice Beach Wines] 529 Rose Ave., Venice, 310.606.2529, venicebeachwines.com. Mon.-Thurs. 4-11 p.m., Fri. 4 p.m.-midnight, Sat. 10:30 a.m.-midnight, Sun. 11:30 a.m.-11 p.m. **WHY** A lovely covered sidewalk patio, worthy wines to drink here or take home, equally worthy beers, and a good weekday happy hour. **WHAT** Part wine shop and part outdoor café, this place was cleverly designed to keep the indoors temperature-controlled for the wine while still having that indoor-outdoor flow so essential to Venice living. The wine-by-the-glass list is relatively short but deeply appealing: an international collection of lesser-known choices at fair prices, including some for under $12. To accompany your Spanish Mencia is a terrific menu that's good enough to attract lunchtime folks who are drinking Pellegrino instead of Pinot. Don't miss the cheeses. **WHO** Mostly locals who can walk here for a drink and a small plate or two. 🍸 ☼

SOUTH BAY TO SOUTH L.A.

[4th Street Vine] 🎭 2142 E. 4th St., Long Beach, 562.343.5463, 4thstreetvine.com. Mon.-Wed. 5-10 p.m., Thurs.-Fri. 5-11 p.m., Sat. 2-11 p.m., Sun. 2-10 p.m. **WHY** Generous pours of good, modestly priced wines and an array of local beers in the middle of vintage-cool Retro Row. **WHAT** 4th Street Vine fast became one of Long Beach's favorite bars, a low-key haunt where the entire city comes for a few sips. Nights usually bring raucous live music to the sleek, loft-like wine bar, but afternoons and early evenings are calm, the ideal time to try a flight of four wines for the eminently reasonable price of $12. **WHO** Pre-dinner wine sippers, tattooed beer drinkers, and wide-eyed movie lovers grabbing a drink after a screening at the Art Theatre. 🎬 ☼

[Friends of the Vine] 221 Ave. Del Norte, Redondo Beach, 310.792.5940, friendsofthevine.net. Tues.-Thurs. 4-11 p.m., Fri.-Sat. 4 p.m.-12:30 a.m. **WHY** A friendly, neighborly spot to sample from a large list of wines. **WHAT** In the late afternoon, this rambling, somewhat cluttered wine shop turns into a lively wine bar, and it feels like a party in a friend's house. Owners Fred and Tracy play their favorite CDs and pour wine by the glass or the flight, or you can buy a bottle, pay a modest corkage, and drink it here. Accompaniments include a generous cheese plate, charcuterie, and a few other snacks. **WHO** PV and south Redondo locals meeting friends for a drink and a cheese plate before moving elsewhere for dinner.

[Phlight] 6724 Bright Ave., Ste. B, Whittier, 562.789.0578,
phlightrestaurant.com. Sun.-Thurs. 5-10 p.m., Fri.-Sat. 5-11 p.m.
WHY An erudite small-plates restaurant that doubles as a wine bar.
WHAT Phlight is an Uptown Whittier gem, an airy and relaxed
place that exudes a casual warmth. Drop in for a quick bite and
you'll find a savvy wine list full of affordable and offbeat varietals
and a concise beer list. Opt for a wine flight and the signature
brown sugar and ginger short ribs and your whole evening will
suddenly seem perfect. **WHO** Savvy wine enthusiasts and couples
looking for a relaxed evening out. ♥

Wine Bars

⛺ GROUPS 🎤 KARAOKE ☼ PATIO ♥ ROMANTIC

Breweries +
Tap Rooms

In the last few years, the brewery scene has exploded in Southern California. San Diego County may be the premier destination, but there's a remarkable amount of good brewing going on closer to L.A., especially in the South Bay. Here are our favorite breweries and tap rooms, where you can taste the good stuff being brewed right in our own backyard. Take note that this is just the beginning for beer bars— head to the Bars + Cocktail Lounges chapter to find dozens of great pubs, beer gardens, and bars that focus on quality craft beers from near and far.

[ESSENTIALLY L.A.]

Angel City Brewery, Little Tokyo/Arts District (PAGE 143)
Beachwood BBQ & Brewing, Long Beach (PAGE 146)
The Brewery at Abigaile, Hermosa Beach (PAGE 146)
Eagle Rock Brewery, Glassel Park (PAGE 143)
El Segundo Brewing Company, Torrance (PAGE 147)
The Golden State, Fairfax District (PAGE 142)
Progress Brewing, El Monte (PAGE 144)
Smog City Brewing, Torrance (PAGE 148)
Stone Company Store, Old Pasadena (PAGE 145)

🏛 GROUPS 🎤 KARAOKE ✷ PATIO ♥ ROMANTIC

CENTRAL CITY

[Beer Belly] 532 S. Western Ave., Koreatown, 213.387.2337, beerbellyla.com. Mon.-Tues. 5-11 p.m., Wed.-Thurs. 5 p.m.-midnight, Sat. noon-1 a.m., Sun. noon-11 p.m. Beer & cider. **WHY** You want a mellow but fun place to share exciting bar snacks (Volcano Chicken Wings!) and drink top-notch beer from local brewers (some of whom you'll find sitting at the stool next to you).
WHAT Owner Jimmy Han curates some of the most interesting beers in the SoCal brewing scene at his cool K-town hangout decorated with colorful graffiti murals. Order duck French dip sandwiches and bacon grilled cheese with maple syrup from the bar. **WHO** Koreatown's hip urbanite set with a taste for craft beer; Wiltern concert-goers stopping by for a pre-show pint. 🏯 ☼

[Blue Palms Brewhouse] 6124 Hollywood Blvd., Hollywood, 323.464.2337, bluepalmsbrewhouse.com. Mon. 4 p.m.-midnight, Tues.-Thurs. 4 p.m.-1 a.m., Fri.-Sat. noon-2 a.m., Sun. noon-midnight. Full bar. **WHY** It's not always easy to find a casual bar in the middle of Hollywood, but this brewpub fills the bill. **WHAT** Adjacent to the Henry Fonda Theater, this basic but friendly pub is a useful stop before a concert or play. With 24 taps concentrating on Southern California craft brews, including a cask ale and a house-brewed beer, the folks at Blue Palms know their suds. A wide variety of styles are thoroughly explained, including alcohol levels and glass types, and the bar food goes down just fine. **WHO** Thirsty showgoers, beer aficionados.

[The Golden State] 🌴 426 N. Fairfax Ave., Fairfax District, 323.782.8331, thegoldenstatecafe.com. Tues.-Sun. noon-10 p.m. Beer & wine. **WHY** Locally sourced foods meet excellent beers at this casual café. **WHAT** A minimalist ode to the joy of pairing craft brews—mostly from the Golden State (that's California for you newcomers)—with food from the state's purveyors, including Scoops' unexpected ice cream flavors (including beer- and wine-inspired tastes), Let's Be Frank dogs and sausages, and naturally raised beef. Don't miss the crunchy fish 'n chips and zingy jalapeño coleslaw. Ask knowledgeable owner Jason Bernstein to help select the perfect beer for the food. **WHO** Daytime families, nighttime clubgoers, and sports fans (there's a TV for the big games). 🐷

EASTSIDE

[Angel City Brewery & Public House] 🌴 216 S. Alameda St., Little Tokyo/Arts District, 213.622.1261, angelcitybrewery.com. Mon.-Thurs. 4-10 p.m., Fri. 4 p.m.-midnight, Sat. noon-midnight, Sun. noon-10 p.m. Beer. **WHY** Enjoy superb house beers, which range from a golden stout to barrel-aged rye lagers, and score some grub from the food trucks outside. **WHAT** This historic brick warehouse houses an entire brewing operation, an art-gallery area, and two expansive levels filled with benches and chairs. Grab a beer and take a load off. **WHO** Downtown residents filling their growlers, or sipping pints and playing board games. 🏠

[Eagle Rock Brewery] 🌴 3056 Roswell St., Glassell Park, 323.257.7866, eaglerockbrewery.com. Wed.-Fri. 4-10 p.m., Sat.-Sun. noon-10 p.m. Beer & wine. **WHY** A place to taste made-in-L.A. beer right at the source...and play board games while you sip. **WHAT** Actually in adjacent Glassell Park, Eagle Rock Brewery is a friendly spot to quaff the brews that are pioneers in L.A.'s craft-beer scene. Manifesto Eagle Rock Wit (wheat beer), Solidarity black mild (a dark beer with a light taste), and Revolution XPA pale ale are just a few of the beers made by father-and-son brewmasters Steve and Jeremy Raub. Food trucks and taco tables pull up in the parking lot, and the brewery holds beer education sessions and supplies dozens of L.A. bars and restaurants. We've been waiting with bated breath for these guys to open an offshoot in the former Fatty's in Eagle Rock, but at press time we were still waiting. **WHO** Eastside bohos and citywide beer geeks. 📷 ☼

[Golden Road Brewing] 5410 W. San Fernando Rd., Atwater, 213.373.4677, goldenroad.la. Mon.-Tues. 11 a.m.-midnight, Weds.-Fri. 11 a.m.-2 a.m., Sat. 10 a.m.-2 a.m., Sun. 10 a.m.-midnight. Beer. **WHY** A veritable theme park of the brewing arts, L.A.'s largest brewery includes a cavernous pub and a beer-friendly menu with plenty of choices for vegetarians. **WHAT** The primary-colored warehouses that house Golden Road beckon from an industrial neighborhood near Glendale and the L.A. River, making it a popular stop for bicyclists on the river trail. Brewery tours and growler fills are available, and while popular beers like Point the Way IPA are widely available in cans, don't miss the special draft selections, like Back Home Gingerbread Stout or El Hefe barrel-aged hefeweizen. **WHO** Bicyclists pulling kid-laden trailers, dog lovers on the patio, craft beer dudes. 🐕 🏠 ☼

[Sunset Beer Company] 1498 Sunset Blvd. #3, Echo Park, 213.481.2337, sunsetbeerco.com. Sun.-Thurs. noon-11 p.m., Fri.-Sat. noon-midnight. Beer. **WHY** A carefully chosen beer selection and all the accoutrements. **WHAT** This offshoot of Eagle Rock's friendly Colorado Wine Shop is smartly located in the heart of craft-beer-adoring Echo Park. Beer expert Alex Macy is in charge of the broad but carefully selected array of beers, with an emphasis on Californian and Belgian breweries. Hang out for informative tastings from the rotating tap selection and beer-friendly snacks, or get advice on which brews to pair with foods. A selection of glassware and accessories will help even the novice hophead look on top of things. **WHO** Eastside beer geeks who enjoy the option of perusing the latest bottle release in the store or enjoying a pint pulled fresh from the tap on the outdoor patio. ✪

SAN GABRIEL VALKLEY

[Ohana Brewing Company] 7 S. 1st St., Alhambra, 626.282.2337, ohanabrew.com. Mon.-Thurs. 4-9 p.m., Fri.-Sat. 11 a.m.-10 p.m., Sun 11 a.m.-5 p.m. Beer. **WHY** An exciting addition to the barren Alhambra beer scene. **WHAT** Although its brewery is in Downtown L.A., Ohana has a new Alhambra tasting room, which is the only place to try all of their creations. Every beer is well done, the service friendly and personable; the only downside is the current permit only allows four four-ounce pours per visit, but plans are in the works to change that. **WHO** Fans of the brewery looking for the freshest offerings possible.

[Progress Brewing] 🌴 1822 Chico Ave., El Monte, 626.552.9603, progress-brewing.com. Sun.-Mon. & Thurs. 3-7 p.m., Fri.-Sat. 3-10 p.m. Beer. **WHY** To taste the best ales crafted in the south San Gabriel Valley. **WHAT** Diego Benitez and Kevin Ogilby are chemists who until not long ago, spent their days working on advanced chemistry, nanotechnology, and quantum mechanics. But they swapped their lab coats for beer goggles and hand-built a brewery in industrial South El Monte. Their parents might not approve of the career change, but L.A. beer drinkers should rejoice: The two create tasty, well-balanced brews, including a few Belgian-style beers, an American amber, and a high-octane imperial stout. The vibe is friendly and prices almost cheap, given the cost of craft beer these days. **WHO** A jovial assortment of East L.A. inhabitants, from construction workers to doctors. 🏷

[Stone Company Store] 🍺 220 S. Raymond Ave., Old Pasadena, 626.440.7243, stonebrew.com. Sun.-Thurs. 11 a.m.-9 p.m., Fri.-Sat. 11 a.m.-10 p.m. Beer. **WHY** The only Stone tap room in L.A. County offers year-round favorites from the great Escondido brewery, as well as special releases, coveted one-offs, and brewery swag. **WHAT** The best way to drink beer is straight from the source, so it doesn t get any better than this for Angelenos. The Pasadena store stocks Stone's newest beers to try, holds week-long events featuring variations on favorites, and sells growler fills (refillable jugs) of beer to enjoy at home. Its Enjoy By double IPA beer is sure to please even the bitterest of hopheads. **WHO** Devout fans of arrogance, gargoyles, and of course, hops. 📷 ☼

WEST VALLEY

[The Lab Brewing Co.] 3015 Agoura Rd., Agoura Hills, 818.735.0091, labbrewingco.com. Sun.-Mon. 11 a.m.-10 p.m., Tues.-Wed. 11 a.m.-11 p.m., Thurs. 11 a.m.-midnight, Fri.-Sat. 11 a.m.-2 a.m. Beer. **WHY** Solid in-house brews are served alongside some 25 other microbrews on tap. **WHAT** Roger Bott calls himself "Dr. Hops," and his graduation from home brewer to commercial brewery owner means he's earned it. His Bad Influence IPA is tasty, and all the beers, whether his own or from other small producers, go well with the good cooking. There's live music some nights, and it can get loud after 9 or so, so if you want to talk 'n' drink, come early. **WHO** Families and serious beer buffs in the early hours, and more of a well-dressed party crowd as the night develops. ☼

[Ladyface Alehouse & Brasserie] 29281 Agoura Rd., Agoura Hills, 818.477.4566, ladyfaceale.com. Daily 11 a.m.-9 p.m. Beer. **WHY** The best Belgian- and French-inspired beer in the Valley, with pretty good food, too. **WHAT** While the strip-mall location leaves a bit to be desired, Ladyface's bar and restaurant are beautiful and spacious. Try the La Grisette farmhouse wheat on a hot day, a barrel-aged sour if you're feeling more adventurous, or the rotating "real ale," which is cask-conditioned and served near room temperature. **WHO** Those with a taste for the complexities of European ales. 👥 ☼

👥 GROUPS 🎤 KARAOKE ☼ PATIO ♥ ROMANTIC

SOUTH BAY TO SOUTH L.A.

[Beachwood BBQ & Brewing] 🌴210 E. 3rd St., Long Beach, 562.436.4020, beachwoodbbq.com. Tues.-Wed. 11:30 a.m.-11 p.m. Thurs.-Sun. 11:30 a.m.-midnight. Beer & wine. **WHY** One of Southern California's—and maybe the nation's—top beer bars. **WHAT** A hophead's heaven, Beachwood is home to two-dozen rotating taps (viewable at any hour via the online HopCam) that feature the best local, national, and imported craft beers as well as some of the most rare and unique brewery collaborations. And under the helm of owner Gabe Gordon and head brewer Julian Shrago, Beachwood continues to produce award-winning beers of its own, too—all the better to pair with that beer- and coffee-glazed smoked ham. **WHO** Craft-beer geeks from all over the country. 🏚 ☼

[Brewco] 124 Manhattan Beach Blvd., Manhattan Beach, 310.798.2744, brewcomb.com. Sun.-Thurs. 11:30 a.m.-11 p.m., Fri.-Sat. 11:30 a.m.-1 a.m. Full bar. **WHY** House-brewed beers, cozy booths, and food that's better than the pub norm, all an easy walk from the pier and the beach. **WHAT** The beer brewed onsite in large copper vats isn't as good as some of the others around SoCal, but their hefeweizen and Manhattan Beach Blonde go down great after a walk on the beach. Regulars crowd into the small four-top booths to share pizzas, sesame ahi tuna, fish tacos, and pesto-shrimp salad, and sometimes watch a game on the big TV. **WHO** Sun-washed folks in their 20s and 30s who've had a good day at the beach. 📺 ☼

[The Brewery at Abigaile] 🌴1301 Manhattan Ave., Hermosa Beach, 310.798.8227, abigailerestaurant.com/brewery. Sun.-Thurs. 5-10 p.m., Fri.-Sat. 5-10:30 p.m. Full bar. **WHY** For great house-brewed beers in a handsome setting (including a fireplace-warmed terrace) with excellent food. **WHAT** Running the largest brewpub in the South Bay, Brian Brewer (yep, that's his real name) used to brew for Stone, where he became a master of creativity and consistency. Don't miss the Cacophony IPA, a once-a-year west coast–style brew made with a special hops blend created by several brewmasters, and Dark Matter, a fantastic Belgian-inspired dark ale. **WHO** Hermosa pub crawlers and the occasional pro athlete (the Kings partied here before the Stanley Cup). 🏚 ☼

🌴 ESSENTIALLY L.A.   ↘ DIVE   🍸 QUIET   ⑤ VALUE

[The Dudes' Brewing Company] 1840 W. 208th St., Torrance, 424.271.2915, thedudesbrew.com. Beer. **WHY** Tasty, hearty Double Trunk IPA and a promised taproom to sip it in. **WHAT** Coming soon, but not open at press time, is a taproom at this large South Bay brewery founded by a group of beer, well, dudes. They take their brewing seriously, and their dark, rich, alcoholic Double Trunk is showing up at taps all over L.A., as are their Juicebox fruit-focused beers. **WHO** Serious beer buffs.

[El Segundo Brewing Co.] 🌴 140 Main St., El Segundo, 310.529.3882, elsegundobrewing.com. Mon.-Thurs. 5-9 p.m., Fri. 5-10 p.m., Sat. 4-10 p.m., Sun. noon-7 p.m. Beer. **WHY** If hoppy, mouth-puckering beers sound appealing, you'll find these beers the best in the bourgeoning South Bay beer scene, and possibly in all of L.A. **WHAT** Although it makes a wide range of styles, El Segundo is best known for its APAs and west coast IPAs (American/Indian pale ales). Try the White Dog IPA for a lighter, cleaner take on the classic; the ultra-bitter Two 5 Left Double IPA; the Hop Tanker; or the Blue House Citra Pale, a fruity but full-bodied ale that gained fame for being one of the only local beers to have been served at Dodger Stadium. **WHO** Beer lovers making that bitter beer face. 🍺 🏠

[Monkish Brewing Co.] 20311 S. Western Ave., Torrance, 310.295.2157, monkishbrewing.com. Thurs.-Fri. 4-9 p.m., Sat. 1-8 p.m., Sun. 1-6 p.m. Beer. **WHY** The best Belgian-style ales in the South Bay. **WHAT** While it's a fact that Southern California brews some of the best pale ales and IPAs in the world, Monkish stays true to its name, churning out year-round and specialty ales that would be welcome in any Belgian abbey. The quaint tap room is the perfect spot to sample some of our favorites, such as the Feminist, a tripel brewed with hibiscus flowers, and the Shaolin Fist, a dubbel amped up by tongue-tingling Sichuan peppercorns. **WHO** Fans of funky yeast strains and imaginative twists on the Belgian classics. 🍺 🏠

[Naja's Place] 154 International Boardwalk, Redondo Beach, 310.376.9951, najasplace.com. Mon.-Tues. 2 p.m.-midnight, Wed.-Thurs. 2 p.m.-1 a.m., Fri.-Sat. noon-2 a.m., Sun. noon-midnight. Beer & wine. **WHY** Eighty-eight beers on tap and cool ocean breezes.

WHAT The beer list here isn't the most esoteric, but that's what makes Naja's such a recommendable place: a beer bar built not just for high-IBU enthusiasts, but for those who simply want an easy-drinking session beer…or three. Occasional tap takeovers liven things up just in case you somehow tire of almost 100 different beers. Some nights bring live music, and it gets loud.
WHO South Bay beach bums, beer bros, and thirsty thirtysomethings.

[Smog City Brewing] 🌴 1901 Del Amo Blvd., Torrance, 310.320.7664, smogcitybrewing.com. Wed.-Fri. 4-9 p.m., Sat. noon-8 p.m., Sun. noon-6 p.m. Beer. **WHY** Named the best new business in Torrance in 2013 for good reason—it makes some of the tastiest beer in the L.A. area. **WHAT** Led by brewmaster Jonathon Porter (who was obviously was born to brew), the team at this South Bay powerhouse produces A-grade beers of all types. Standouts include their IPAs (Amarilla Gorilla, Hoptonic, and Grape Ape), coffee-infused porters (Chip Shot and Groundworks Coffee Porter), inventive farmhouse ales (the L.A. Saison brewed with sour cherries, peaches, or mango), and a double chocolate imperial stout dubbed The Nothing. The rare barrel-aged offerings are even more impressive, so be sure to swing by the tap room often, as they go fast. **WHO** An ever-increasing number of beer geeks. 🏖

[Strand Brewing Company] 23520 Telo Ave., Torrance, 310.517.0900, strandbrewing.com. Thurs.-Fri. 4-9 p.m., Sat. noon-8 p.m., Sun. noon-5:00 p.m. Beer. **WHY** Stellar, under-the-radar craft beer. **WHAT** Despite its lower profile, Strand Brewing Company is one of L.A.'s best. The beachy brewery consistently produces excellent beers, and its tap room is where to go for rare and seasonal releases. While you're there, make sure to try the toasty and unique Musashi Black IPA. **WHO** Bearded beer geeks and surfers fresh from the ocean. 🏖

SANTA CLARITA

[Wolf Creek Brewery] 25108 Rye Canyon Loop, Valencia, 661.294.9977, wolfcreekbrewingco.com. Wed.-Thurs. 4-9 p.m., Fri. 3-9 p.m., Sat. noon-9 p.m., Sun. noon-5 p.m. Beer. **WHY** A rare family-friendly brewery that crafts delicious beers. **WHAT** This long-established brewery is successful for good reasons: All beers cost just $5 and are served in appropriate glassware; workers are jovial and chatty; and there are cornhole, card, and table games for fun. Sodas and snacks keep the kids happy, and they also allow outside food. There's a full-service restaurant in Santa Clarita. **WHO** Valencia beer lovers and parents looking to unwind after a long day at Magic Mountain. 📷 🏛 ☼

[**Wolf Creek Restaurant & Brewing Co.**] 27746 McBean Pkwy., Santa Clarita, 661.263.9653, wolfcreekbrewingco.com. Mon.-Thurs. 11 a.m.-10 p.m., Fri.-Sat. 11 a.m.-11 p.m., Sun. 10:30 a.m.-9:30 p.m. Beer & wine. **WHY** House-crafted beers served in a warm, friendly restaurant. **WHAT** The flagship of the three-location Wolf Creek brewing empire, this is a full-service restaurant that showcases their very good (and affordable) beers and lots of good food to go with them—and a decent wine list for the haters. You could do far worse than a discounted Dogtown Dunkelweizen and the $5 empanadas out on the terrace at happy hour. **WHO** Longtime regulars and young suburbanite families. 📷 🏛 ☼

INLAND EMPIRE

[**Hangar 24 Brewery**] 1710 Sessums Dr., Redlands, 909.389.1400, hangar24brewery.com. Sun.-Thurs. 11 a.m.-10 p.m., Fri.-Sat. 11 a.m.-midnight. Beer. **WHY** Their refreshing Orange Wheat beer is perfect after a day hiking in the local mountains. **WHAT** Surrounded by groves of orange trees and located next door to a small airport, this Redlands brewery offers awesome views from its warehouse-style tap room. Its beers, which include a variety of worthy IPAs, are excellent, too. **WHO** Local brewers and hobbyists and East SGV bros fresh off a day of BMX riding. ☼

Coffee, Tea + Boba

In case you hadn't noticed, L.A. has gone mad for coffee. Oh sure, you may decry the prevalence of handlebar-mustachioed baristas laboring for ages over $6 siphon coffees and foam-art lattes, but there's no doubting that the good stuff is not just in the Pacific Northwest and the Bay Area anymore. And it's not just good coffee that we're blessed with—L.A. has world-class tea emporiums and, thanks to our vibrant Asian community, lots of great boba. This chapter showcases our favorites.

[ESSENTIALLY L.A.]

Aroma Coffee & Tea Company, Studio City (PAGE 170)
Balconi Coffee Company, West L.A. (PAGE 175)
Bar Nine Collective, Culver City (PAGE 172)
Bird Pick Tea & Herb, Old Pasadena (PAGE 164)
Blue Bottle Coffee, Little Tokyo/Arts District (PAGE 157)
Caffé Luxxe, Santa Monica (PAGE 175)
The Conservatory, Culver City (PAGE 173)
De Café Baristas, Monterey Park (PAGE 166)
Dragon Herbs, Santa Monica (PAGE 176)
Euro Caffé, Beverly Hills (PAGE 173)
Funnel Mill, Santa Monica (PAGE 176)
Go Get Em Tiger, Hancock Park (PAGE 153)
Half & Half Tea House, Monterey Park (PAGE 166)
Hwa Sun Ji, Koreatown (PAGE 154)
Intelligentsia Coffee, Silver Lake (PAGE 160)
Intelligentsia Venice Coffeebar, Venice (PAGE 178)
Jones Coffee Roasters, Pasadena (PAGE 168)
Klatch Coffee, San Dimas (PAGE 183)
Portfolio Coffeehouse, Long Beach (PAGE 182)
République Café, Miracle Mile (PAGE 155)
Tearoom at the Langham Huntington, Pasadena (PAGE 169)
Ten Ren's Tea Time, Chinatown (PAGE 163)
Tierria Mia Coffee, South Gate (PAGE 182)
Two Guns Espresso, Manhattan Beach (PAGE 183)

Coffee, Tea &
Boba

🏠 GROUPS   🎤 KARAOKE   ☼ PATIO   ♥ ROMANTIC

CENTRAL CITY

[Alfred Coffee & Kitchen] 8428 Melrose Pl., Melrose, 323.944.0811, alfredcoffee.com. Mon.-Sat. 7 a.m.-7 p.m., Sun. 8 a.m.-6 p.m. **WHY** Stumptown coffee, Farmshop baked goods, chilly baristas. **WHAT** During peak morning hours, it's a stereotypically L.A. scene at this European-style café. Order your caffeine at the subterranean counter then wander upstairs to find a table (hopefully outside) so you can discreetly gawk at 23-year-olds carrying thousand-dollar handbags and impossibly toned women pushing strollers that cost as much as a used car. After all, you've got a ringside seat for Melrose Place, the street made famous by Aaron Spelling's hilariously over-the-top '90s soap opera. **WHO** People who believe in pressed juice, colonics, and bar method classes but can't resist the occasional secret cigarette after a couple of glasses of overpriced Pinot. And on Sunday mornings, shoppers from the small but pleasant farmers' market. ☼

[Andante Coffee Roasters] 7623 Beverly Blvd., Fairfax District, 323.525.0355. Mon.-Sat. 7 a.m.-9 p.m., Sun. 8 a.m.-8 p.m. **WHY** House-roasted beans, careful brewing, and free WiFi. **WHAT** There's a serenity to this high-ceilinged coffeehouse, with a communal table, a regular clientele of laptop people, and a menu of pour-over coffees, espresso drinks, tea lattes, and a few sandwiches and baked goods. **WHO** Independent contractors who can work anywhere. ☽

[BrewWell] 3525 W. 8th St., Koreatown, 213.384.0884. Mon.-Fri. 8 a.m.-10 p.m., Sat. 10 a.m.-10 p.m. **WHY** A cheerful place to study or work while enjoying a lavender-infused cappuccino. **WHAT** In the heart of K-town behind an Assi Supermarket, BrewWell has a large selection of coffees, lattes, and teas. The herbal options—the PJL (passionfruit, jasmine, and lychee iced tea) and lavender cappuccino—set them apart. The colorful décor and friendly baristas make for a cheerful vibe. Bring your laptop and work at the counter or one of many tables. **WHO** Koreans from the neighborhood, college students.

[Bricks & Scones] 403 N. Larchmont Blvd., Hancock Park, 323.463.0811, bricksandscones.com. Mon.-Fri. 7:30 a.m.-9 p.m., Sat.-Sun. 8 a.m.-8 p.m. No booze. **WHY** House-baked pastries, good sandwiches, Intelligentsia coffee, Lupicia teas, and tomb-like quiet for working. **WHAT** With a no-talking upstairs study area and a

Coffee, Tea & Boba

quiet downstairs lounge, plus a leafy patio with plenty of shade
umbrellas and no restriction on chatting, Bricks & Scones appeals
to serious students and screenwriters as well as ladies who lunch
and have afternoon tea. We aren't partial to the heavy, salty scones
that everyone seems to adore, but the muffins and sandwiches are
quite good (try the mango curried chicken salad sandwich).
WHO Laptop-toters and people fresh from yoga class. 🎧 ☼

[Bru Coffeebar] 1866 N. Vermont Ave., Los Feliz, 323.664.7500,
brucoffeebar.com. Mon.-Sat. 7 a.m.-8 p.m., Sun. 7 a.m.-8 p.m.
WHY Quality Ritual coffee drinks, free parking (in back) in a
parking-poor neighborhood, and WiFi. **WHAT** Pour-over coffee
comes to Los Feliz in this minimalist, high-ceilinged café, where
the baristas are friendly, the atmosphere is quiet, and the coffee is
made with care. **WHO** The same folks you see on the sidewalk at
Figaro and browsing in Skylight.

[C+M] Los Angeles County Museum of Art, 5905 Wilshire Blvd.,
Miracle Mile, 323.857.6180, patinagroup.com/c+m. Mon.-Tues. &
Thurs. 10 a.m.-5 p.m., Fri. 10 a.m.-7 p.m., Sat.-Sun. 10 a.m.-6 p.m.
WHY Coffee that's much better than at most museums, plus
creative sweets. **WHAT** Coffee plus milk is a winning formula at
this Patina Group coffee and pastry stop in the LACMA courtyard.
Lemon, bacon, or Nutella pop-tarts are the perfect post-art snack
with an Intelligentsia cappuccino, or try the housemade organic
milk sorbet in an ice cream sandwich, or perhaps an espresso
affogato. **WHO** Art- and caffeine-loving museum-goers; well-
dressed docents.

[Coffee Commissary] 801 N. Fairfax Ave. #106, West Hollywood, 323.782.1465, coffeecommissary.com. Daily 7 a.m.-8 p.m.
WHY A nice coffee break and people-watching spot in the
mid-Fairfax rush. **WHAT** Less obnoxious than many of its West
Hollywood neighbors, this place boasts great coffee and a lot of
delicious complementary pastries. Modest outdoor seating fills up
fast and tends to spill over into that of the café next door.
WHO That super-buff guy from the gym, and that girl from the re-
ality show, and was that Zac Efron? Plus lots of trendy Hollywood
types who live in the swanky building upstairs. ☼

[Go Get Em Tiger] 🎋230 N. Larchmont Blvd., Hancock Park,
323.380.5359, ggetla.com. Daily 7 a.m.-6 p.m. **WHY** Hipster coffee
for the bougie set. **WHAT** The Larchmont outpost of G&B Coffee

has the same sleek bar setup as the Grand Central Market location, with added wooden boxes for extra-modern, less-than-comfortable seating. It's still all about the homemade almond milk here, or the seriously deadly Gget Shake, with two shots of espresso and vanilla ice cream. Pastries are made in-house, and it shows.
WHO A sea of Lululemon apparel.

[Graffiti Sublime Coffee] 180 S. La Brea Ave., Hancock Park, No phone. Daily 9 a.m.-8 p.m. **WHY** For a soothing, distraction-free place to catch up on work. **WHAT** The solely black-and-white decor, backlit peace sign, and enormous hanging mobile give this gallery-like space a chic, sleek look. Though it may be trying a bit too hard, the beverages are great, albeit expensive. The Sister Midnight, shaken with chocolate ganache, takes your basic iced mocha up a notch. Best not to bring the kids along, as this coffee shop has a no-nonsense policy about preserving its chi. **WHO** Mac-owning young professionals, hipster coffee snobs. 🍸 ☼

[Groundwork] 1501 N. Cahuenga Blvd., Hollywood, 323.871.0107, groundworkcoffee.com. Mon.-Wed. 6 a.m.-7 p.m., Thurs.-Fri. 6 a.m.-10 p.m., Sat. 7 a.m.-10 p.m., Sun. 7 a.m.-7 p.m. **WHY** Organic drip coffee (Ethiopian Nile) good enough to convert a latte lover; friendly baristas who know their foam drawings. **WHAT** A small, hip, L.A. coffee roaster with a social conscience and locations in areas that need them most—like this heart-of-Hollywood spot. Good coffee and perfectly decent pastries. **WHO** Hollywood night owls straggling in late in the morning for a hangover-killing jolt of java. 🍸 ☼

[The Helio Café] 710 N. Heliotrope Dr., East Hollywood, 323.662.2302, theheliocafe.com. Mon.-Fri. 8 a.m.-4 p.m., Sat. 9 a.m.-4 p.m., Sun. 10 a.m.-2 p.m. **WHY** Warm, friendly people making simple, quality coffee. **WHAT** The former Cafecito Organico is now Helio, and it's found a devoted clientele for its friendliness, its cold brew coffee, its espresso drinks, and its excellent Vietnamese coffee with sweet condensed milk. Prices are very fair for the quality; beans come from places like Ritual and Four Barrel. The food's good, too—try the quiche if they have it. **WHO** LACC students and faculty, East Hollywood denizens, Los Feliz folks willing to drive south for a great coffee at a good price. 🍸 🗑 ☼

[Hwa Sun Ji] 🌴3690 Wilshire Blvd., Ste. 100, Koreatown, 213.382.5302. Mon.-Sat. noon-midnight, Sun. noon-11 p.m.

WHY A Zen-like, truly Korean tea experience. **WHAT** Hiding in a nondescript Koreatown strip mall (like all the best places around here), this tea lounge has overcome its drab architecture to become a peaceful oasis, complete with an indoor fountain. The high-end tea options, served in beautiful, traditional wares, claim lofty health benefits; whether they reach these or not, the experience is worth the gamble. **WHO** Older Korean businesspeople and younger folks on dates.

[Insomnia Café] 7286 Beverly Blvd., Beverly/Third, 323.931.4943. Daily 10 a.m.-1 a.m. **WHY** A convenient location, comfy furniture, and a no-cell-phone policy make this a good spot for working or meeting someone, although parking can be tricky, and the WiFi's not free. **WHAT** This longtime caffeination station is a relaxed, friendly, and very quiet place, with decent coffee drinks and snacks. Best of all, it's open until 1 a.m. **WHO** Screenwriters, freelance writers, students, and a post-theater crowd. 🍵 ☕

[République Café] 🍴 624 S. La Brea Ave., Miracle Mile, 310.362.6115, republiquela.com. Daily 8 a.m.-3 p.m. **WHY** For Margarita Manzke's dreamy blueberry brioche and pain au chocolat and a chance to sit in this amazing space without the nighttime mobs. **WHAT** L.A.'s hottest French restaurant is more peaceful in the morning, when locals stop in for carefully pulled espresso drinks, tea lattes, and a gorgeous array of baked goods. By the time you read this, a full breakfast may be offered, but for now it's just coffee, tea, and pastries, and that's enough for us. **WHO** Agents, businesspeople, and Hancock Park moms. ♥

[Sabor y Cultura] 5625 Hollywood Blvd., Hollywood, 323.466.0481, flavorandculture.wordpress.com. Mon.-Fri. 6:30 a.m.-11 p.m., Sat.-Sun. 7:30 a.m.-10 p.m. **WHY** A friendly vibe, fairly easy street parking, free wireless, and skilled baristas. **WHAT** A double-wide storefront in Little Armenia, this spacious, inviting coffeehouse doesn't display the sort of Latin influences you might expect from its name. It's just an all-around good place to hang out over a latte, hot breakfast sandwich, or frozen yogurt. Check for events: art openings, music, perhaps even flamenco dance. **WHO** A typical coffeehouse crowd, East Hollywood style. 🍵 ☼

[Sanjang Coffee Garden] 101 S. Virgil Ave., East Hollywood, 213.387.9190. Mon.-Fri. 5 p.m.-2 a.m., Sat. 5 p.m.-2 a.m., Sun. 5 p.m.-midnight **WHY** Good coffee, boba, Korean snacks, desserts, and sandwiches. Drink prices are on the high side because many patrons stay for hours just ordering one drink. **WHAT** This lavish space catering to the Korean community features several heated outdoor areas, including one with a fire pit. All the amenities are provided, including free WiFi and blankets for snuggling by the fire, and it's open until 2 a.m. **WHO** Young Koreans—mostly smokers—and the occasional curious non-Korean. ☼

[Single Origin Coffee at Short Cake] Farmers Market, 6333 W. 3rd St., Stall 316, Beverly/Third, 323.761.7976, socoffeela.com. Mon.-Sat. 8 a.m.-9 p.m., Sun. 8 a.m.-7 p.m. **WHY** You're looking for authentic Verve coffee and don't want to drive all the way up to Santa Cruz. **WHAT** Little more than a counter among many others at the Farmers Market, Short Cake specializes in espresso and pastries. The friendly baristas will be happy to give you a detailed explanation of their coffee, which is, unsurprisingly, sourced from a single geographic origin. **WHO** Tired tourists and screenwriters and other Farmers Market regulars. ☼

[Stir Crazy Coffee Shop] 6903 Melrose Ave., Melrose, 323.934.4656. Mon.-Thurs. 7 a.m.-11 p.m., Fri. 7 a.m.-midnight, Sat. 8 a.m.-midnight, Sun. 8 a.m.-11 p.m. **WHY** A mellow (despite the name) hangout with good coffee and smoothies. **WHAT** A friendly neighborhood coffeehouse with free WiFi, lots of laptop people, dogs (and smokers) on the patio, and good coffee made until midnight on weekends. **WHO** Writers and locals who want to look like writers, tapping away on their MacBooks while sipping nonfat lattes. 🖘 ☼

[T (Farmers Market)] Farmers Market, 6333 W. 3rd St., Stall 212, Fairfax District, 323.930.0076, teashopla.com. Mon.-Fri. 9 a.m.-9 p.m., Sat. 9 a.m.-8 p.m., Sun. 10 a.m.-7 p.m. **WHY** Bypass the chains for this charming stall with hundreds of bulk teas, as well as tea drinks to enjoy in the Farmers Market bustle. **WHAT** Have a cuppa and a sandwich or take home a few exotic varieties of herbal and traditional teas. ☼

[Urth Caffé] 8565 Melrose Ave., West Hollywood, 310.659.0628, urthcaffe.com. Sun.-Thurs. 6:30 a.m.- 11:30 p.m., Fri.-Sat. 6:30 a.m.-midnight. **WHY** Spanish lattes, tea lattes, and all-around good drinks, most of which are organic and/or sustainably produced. Don't mind the poseurs and enjoy the coffee and excellent oatmeal or pumpkin pie. **WHAT** Sure, it's a Hollywood scene, and the park-

Coffee, Tea & Boba

ing is terrible, but you could do far worse in this 'hood for coffee, tea and/or a light meal. The baristas are skilled, the products are good, and the patio is a fine place to catch up with an old friend. **WHO** Actors, screenwriters, the gluten-phobic—a stereotypical L.A. crowd. ☼

EASTSIDE

[Barista Society Coffee Boutique] US Bank Tower, 633. W. 5th St., 2nd Fl., Downtown, 213.444.3389, baristasociety.com. Mon.-Fri. 7 a.m.-6 p.m. **WHY** A former Starbucks is now an indie place that makes first-rate Kyoto cold-brew coffee and other good caffeine drinks. **WHAT** Friendly, well-trained baristas make drinks from quality beans (including Stumptown, Klatch, and Blue Bottle). It's the real deal. Sit inside or out or take it back to your marketing meeting. **WHO** Grateful office workers. ☼

[Blue Bottle Coffee] 🎋 582 Mateo St., Little Tokyo/Arts District, bluebottlecoffee.com. Daily 7 a.m.-6 p.m. **WHY** For the meticulously (fanatically?) roasted and prepared coffee that's had Bay Area folks swooning for years. **WHAT** This SoCal outpost of the Oakland-based coffee roaster still wasn't open at press time, but we're including it anyway, because it's coming very soon and it's going to be a big deal. Occupying the former Handsome Coffee location in the Arts District (actually, the two companies merged), it's sure to become the go-to caffeine destination for Arts District lofties. **WHO** Pilgrims. 🎧

[Boba 7] 518 W. 7th St., Downtown, 213.538.8022, labobatory.com. Sun.-Wed. noon-9 p.m., Thurs.-Sat. noon-10 p.m. **WHY** For the Green-TeaHeineken and other alcohol-boba cocktails with clever names (such as the Pokemon-theme Bobasour and Sricharizard), or the Bobatella (milk tea with honey boba) if you're not feeling something alcoholic. **WHAT** You'd think more people would be daring enough to try mixing boba with sweet alcoholic drinks, but Boba 7 remains a unique treat. You'll find this artsy, speakeasy-style boba joint at the back of a Thai restaurant near 7th & Grand. It was started by a USC graduate with a fondness for puns. **WHO** Hip young Downtowners, USC students, and geeks who wants a drink named after their favorite childhood video game.

[Broome St. General Store] 2912 Rowena Ave., Silver Lake, 323.570.0405, broomestgeneral.com. Mon.-Sat. 8 a.m.-7 p.m.,

Sun. 9 a.m.-5 p.m. **WHY** No-crowd premium coffee and a great
NY-inspired general store for gifts. **WHAT** On a quieter stretch of
Rowena Blvd., find this quaint shop and patio selling NY favorite
Gimme! Coffee along with a good selection of home goods and
classic prep clothing. Don't expect to eat a full meal or find
reliable WiFi, but relax on the underused patio when the sun's out.
WHO The wealthier side of Silver Lake. ☼

[Café de Leche] 5000 York Blvd., Highland Park, 323.551.6828,
cafedeleche.net. Sun.-Thurs. 7 a.m.- 6 p.m., Fri.-Sat. 7 a.m.-7 p.m.
WHY This café is everything that this gentrifying neighborhood
is becoming: accessible, affordable, and full of adorably attired babies. **WHAT** At the corner of York and Avenue 50, this is a perfect
little coffeehouse in a neighborhood that needed it. The menu is
small, but everything is delicious (try the jalapeño bagels). There's
a fantastic selection of organic teas, as well as the expected lattes
and mochas—and an amazingly creamy hot chocolate that's full
of spices. A row of little tables is perfect for laptops, and there are
enough outlets for them all—plus free wireless. **WHO** Twentysomethings working at their laptops and indie parents with cute
indie children. 🐿

[Cafecito Orgánico] 534 N. Hoover St., Silver Lake,
213.537.8367, cafecitoorganico.com. Mon.-Fri. 6 p.m.-7 p.m., Sat.-
Sun. 7 a.m.-7 p.m. **WHY** A mellow alternative to Silver Lake's
over-caffeinated coffee scene. **WHAT** Housed in a faux-lighthouse
building on none-too-gentrified Hoover Street, this place started
selling organic fair-trade beans at local farmers' markets before
opening the café. With free WiFi, a large covered patio, and baked
goods from Echo Park's Delilah Bakery, it's a funky and calm
place for a cappuccino or the special house Cafecito, made with
steamed milk and sugar cane juice. All the freshly roasted beans
are available by the pound. ☼

[Caffè Vita] 4459 W. Sunset Blvd., Silver Lake, 323.663.6340,
caffevita.com. Mon.-Fri. 6 a.m.-10 p.m., Sat.-Sun. 8 a.m.-9 p.m.
WHY Excellent coffee without the pretension, jaunty hats, or long
lines found at Intelligentsia just up the street. **WHAT** At the massive intersection of Sunset and Hollywood, the friendliest baristas
on the eastside serve up some of the best coffee and espresso
drinks around; best of all, iced coffee is on tap. If you can snag
a chair, the sparse outdoor seating is ideal for people-watching;
inside, décor is minimal and tables are mostly full of laptops. The

only California location of this Seattle-based roaster, it's the perfect place for a pick-me-up to ensure you stay awake at the movies—the Vista Theater is right across the street. **WHO** Hairdressers and patrons of Rudy's Barbershop next door, aspiring screenwriters typing away. Always a motorcycle or two parked out front.

[The Coffee Table] 1958 Colorado Blvd., Eagle Rock, 323.255.2200, coffeetablebistro.com. Daily 7 a.m.-10 p.m. Beer & wine. **WHY** Breakfast burritos are a favorite, and the wide selection of Sweet Lady Jane cakes makes a good accompaniment to coffee drinks. **WHAT** Chat or work in this Eagle Rock offshoot of the now-closed Silver Lake screenwriter's hangout. Thanks to the liquor license and adjacent bar and lounge, it's easy to move from coffee to evening entertainment. **WHO** Eagle Rock artists, writers, entrepreneurs, and families. 🍵

[Demitasse] 135 S. San Pedro St., Little Tokyo/Arts District, 213.613.9300, cafedemitasse.com. Mon.-Fri. 7 a.m.-10 p.m., Sat.-Sun. 8 a.m.-10 p.m. **WHY** Intensely sweet hot chocolate and coffee-geek coffee in a great Little Tokyo location. **WHAT** Service can tend toward the surly, and the prices are on the high side, but there's still much to recommend this place: carefully made siphon coffee, intense "sipping chocolate," lovely lattes, an excellent iced tea and iced Kyoto coffee, free WiFi, and comfortable seating inside and out. **WHO** Little Tokyo coffee snobs. ☼

[Fix Coffee] 2100 Echo Park Ave., Echo Park, 323.284.8962, fixcoffeeco.com. Daily 7 a.m.-7 p.m. **WHY** A picturesque patio for an afternoon catch-up or freelance working, perhaps with your dog curled at your feet. **WHAT** Located way up on Echo Park Boulevard, the patio here (complete with twinkly lights in the evening) is a coffee oasis in the midst of lush foliage and a quiet residential neighborhood. It serves coffee from such favorite local roasters as Intelligentsia and Verve, and there's no better place in Echo Park to get your fix than on this shady patio. **WHO** Young Echo Park families, indie musicians, Elysian Park hikers—a rotating group that all seems to know each other. 🐾 ☼

[Four Leaf] 318 E. 2nd St., Ste. 8, Little Tokyo/Arts District, 877.797.4532. Tues.-Thurs. noon-9 p.m., Fri.-Sat. Sun, noon-1 a.m., Sun. noon-10 p.m. **WHY** Little Tokyo doesn't have as many boba offerings as your other Asian enclaves, but Four Leaf remains a solid choice. The crêpes are great too. **WHAT** This slightly artsy café has a variety of teas with or without milk, fruit teas (with bits of fruit mixed in!), and artful flower teas. The creatively named crêpes come in both sweet and savory varieties. **WHO** Visitors to Little Tokyo and residents from the nearby apartments.

[G&B Coffee] Grand Central Market, 324 S. Hill St., Ste. C19, Downtown, No phone, gandbcoffee.com. Daily 7 a.m.-6 p.m. **WHY** The housemade almond-macadamia milk and the extra-premium coffee selection. **WHAT** Sidle up to this true coffee bar in the bustling, evolving Grand Central Market and enjoy a super-smooth coffee while chatting with the knowledgeable baristas or watching Downtown go by. The bar setup does not make for the most efficient service, but this open-air spot is great for a semi-quick coffee break and some amazing pastries, like the cheddar prosciutto muffin, made at their Larchmont sister café, Go Get Em Tiger. **WHO** Downtown worker bees and coffee snobs.

[Groundwork] 108 W. 2nd St., Little Tokyo/Arts District, 213.620.9668, groundworkcoffee.com. Mon.-Fri. 6 a.m.-5 p.m., Sat.-Sun. 8 a.m.-1 p.m. **WHY** A worthy member of the Groundwork family in a cool old Downtown building. **WHAT** On the western edge of Little Tokyo, this is a good place to know about for folks who work on the north end of Downtown, and it's a godsend for people on jury duty nearby. Good house-roasted coffee, free WiFi, and fair prices. **WHO** Laptop people upstairs and on-the-go Downtowners, cops, and City Hall workers downstairs. 🌴 ☼

[Holy Grounds Coffee & Tea] 5371 Alhambra Ave., El Sereno, 323.222.8884, holygroundscoffeeandtea.com. Mon.-Fri. 6:30 a.m.-9 p.m., Sat.-Sun. 8 a.m.-6 p.m. **WHY** For the large, lush patio, complete with a fountain, and the Café de Olla, a brewed coffee with cinnamon and *piloncilo* (a Mexican brown sugar). **WHAT** A sweet, community-focused coffeehouse, Holy Grounds combines a hip Latino look with good coffee, a serene garden, and baked goods from such worthy vendors as Homeboy. **WHO** Artists, Cal State L.A. students, and El Sereno, Lincoln Heights, and Monterey Hills residents. 🌴 ☼

[Intelligentsia Coffee] 🌴 3922 W. Sunset Blvd., Silver Lake, 323.663.6173, intelligentsiacoffee.com. Sun.-Wed. 6 a.m.-8 p.m., Thurs.-Sat. 6 a.m.-11 p.m. **WHY** A very serious approach to coffee, but with less of the snobbiness seen at some other Clover-stocked joints. **WHAT** Silver Lake's intelligentsia—those who can afford

Coffee, Tea & Boba

your higher-end coffees, that is—belly up to the bar or snag a Sunset Junction patio table to linger over aromatic, beautifully prepared Clover coffee or espresso drinks. **WHO** Silver Lake cool people—and isn't everyone who lives in Silver Lake cool? ☼

[**Kaldi**] 3147 Glendale Blvd., Atwater, 323.660.6005, kaldicoffeeatwater.com. Mon.-Fri. 6:30 a.m.-8 p.m., Sat.-Sun. 7:30 a.m.-8 p.m. **WHY** Smaller than the South Pasadena location, this funky coffeehouse offers free WiFi and sidewalk tables that are prime for people-watching. **WHAT** This is the place to come for sturdy cappuccinos and plenty of other coffee and tea permutations, but don't come hungry—food selections are minimal. **WHO** Trendy young couples and families from hipsterfying Atwater. 🗺 ☼

[**Lamill Coffee Boutique**] 1636 Silver Lake Blvd., Silver Lake, 323.663.4441, lamillcoffee.com. Daily 7 a.m.-10 p.m. **WHY** For an obsessive approach to perfect coffee, made in a Clover or tableside via Chemex, served in the swankiest coffee shop in town. Excellent cold-brewed iced coffee, too. **WHAT** Is it a coffeehouse or a restaurant? The answer seems to be the latter, thanks to the menu by consulting chef Michael Cimarusti (Providence). But you can still come here just for a cup of hand-brewed coffee or a meticulously crafted latte, though you'll have to order it from a waiter instead of at a counter, and you'd better not be in a rush. If you're a serious coffee person, you've probably already been here. If you're not, it's probably not worth it just for a cup of coffee—but it might be worth it for a good lunch. **WHO** People who can order a $7 cup of coffee and live with themselves. ☼

[**The Novel Café**] 811 Traction Ave., Little Tokyo/Arts District, 213.621.2240. Mon.-Fri. 7 a.m.-6:30 p.m., Sat.-Sun. 8 a.m.-6:30 p.m. **WHY** Good-enough Groundworks coffee, a hang-as-long-as-you-like vibe, and a location in the Arts District **WHAT** This ahead-of-the-curve Arts District coffeehouse is an offshoot of Venice's expanding Novel Café. It's scruffily pleasant, staffed by heavily tattooed young folks, and it has a big menu of wraps, pastries and salads—although we stick to the coffee and do our eating on the next block at Wurstküche. **WHO** Rocker-artist loft kids, casual-Friday types getting their dogs out of the loft for a walk, and people who find Stumptown and Blue Bottle too pretentious. 🗺 ☼

[**Ozero Tea & Desserts**] 131 Central Ave., Little Tokyo/Arts District, 213.626.8889. Sun.-Thurs. noon-11 p.m., Fri.-Sat. noon-

midnight. **WHY** For the soft, chewy boba, and a highly customiz-
able menu featuring tea, coffee, shaved ice, and yogurt drinks.
Also consider the unique Fluffy Milk Teas—aerated milk foam
above tea or milk tea. **WHAT** This hip tea and boba spot among
Little Tokyo's many eateries also offers brick toast in a variety of
flavors, cakes, shaved ice, and tea–ice cream floats, as well as free
WiFi. Ozero's drinks come in particularly sturdy plastic cups, and,
as part of their effort to be environmentally responsible, they ask
that you save your cup and bring it back for a discount on your
next beverage. **WHO** College students, Little Tokyo residents, and
visitors coming in for their boba fix after a meal at Shinsengumi
across the street or the Japanese Village Plaza around the corner.

[Primera Taza Coffee House] 1850 1/2 1st St., Boyle Heights,
323.780.3923, primerataza.com. Mon.-Fri. 7 a.m.-7 p.m., Sat. 8 a.m.-
5 p.m., Sun. 8:30 a.m.-1:30 p.m. **WHY** A place to hang in bitchin'
Boyle Heights. **WHAT** This funky, rather cramped joint is em-
blematic of the gentrification of Boyle Heights (in case you didn't
know, it's the new Highland Park, which in turn was the new
Echo Park only yesterday), thanks in part to the Metro station out
front. It has all the essentials: free WiFi, art-for-sale on the walls,
occasional live music, and the expected coffee drinks, smoothies,
pastries, and light dishes. Try the Taza de Mocha, a latte made
with Mexican cocoa. **WHO** Boyle Heights cool people and east
Downtowners making the trek over the 1st Street bridge. 📷 ☾

[Stumptown Coffee Roasters] 806 S. Santa Fe Ave., Little
Tokyo/Arts District, 213.337.0936, stumptowncoffee.com. Daily 7
a.m.-7 p.m. **WHY** Experience Portland's finest in industrial Downtown. **WHAT** The first L.A. outpost of Portland's coffee pioneer,
this place has much in common with its Arts District neighbor,
Blue Bottle, from its minimalist design to in-house roaster and
limited seating. Post up at the awkward-level counter or take your
premium java for a nice walk around the fascinating and rapidly
gentrifying neighborhood next to the L.A. River. **WHO** Fashionis-
tas, artists, and explorers of this fast-changing warehouse district
near the produce mart.

[Swork] 2160 Colorado Blvd., Eagle Rock, 323.258.5600, swork.
com. Daily 6 a.m.-9 p.m. **WHY** Dark-roast Truck Driver blend coffee, free WiFi, and kids' drinks like the Princess Potion.
WHAT Well more than a decade ago, this corner storefront with an
Ikea-style décor brought good coffee, free WiFi, and a stylish yet

family-friendly vibe to Eagle Rock, which has since gone on to become a shabby-chic hip spot. **WHO** Moms and dads drawn by the irresistible combo of strong caffeine and a kids' play area; loyal locals with laptops or screenplays to read. ☼

[Ten Ren's Tea Time] 🌴 727 N. Hill St., Ste. 136, Chinatown, 213.626.8844, tenren.com. Daily 9:30 a.m.-7 p.m. **WHY** Bulk teas, ginseng and hot teas, iced teas, and iced milk teas to sip in the shop. **WHAT** This Chinatown branch of the international tea company has a loyal following for its bulk teas from around the world: green, jasmine, black, Pouchong, Ti Kuan, organic teas, flavored teas, and more. Take a break and sit down with an iced bubble (boba) tea or a pot of King's Tea. 🍵

[Tierra Mia Coffee] 1202 N. Alvarado St., Echo Park, 213.483.3955, tierramiacoffee.com. Daily 6:30 a.m.-10 p.m. **WHY** You want high-quality coffee and you want to know where it came from and how it was made. **WHAT** The décor is understated, featuring bare wooden tables and photographs of the harvest, but that's fine; the focus is on coffee. And it's the real deal—each cup is rich and individually brewed. You'll also find worthwhile sweet drinks; the house specialty is the Mocha Mexicano, a delicious, cinnamony take on the mocha latte. **WHO** Young creative types, Latino families, Echo Park locals. ☼

[Urth Caffé] 451 S. Hewitt St., Little Tokyo/Arts District, 213.797.4534, urthcaffe.com. Sun.-Thurs. 6 a.m.-11 p.m., Fri.-Sat. 6 a.m.-midnight. **WHY** Spanish lattes, tea lattes, and all-around good drinks, most of which are organic and/or sustainably produced. And did we mention free guarded parking? In the heart of Downtown's Arts District? **WHAT** It's pricey and sometimes too crowded, but when you factor in the free parking, free WiFi, and high-quality food (try the turkey burger and pumpkin pie), you could do far worse Downtown. The baristas are skilled, the bakery is good, and the patio is a pleasant place to talk shop. **WHO** Young Downtowners who look like they'd live in Santa Monica. ☼

SAN GABRIEL VALLEY

[AU 79 Teahouse] 1635 S. San Gabriel Blvd., San Gabriel, 626.569.9462, au79teahouse.com. Mon.-Wed. noon-midnight, Thurs. noon- 12:30 a.m., Fri. noon-1:30 a.m., Sat. 11 a.m.-1:30 a.m., Sun. 11 a.m.-midnight. **WHY** A huge selection of tea drinks and bobas;

we love the lavender infusion. **WHAT** A happening Taiwanese tea and boba hangout, with a TV blaring by day, music playing by night, and very good tea drinks all the time. **WHO** Young Taiwanese hipsters in animated conversation.

[Bean Town Coffee Bar] 45 N. Baldwin Ave., Sierra Madre, 626.355.1596, beantowncoffeebar.com. Mon.-Wed. 5:30 a.m.-9 p.m., Thurs.-Sat. 5:30 a.m.-10 p.m., Sun. 6 a.m.-10 p.m. **WHY** Because it makes you want to move to Sierra Madre just to make this place your local coffeehouse. **WHAT** This just might be the perfect coffeehouse—robust, no-frills java, funky-but-comfortable furniture, and a terrifically diverse crowd. All that plus bluegrass and folk music on the weekends, WiFi, board games, sidewalk tables, and homemade baked goods. **WHO** Book clubbers, retirees, moms with strollers, teens, dogs. 🎵 📺 ☼

[Bird Pick Tea & Herb] 🌴 10 S. De Lacey Ave., Old Pasadena, 626.773.4372, birdpick.com. Mon.-Thurs. 9 a.m.-9 p.m., Fri.-Sat. 10 a.m.-10 p.m., Sun 10 a.m.-7 p.m. **WHY** In a world dominated by the coffee shop, this serene and beautiful shop is a tea lover's dream. **WHAT** With an abundant selection of loose leaf, prepackaged, and blossoming teas, this lovely shop provides a full tea service for four, or sit at the bar for an iced lychee oolong. **WHO** Aesthetes, women in yoga wear, professorial sorts. ☼

[Buster's Ice Cream and Coffee Stop] 1006 Mission St., South Pasadena, 626.441.0744. Mon.-Fri. 6:30 a.m.-7 p.m., Sat.-Sun. 7 a.m.- 7 p.m. **WHY** Lime rickeys, Fosselman's ice cream, and gentle baristas. **WHAT** A few steps from the Gold Line, this colorful neighborhood hub offers prime people-watching from a handful of sidewalk tables. Or grab an inside table (upstairs or down) to sip a latte or savor a scoop of mint chip. **WHO** Kids, commuters, local loft-dwellers, and music fans (performances on weekends). 📺 ☼

[Cha for Tea] 2 E. Main St., Alhambra, 626.576.1209, chafortea. com. Sun.-Thurs. 10 a.m.-1 p.m., Fri.-Sat. 10 a.m.-2 a.m. **WHY** Tasty tea creations (the mango green tea is their most popular), honey boba, and a nice local hangout spot. **WHAT** Since it's both a teahouse and a restaurant, some folks come for a meal while others do the sip-a-drink-and-surf-the-web thing. The teas are good quality; food includes noodle soups and Chinese dishes cooked with tea. It can get busy with groups hanging around for hours studying, but the servers are accommodating and even keep a waiting list for outlets. **WHO** Local high schoolers and college students cramming over plates of crispy chicken and iced milk tea.

[Chado Tea Room] 79 N. Raymond Ave., Old Pasadena, 626.431.2832, chadotea.com. Daily 11:30 a.m.-7 p.m. **WHY** More than 200 varieties of tea, and a yellow-coconut cake that you'll want to lie down in, because it's so hypnotically sweet and moist. **WHAT** An afternoon tea room with an English look, knowledgeable servers, full high-tea service, and many good teas. For a fun education, sign up for the $20 tea tasting. **WHO** Lots o' women, celebrating birthdays, taking their teens out for a treat and pausing for an Old Town shopping break. 🎵

[Class 302] 1015 S. Nogales St., Ste. 125, Rowland Heights, 626.965.5809. Daily 11 a.m.-midnight. **WHY** A uniquely nostalgic Taiwanese café that serves all manner of sweet drinks in what's meant to look like an aging classroom. **WHAT** If you've ever wanted to go back to school, Class 302 is for you. Take a seat at a desk and feel like a kid again with a slushy peach smoothie, a fruity milk tea, a blended mocha with boba or an iced pudding green tea. Then have dessert for dinner with one of Class 302's mountains of shaved snow. Cash only. **WHO** Young Asian-American families and partiers beset by the munchies. 🏠

[The Coffee Gallery] 2029 N. Lake Ave., Altadena, 626.398.7917, coffeegallery.com. Mon.-Fri. 6 a.m.-10 p.m., Sat.-Sun. 7 a.m.-10 p.m. **WHY** You can hang out as long as you like, and the private room is great for a committee meeting. **WHAT** Maybe the coffee's not so great—and the service is often bizarrely slow—but there's something endearing about this appealingly scruffy place anyway. For one thing, the live music in the separate concert room is often amazing. **WHO** A cast of Altadena characters, from local politicians to aging hippies to moms 'n kids. 🎵 📻 🏠 ☼

[Copa Vida] 70 S. Raymond Ave., Old Pasadena, 626.213.3952, copa-vida.com. Mon.-Thurs. 7 a.m.-8 p.m., Fri. 7 a.m.-10 p.m., Sat. 8 a.m.-10 p.m., Sun. 8 a.m.-9 p.m. **WHY** Gorgeous coffee and tea drinks, a few excellent salads and sandwiches, and a cool, chic setting. **WHAT** The guys behind Copa Vida are very serious about their coffees (single-origin espressos, meticulously crafted lattes, delicious cold coffees) and mostly organic teas, and they pay just as must attention to the sandwiches, which are made on house-baked bread. Savvy regulars set up their laptops in front of the windows, so the parade of passersbys makes it easy to neglect their work. **WHO** Rows of silent people on MacBook Airs. 🎧

[De Café Baristas] 🌴 500 N. Atlantic Blvd., Ste. 121, Monterey Park, 626.872.6302. Mon.-Wed. 7 a.m.-9 p.m., Thurs.-Fri. 7 a.m.-11 p.m., Sat. 8 a.m.-11 p.m., Sun. 8 a.m.-9 p.m. **WHY** Because a latte without an awesome foam design just doesn't cut it. **WHAT** De Café Baristas' approach to coffee is truly artistic. The baristas understand that each beverage requires a unique brewing process—and they're happy to geek out about their craft with you. It's a little on the pricey side but worth it, as you won't find better coffee within a 15-mile radius. The pastries are delicious as well. **WHO** Students, couples, groups.

[Factory Tea Bar] 323 S. Mission Dr., San Gabriel, 626.872.2969, factoryteabar.com. Tues.-Sun. 1 p.m.-midnight. **WHY** A comfortable hangout or study spot with tasty flavored milk and tea combinations, or the flavored Red Bull combos for tired students there to cram. **WHAT** This popular tea and boba house is beloved for its quality teas and cozy ambiance. There's also a food menu with offerings typical at a tea-and-boba café: popcorn chicken, fries, brick toast with condensed milk. **WHO** A youngish, predominantly Asian crowd spending time with friends or studying. ⚙

[Fresh Roast] 308 S. San Gabriel Blvd., San Gabriel, 626.451.5918. Daily 7 a.m.-11 p.m. **WHY** Roasted-on-site coffee, in bulk or to drink here, prepared by the Chinese-American owner, Jimmy, who's brought his passion for coffee to a neighborhood that needed it. Great prices, too. Oh, and the Hong Kong pancake. **WHAT** This coffee roaster, coffeehouse, and juice bar is a real find, run by a friendly guy who wants everyone to love coffee as much as he does. Fresh-roasted beans are just $10 to $12 a pound; espressos and lattes are carefully made; and the juice selection (coconut, orange, sugarcane) is seductive. Best of all, each cup of brewed coffee is made to order—Jimmy doesn't believe in having coffee sit around. Try the Vietnamese coffee. **WHO** A devoted crowd of mostly Asian regulars. 💲⚙

[Half & Half Tea House] 🌴 141 N. Atlantic Blvd., Ste. 112, Monterey Park, 626.872.0200. Daily noon-12:30 a.m. **WHY** For the ever-popular Half & Half honey boba and iced milk drinks: icy, fresh milk mixed with a range of combinations, such as caramel, custard pudding, or strawberries. **WHAT** This wildly popular boba

Coffee, Tea & Boba

🌴 ESSENTIALLY L.A.   ↘ DIVE   🎧 QUIET   💲 VALUE

joint offers a large menu of tea, milk tea, and coffee combinations as well as some food offerings such as crispy chicken bites and brick toast. It's known for distinctly shaped cups: short and wide, which is supposed to make for better mixing of the drink when you shake it up. Just don't expect it to fit in your cupholder. It's a busy place, especially at night in the after-dinner-hours, so be prepared for a wait. **WHO** High schoolers, college students, and Asian twentysomethings in need of their late-night boba fix. ☼

[Home Brewed Bar] 39 N. Arroyo Pkwy., Old Pasadena, 626.397.2887, homebrewedbar.com. Mon.-Fri. 8 a.m.-6 p.m., Sat. 10 a.m.-8 p.m., Sun. 10 a.m.-5 p.m. **WHY** Great cold brew coffee, Vietnamese coffee, and boba teas on the quiet edge of Old Pasadena, away from the Intelligentsia hipsters. **WHAT** This great little find next to King Taco lacks the preciousness of such coffee temples as Copa Vida and Intelligentsia, but it nonetheless is serious about the quality of its drinks. Fans of Vietnamese coffee and almond-tea boba go out of their way to come here. **WHO** Young folks caffeinating after a taco binge, boba buffs, prowlers of Old Pasadena's side streets.

[Intelligentsia Pasadena] 55 E. Colorado Blvd., Old Pasadena, 626.578.1270, intelligentsiacoffee.com. Sun.-Thurs. 7 a.m.-8 p.m., Fri.-Sat. 7 a.m.-midnight. Beer & wine. **WHY** A coffee-and-wine café with indie cred in the midst of corporate Old Pasadena. **WHAT** Of course, Intelligentsia Pasadena has its own pour-over coffees, a gleaming espresso machine, and practiced baristas. But this location, in a historic brick building furnished with reclaimed church pews and electric blue walls, also has a beer and wine bar at the back with a thoughtful selection of pours. Eagle Rock Brewery supplies on-tap selections like Stimulus, a beer brewed with coffee. With pastries and desserts too, this groovy temple of caffeine is good to go from early morning until 8 on weeknights, midnight on weekends. **WHO** Wins the most-likely-to-see-a-handlebar-mustache award in Pasadena. ☼

[Jameson Brown Coffee Roasters] 260 N. Allen Ave., East Pasadena, 626.395.7585, jamesonbrown.com. Mon.-Fri. 7 a.m.-7 p.m., Sat. 8 a.m.-6 p.m. **WHY** First-rate house-roasted beans or coffee to drink onsite in a spacious, peaceful setting. **WHAT** Can't find a seat at Jones? Then head to this fine coffeehouse, which also roasts its own beans (they're excellent) and has more room to hang out than its west Pasadena competitor. Founded by coffee-obsessed business partners Ryan Hamlin and David Ross, it has a community-ty focus, free WiFi, and an almost studious vibe. **WHO** Fuller and Caltech students, seniors meeting friends, and creative/tech types looking for a place to write or think or code... with coffee. 🎧

[Jones Coffee Roasters] 🌴 693 S. Raymond Ave., Pasadena, 626.564.9291, thebestcoffee.com. Mon.-Fri. 6:30 a.m.-6 p.m., Sat. 7 a.m.-5 p.m., Sun. 8 a.m.-5 p.m. **WHY** Rich, intense lattes, great house-roasted beans, and frequent live music. **WHAT** One of Pasadena's premier coffee roasters (the other is Jameson Brown), Jones has a globe-hopping selection of roasted beans (including organic choices) as well as green beans for home-roasting and offerings from the proprietors' Guatemalan coffee plantation. And the espresso drinks are exquisitely crafted. Extras include a daily sandwich, tamales on Fridays, regular live music. **WHO** Writers, moms, artists, Art Center profs and students, Huntington docs... everyone who's anyone in Pasadena, unless they want WiFi—they don't have it on purpose. 💲 ☼

[Kaldi] 1019 El Centro St., South Pasadena, 626.403.5951. Mon.-Fri. 7 a.m.-9:30 p.m., Sat.-Sun. 7:30 a.m.-9 p.m. **WHY** An authentic and appealing slice of European-style café life, right in the middle of Small Town, U.S.A. **WHAT** The sultry purple neon sign beckons passersby into this popular hangout in a handsome old brick building across from the library. On the menu: respectable espresso drinks and sunny sidewalk tables, but not much to eat. **WHO** Students and game players who favor the outdoor tables; freshly coiffed patrons of the salon next door; errand-runners and library patrons. 🎧 ☼

[Lavender & Honey] 1383 E. Washington Blvd., Pasadena, 626.529.5571, lavenderandhoneyespresso.com. Mon.-Sat. 7 a.m.-5 p.m., Sun. 8 a.m.-4 p.m. **WHY** For tasty coffee drinks and lovely atmosphere in north Pasadena. **WHAT** At this popular new Washington Boulevard spot, you'll find a menu with espresso drinks, hot chocolate, fancy toast, and sandwiches. The idea is to create your own drink with a base of Klatch coffee and L&H's special add-ins, like lavender (of course) or toasted marshmallow. The basic cappuccino is decent, but the lavender lemonade is really special. **WHO** Lululemon-clad women, accompanied by their laptops, friends, or kids. ☼

[Peet's Coffee & Tea] 605 S. Lake Ave., Pasadena, 626.795.7413, peets.com. Mon.-Fri. 5 a.m.-10 p.m., Sat.-Sun. 6 a.m.-10 p.m. **WHY** Major Dickason's blend. **WHAT** If you must drink at a chain, this estimable Bay Area institution is the one to pick. The coffee drinks are robust and made by actual baristas, the take-home beans are addictive and thoughtfully ground, and all the locations were carefully chosen to showcase Peet's' outdoor tables in lively, people-watching neighborhoods. Delectable baked goods, too. **WHO** Parents after drop-off at Pasadena's nearby Poly-technic School; Lake Avenue shoppers; Caltech profs; homesick Northern Californians. 🌙 ☼

[Perry's Joint] 2051 Lincoln Ave., Pasadena, 626.798.4700, perrysjoint.com. Mon.-Fri. 8 a.m.-6 p.m., Sat. 10 a.m.-5 p.m. **WHY** Can't beat the soundtrack—great jazz on the stereo. **WHAT** A sophisticated, spacious spot, Perry's is a terrific place to hold small business meetings or to work on your laptop (free WiFi). Good coffee, tasty sandwiches, and Dreyer's ice cream. **WHO** The hipper sorts of Northwest Pasadenans, after-school kids, and employees of local nonprofits. 🌙 📷 🏠

[Tearoom at the Langham Huntington] 🌴 1401 S. Oak Knoll Ave., Pasadena, 626.585.6218, pasadena.langhamhotels.com. Mon.-Sat. noon-4 p.m. **WHY** A proper silver tea service, and, for those who must, good Champagne. **WHAT** The swankiest afternoon tea east of Beverly Hills is served in the lobby lounge at this love-ly Pasadena landmark. White linens, formal service, and an array of pinkies in the air all reassure one that the barbarians are safely on the other side of the gates. The price may cause a heart attack, but what a way to go! **WHO** Blue-blood grandmothers taking their granddaughters to tea. 🌙 ♥

[Ten Ren & Tea Station] 154 & 158 W. Valley Blvd., San Gabriel, 626.288.1663, tenren.com. Daily 9:30 a.m.-7 p.m. **WHY** A good range of teas, delicious fried tofu, and tasty taro balls. **WHAT** This tea-dealing chain is part retail store, part Chinese tea room. You can buy bulk green, jasmine, black, Pouchong, flavored, organic, and pretty much any kind of tea, or sit down next door with a properly brewed cup or a refreshing boba. 📷

[Ten Ren's Tea Time] 111 W. Garvey Ave., Monterey Park, 626.288.2012, tenren.com. Daily 9:30 a.m.-7 p.m. **WHY** Bulk teas, ginseng and hot teas, iced teas, and iced milk teas to sip in the

shop. **WHAT** A branch of the international tea company has a loyal
following for its bulk teas from around the world: green, jasmine,
black, Pouchong, Ti Kuan, organic teas, flavored teas, and more.
Take a break and sit down with boba or a pot of King's Tea. 🌙 ☞

[Zona Rosa Caffé] 15 S. El Molino Ave., Pasadena,
626.793.2334, zonarosacoffe.com. Mon. 7:30 a.m.-9 p.m., Tues.-
Thurs. 7:30 a.m.-11 p.m., Fri.-Sat. 7:30 a.m.-midnight, Sun. 9 a.m.-
11 p.m. **WHY** Heavenly Mexican hot chocolate to sip in the charming and romantic upstairs room. **WHAT** Tiny and vividly colorful,
this coffeehouse has Mexican flair and a prime location next to
the Pasadena Playhouse. In summer they host live music in the
adjacent alley. **WHO** Shoppers, strollers, readers, and theatergoers — in addition to the Playhouse next door, there's an art-house
Laemmle multiplex and the great bookstore Vroman's just around
the corner. 🌙 ♥

EAST VALLEY

[Aroma Coffee & Tea Company] 🌴 4360 Tujunga Ave.,
Studio City, 818.508.7377, aromacoffeeandtea.com. Mon.-Sat. 6 a.m.-
11 p.m., Sun. 7 a.m.-10 p.m. **WHY** Well-made iced lattes, cappuccinos, and chai drinks to drink on a patio of tremendous charm.
WHAT Owned by the same folks behind Alcove in Los Feliz, this
café/coffeehouse is in a fetching old cottage with a lovely enclosed
brick patio. The menu is extensive, but it's fine to just have coffee.
Partial table service (order at the counter) can be spotty and a
little full of attitude, and you'll have to wait at peak times, but the
coffee, food, and setting are usually worth it. **WHO** Studio City
beautiful people, including lots of writers toiling away. 🌙 ✿♥

[Coffee Commissary] 3121 W. Olive Ave., Burbank,
818.556.6055, coffeecommissary.com. Daily 7 a.m.-8 p.m. **WHY** The
best coffeehouse in Burbank. Plus a great breakfast burrito.
WHAT This small but growing L.A. chain has found a warm
welcome in Burbank (Toluca Lake–adjacent), where quality coffee
had been surprisingly scarce. The cold brew coffee is good, the
seating is comfortable, and the WiFi is free. **WHO** Young Mac-
Book Air zombies, TV actors, below-the-line studio workers. ✿

[The Coffee Roaster] 13567 Ventura Blvd., Sherman Oaks,
818.905.9719, thecoffeeroaster.net. Mon.-Fri. 7 a.m.-6 p.m., Sat.
7 p.m.-5 p.m. **WHY** Roasted-onsite beans sold by the pound, and

robust coffee drinks to take away or drink in the tiny café.
WHAT This longstanding Valley shop roasts beans to sell both
retail and wholesale. That's its main business, but it also makes
lattes, mochas, and brewed blends. **WHO** Unpretentious Valley
coffee lovers.

[M Street Coffee] 13251 Moorpark St., Sherman Oaks,
818.907.1400, mstreetcoffee.com. Mon.-Fri. 7 a.m.-6 p.m., Sat.-Sun.
8 a.m.-5 p.m. **WHY** Nice people, good organic coffee, smoothies,
and chai, copies of the *L.A. Weekly*, and free WiFi. **WHAT** A bright
yet soothing space done in earth tones makes for a comfortable
spot to sit with a cappuccino or an iced chai latte. Interesting art-
for-sale, too. **WHO** Writers, artists, friends meeting to chat quietly
and assorted Starbucks refugees. ✿

[Priscilla's Gourmet Coffee and Tea] 4150 W. Riverside Dr.,
Toluca Lake, 818.843.5707, priscillascoffee.com. Mon.-Fri. 6 a.m.-
11 p.m., Sat.-Sun. 7 a.m.-11 p.m. **WHY** A lovely, relaxed neighborhood hangout, and good cinnamon streusel, too. **WHAT** We wish
the coffee were better, but we forgive Priscilla's any faults. It
still has a lot more personality, not to mention better coffee, than
Starbucks. Free WiFi, amusing industry eavesdropping, and good
coffeehouse snacks. **WHO** TV writers, production people, beautiful
actress/moms—the usual Toluca Lake crowd. ✿

WEST VALLEY

[Beanscene Espresso] 610 N. Lindero Canyon Rd., Oak Park,
818.991.0910, beansceneespresso.com. Mon.-Thurs. 6 a.m.-8 p.m.,
Fri. 6 a.m.-9 p.m., Sat. 6:30 a.m.-10 p.m., Sun. 7 a.m.-7 p.m.
WHY Honest espresso drinks in the chain-filled West Valley.
WHAT A West Valley find with personality and charm. The lattes
and Americanos are fine, and at night, they add wine to the mix.
WHO Desperate housewives, teenagers, and other locals who
prefer the indie place to the neighboring Starbucks. ✿

[Peet's Coffee & Tea] 18973 Ventura Blvd., Tarzana,
818.401.0263, peets.com. Mon.-Fri. 5 a.m.-9 p.m., Sat.-Sun.
6 a.m.-9 p.m. **WHY** True neighborhood coffeehouses are as rare
as cool summer days in the West Valley, so Peet's is the next
best thing—or the best thing, depending on how hooked you are
on Major Dickason's Blend. **WHAT** If you must drink at a chain,
this estimable Bay Area institution is the one to pick. The coffee

Coffee, Tea & Boba

drinks are robust and made by actual baristas, the take-home beans are addictive and thoughtfully ground, and all the locations were carefully chosen to showcase Peet's' outdoor tables in lively, people-watching neighborhoods. Delectable baked goods, too. **WHO** Quiet laptop people and social small groups. ☼

WESTSIDE: CENTRAL

[American Tea Room] 401 N. Cañon Dr., Beverly Hills, 310.271.7922, americantearoom.com. Mon.-Sat. 10 a.m.-6 p.m., Sun. noon-5 p.m. **WHY** A beautiful space with both a retail operation and a tea room in the heart of Beverly Hills. **WHAT** Beverly Hills is the obvious location for a tea boutique of this quality and price level. Indulge in brewed tea and lovely petits fours at the counter, shop for a swank gift for a tea-loving friend, or take home a tin of a rare blend. **WHO** BevHills matrons, tourists from around the world, and tea buffs with full wallets.

[Bar Nine Collective] 🌴 3515 Helms Ave., Culver City, 310.837.7815, barninecollective.com. Mon.-Fri. 7 a.m.-6 p.m., Sat.-Sun. 8 a.m.-6 p.m. **WHY** Gorgeous espressos pulled from super-cool Modbar machines built into the wooden counter. **WHAT** The folks in this industrial-chic warehouse space in the Helms complex roast one blend per week, so that's what you'll get when you visit—and if you're into coffee, you should visit. This place is more about drinking (and buying) coffee than hanging out with your laptop, and yet it manages to not be (too) pretentious. Watch the beans roast, admire the Modbar machines, savor your pour-over, and consider selling some stock so you can afford to bring a couple of pounds of beans home. **WHO** Serious coffee people. 🌙 ☼

[Bird Pick Tea & Herb] 6000 Sepulveda Blvd., Culver City, 310.313.4372, birdpick.com. Mon.-Sat. 10 a.m.-9 p.m., Sun. 11 a.m.-7 p.m. **WHY** In a world dominated by the coffee shop, this serene and beautiful shop is a tea lover's dream. **WHAT** With an abundant selection of loose leaf, prepackaged, and blossoming teas, this lovely shop provides a full tea service for four, or sit at the bar for an iced lychee oolong. **WHO** Aesthetes, women in the best yoga wear, professorial sorts. ☼

[Cognoscenti Coffee] 6114 Washington Blvd., Culver City, 310.363.7325, popupcoffee.com. Mon.-Sat. 8 a.m.-5 p.m., Sun. 9 a.m.-2 p.m. **WHY** Perfect cold brewed coffee, baked goods from

Proof, and, on Wednesdays, the Guerrilla taco truck out front.
WHAT Culver City folks like to argue about whether the Conservatory is better than Cognoscenti, or if Bar Nine is better than all of them. We say: Culver City is lucky to have such a problem. We might give the nod for espresso drinks to the Conservatory, and the pour-overs at Bar Nine are impressive, but we'll give the cold brew award to these guys. But really, they're all good. **WHO** Your usual coffeehouse hipster crowd. ☼

[The Conservatory] 🌴 10117 Washington Blvd., Culver City, 310.558.0436, conservatorycoffeeandtea.com. Mon.-Sat. 7 a.m.-6 p.m. **WHY** Subtle, artful roasting in a low-key yet cool environment where the bean is king. Seriously good cocoa, too.
WHAT The onsite roasting makes this a coffeehouse for aficionados. Fans sing the praises of the nuanced brews and drive happily from the Valley or beyond just to buy a pound. The location, across the street from Sony Studios, is a convenient place to caffeinate before a pitch meeting. **WHO** Culver City locals, studio musicians, screenwriters, and anyone with business at that big movie studio across the street. ☼

[Espresso Profeta] 1129 Glendon Ave., Westwood, 310.208.3375. Daily 7 a.m.-7 p.m. **WHY** Just when you think Westwood is nothing but chains, you find this charming spot with rich, creamy espresso pulled by people who love it. **WHAT** In an atmospheric 1927 brick building in the heart of the Village, Espresso Profeta has it all: beautiful coffee drinks made from custom-roasted beans, food from Breadbar and Buttercake Bakery, free if slow WiFi (but no power outlets), and comfy spots to hang out. It's not cheap, but it's worth it. **WHO** Your more sophisticated brand of UCLA student. 🍸 ☼

[Euro Caffé] 🌴 9559 S. Santa Monica Blvd., Beverly Hills, 310.274.9070. Mon.-Sat. 7 a.m.-6 p.m., Sun. 9 a.m.-4:30 p.m.
WHY For true Italian espresso drinks made from a giant brass R2-D2 machine, with good panini and baked goods, too. Our fave coffee stop in Beverly Hills. **WHAT** This small caffé is authentically Italian—which means no hanging around with your laptop for hours. Instead, drink your carefully pulled espresso or glass of Valpolicella (it's an enoteca, too) or eat your prosciutto panini at one of the three sidewalk tables or five indoor tables, and then move on. **WHO** The local Italian expat community, all of whom seem to show up when Italian soccer is on TV, mixed with women

who've had work done and mature men who know their way around a tanning booth. ☼

[**Paper or Plastik Café**] 5772 W. Pico Blvd., Pico-Robertson, 323.935.0268, paperorplastikcafe.com. Daily 7 a.m.-10 p.m. **WHY** It's business in the front and party in the back at this industrial-chic café that's equal parts coffee shrine and performance space. **WHAT** This small, subdued place serves impeccable brews by Intelligentsia and Coava along with sweet and savory treats made in-house or from places like Cake Monkey and Rustico. On the mezzanine level, a shop stocked with Moroccan vases and artisanal Eastern European wares overlooks a large dance studio that husband and wife Yasha and Anya Michelson have transformed into a hub for emerging artists with dance classes, film screenings, and performance salons. Turkish coffee with a hip-hop ballet? Naturally. **WHO** An eclectic mix of dancers, comedians, filmmakers, writers, and performers. 📷 ☼

[**Urth Caffé**] 267 S. Beverly Dr., Beverly Hills, 310.205.9311, urth-caffe.com. Sun.-Thurs. 6:30 a.m.-11:30 p.m., Fri.-Sat. 6:30 a.m.-midnight. **WHY** Organic coffee, excellent teas, and good food with a vegetarian/vegan emphasis. **WHAT** Except for the Lamborghinis parked out front and $200 T-shirts being worn by patrons inside, you could be at any of the other Urth locations. **WHO** Beautiful people, in a Beverly Hills way. ☼

WEST OF THE 405

[**18th Street Coffee House**] 1725 Broadway, Santa Monica, 310.264.0662. Mon.-Thurs. 7 a.m.-7 p.m., Fri. 7 a.m.-6:30 p.m., Sat. 9 a.m.-6 p.m. **WHY** Homemade rugelach and 50-cent refills. **WHAT** This adorable historic brick building, complete with homey outdoor patio, has a folksy, East Bay/East Village vibe (but no, Bob Dylan does not own it, local rumor mill notwithstanding). **WHO** Young moms, students, writers, and people without cell phone addictions (there's an outdoor-calling-only policy). ☼

[**Abbot's Habit**] 1401 Abbot Kinney Blvd., Venice, 310.399.1171, abbotshabitvenice.com. Daily 6 a.m.-10 p.m. **WHY** Mellow vibe, good coffee, amusing people-watching. **WHAT** Try for a coveted sidewalk table at this funky (think Berkeley in the 1970s) place in the heart of ultra-hip Abbot Kinney. Or check out the two inside rooms, where you can grab an everything bagel or settle in for

🌴 ESSENTIALLY L.A.   ⬊ DIVE   🌙 QUIET   💲 VALUE

the afternoon with a laptop or sketchbook. **WHO** A happy mix of upwardly mobile Venice homeowners and hippie stoners. ☼

[Balconi Coffee Company] 🌴 11301 W. Olympic Blvd. #124, West L.A., 310.906.0267, balconicoffeecompany.com. Mon.-Fri. 7 a.m.-10 p.m., Sat.-Sun. 10 a.m.-10 p.m. **WHY** To sit in front of a row of siphons, sip coffee, and talk to the owner about the body, flavor, and other qualities of every coffee he offers. Try the latte flavored with crushed almonds. **WHAT** Don't be in a rush when you come in for a coffee—it takes time to make such a perfect cup, and besides, owner Ray Sato wants his patrons to relax and give their cup o' joe their full attention. And they do, sampling meticulously prepared coffee brewed from a variety of organic, local and/or fair-trade beans. The Japanese-influenced setting is serene, and there's free validated parking. **WHO** People who obsess over their beans. ☼

[Café Bolívar] 1741 Ocean Park Blvd., Santa Monica, 310.581.2344, cafebolivar.com. Mon.-Fri. 7 a.m.-8 p.m., Sat. 8 a.m.-7 p.m. **WHY** It's the perfect place to sit and finish your novel (the one you're reading or the one you're writing), while sipping coffee and eating some addictive *arepas* (stuffed cornmeal patties). **WHAT** This relaxed place is a real find in Ocean Park. It's got an open, modern look and warm Latin music on the stereo, along with excellent coffee and delicious lunches (grilled chicken sandwich with roasted pepper pesto, a true Spanish *jamón serrano*, a vegan torta). Free wireless, too. **WHO** Art lovers and poets drawn to the openings and readings that occasionally liven things up; friends looking for a good spot to catch up. 🍴

[Caffé Luxxe] 🌴 925 Montana Ave., Santa Monica, 310.394.2222, caffeluxxe.com. Mon.-Fri. 6 a.m.-6 p.m., Sat.-Sun. 6:30 a.m.-6 p.m. **WHY** Each cup is a work of art. **WHAT** This place makes the best cappuccino—the espresso creamy and almost sweet, the milk steamed with precision—in Santa Monica (calm down—Intelligentsia is in Venice). The setting is serene and European, with high ceilings and framed mirrors. Its menu has broadened since the days of espresso drinks only; now you can get pour-over brewed coffee and organic teas. To eat are a few high-quality baked goods. **WHO** Serious coffee lovers.

[Coffee Tomo] 11309 Mississippi Ave., West L.A., 310.444.9390, coffeetomo.com. Mon.-Thurs. 7:30 a.m.-10 p.m., Fri. 7:30 a.m.-10:30 p.m., Sat. 9 a.m.-10:30 p.m., Sun. 9 a.m.-9 p.m. **WHY** Precisely made

Coffee, Tea & Boba

espresso drinks and matcha tea lattes with teddy bears sketched into the foam. **WHAT** A small, mostly quiet café where you can sip top-notch drip coffee while tapping away on your laptop. Located near the heart of West L.A.'s bustling Sawtelle Boulevard, which has in the last few years become a restaurant hub, it serves such specialty coffee drinks as lattes made with condensed milk alongside such snacks as pretzels filled with red bean paste and mozzarella. **WHO** Coffee snobs, students, residents of Little Osaka who want a sweet potato latte that doesn't taste like chemical detritus.

[Demitasse] 1149 3rd St., Santa Monica, 310.260.6308, cafedemitasse.com. Mon.-Wed. 7 a.m.-8 p.m., Thurs.-Fri. 7 a.m.-10 p.m., Sat. 8 a.m.-10 p.m., Sun. 8 a.m.-8 p.m. **WHY** Intensely sweet hot chocolate and coffee-geek coffee in a great location just off the 3rd Street Promenade. **WHAT** The prices are on the high side, but there's still much to recommend this place at the site of the former Infuzion: carefully made siphon coffee, intense lavender-infused "sipping chocolate," lovely lattes, an excellent iced tea and iced Kyoto coffee, elegant pastries from Jin, free WiFi, and fire pits on the patio. **WHO** Chocolate lovers and coffee snobs. ☼

[Dragon Herbs] 🌴 315 Wilshire Blvd., Santa Monica, 310.917.2288, dragonherbs.com. Daily 11 a.m.-7 p.m. **WHY** For herbal tea drinks that just might cure what ails you. **WHAT** All sorts of Chinese herbs and teas are served at the tonic bar in this retail herb emporium. Tell them what you're seeking (more energy, less weight, fewer hot flashes), and they'll fix you up with a drink that just might help. **WHO** The seriously health conscious.

[Espresso Cielo] 3101 Main St., Santa Monica, 310.314.9999, espressocielo.com. Daily 7 a.m.-7 p.m. **WHY** The robust, refreshing iced coffee is just the thing after a day at the beach or shopping Main Street. **WHAT** A respectable little coffeehouse on Main Street, with a French country look and good espresso drinks and hot chocolate. **WHO** Ocean Park locals who (despite the free WiFi) aren't always on laptops—sometimes they're talking to a friend and sometimes, gasp, even reading a book. 🌙 ☼

[Funnel Mill] 🌴 930 Broadway, Santa Monica, 310.393.1617, funnelmill.com. Mon.-Fri. 9 a.m.-7 p.m., Sat. 10 a.m.-7 p.m. **WHY** Siphon coffee and cold-water-infusion iced coffee, made with quality beans—you can taste the layers of flavor in the Sumatra Mandheling like a good bar of chocolate. **WHAT** Coffee is taken very seriously at this soothing spot, where a waterfall burbles and people work quietly on laptops (free WiFi). You can choose from a global menu of coffee beans to have ground and brewed in a glass siphon at your table, or explore the exceptional collection of teas, including an authentic Indian chai and fresh ginseng. Know that there are no takeout drinks, and expect to wait a good ten minutes while your coffee brews—it's worth the wait. The four-coffee sampler tray is a great way to expand your java palate. **WHO** Studious sorts who love the quiet, but mostly people who are *really* into their coffee or their tea. 🔊

[Groundwork] 2908 Main St., Santa Monica, 310.452.8925, groundworkcoffee.com. Mon.-Thurs. 6 a.m.-6 p.m., Fri. 6 a.m.-7 p.m., Sat. 7 a.m.-7 p.m., Sun. 7 a.m.-6 p.m. **WHY** For house-roasted organic coffee, properly robust, to take home by the pound or order in a cup. **WHAT** Don't expect to hang out in this miniature storefront—it's a place to buy good whole beans to take home or a tasty brewed cup or latte to take with you. **WHO** Locals who walk here. 🐷

[Groundwork] 3 Westminster Ave., Venice, 310.450.4540, groundworkcoffee.com. Mon.-Thurs. 6 a.m.-6 p.m., Fri.-Sat. 6 a.m.-7 p.m., Sun. 7 a.m.-7 p.m. **WHY** Good coffee on the Venice boardwalk. **WHAT** This L.A. native roastery runs a number of small cafés around town, and this tiny one is a favorite for its great location. A Mexican mocha or cold brew coffee will be just the thing to fuel you for a long bike-path ride. **WHO** Locals in the early hours, tourists in the afternoon. ☼

[Gunpowder] 202 S. Main St., Venice, 310.422.6138, drinkgunpowder.com. Daily 6:30 a.m.-midnight. **WHY** Because coffee just isn't cutting it anymore, and you're looking for an energy alternative that's been used by Amazonian hunters for 2,000 years. **WHAT** This Venice café is one of only a few places in the country that brews guayusa, a caffeine-packed Ecuadorian herb. The taste takes some getting used to, but it isn't totally unpleasant. It also has a variety of bottled cold beverages (think tea meets energy drink) in flavors like ginger-lemonade and hibiscus-mint. You can sit on an actual indoor grassy knoll, but you'll also find comfy chairs and a long conference table if traditional seating is more your thing. **WHO** Young professionals working at the conference table, health nuts, surfer dudes.

[Intelligentsia Venice Coffeebar] 🌴 1331 Abbot Kinney Blvd., Venice, 310.399.1233, intelligentsiacoffee.com. Mon.-Fri. 6 a.m.-8 p.m., Fri. 6 a.m.-10 p.m., Sat. 7 a.m.-10 p.m., Sun. 7 a.m.-8 p.m. **WHY** So you can be greeted by your own personal barista. **WHAT** When this offshoot of the Chicago-by-way-of-Silver-Lake coffeehouse opened on Abbot Kinney, you'd have thought the Obamas themselves were pulling espressos from the Synesso machines. Coffee geeks walk into this light-filled industrial space and begin hyperventilating at the sight of the Mazzer grinders and array of contraptions, from Siphon to Chemex—but the gentle guidance of their personal barista soon calms the feverish excitement. Said baristas escort each guest through the space, guiding him or her to the station that best suits his or her desires (espresso, brewed, pressed). Yes, it's dreadfully precious, but the coffee is damn good. Seating is on uncomfortable stadium-style benches. **WHO** The sort of people who can argue about whether the overtones in a particular brew suggest cherries or tamarind.

[Menotti's Coffee Stop] 56 Windward Ave., Venice, 310.392.7232, menottis.com. Daily 8 a.m.-8 p.m. **WHY** For a quick pick-me-up before you hit the boardwalk. **WHAT** Menotti's is tiny and stark, but if you're grabbing a quick drink, it gets the job done, and does it well. Throw back an espresso à l'italien and you'll be ready for the two-mile walk to Santa Monica. The baristas know their stuff and take pride in their work. Vinyl records playing on vintage speakers and a stuffed armadillo behind the counter lend an undeniably hip vibe. **WHO** Young coffee enthusiasts, Venice hipsters, beach-bound tourists.

[Primo Passo Coffee Co.] 702 Montana Ave., Santa Monica, 310.451.5900, primopassocoffee.com. Daily 6:30 a.m.-6:30 p.m. **WHY** Good Americanos, baked goods from Tavern, and nice sidewalk tables. **WHAT** As chic (and pricey) as you would expect an artisanal coffee joint on Montana to be, Primo Passo uses Stumptown beans, makes worthy iced concoctions, and plays good music, but not too loudly. A fine stop on a Montana shopping walk. **WHO** North-of-Montana locals, including yoga-pants moms and on-hiatus TV writers; the ones with dogs sit outside. ☼

[Tanner's Coffee Co.] 200 Culver Blvd., Playa del Rey, 310.574.2739. Mon.-Fri. 6 a.m.-8 p.m., Sat. 6:30 a.m.-8 p.m., Sun. 6:30 a.m.-7 p.m. **WHY** The most acceptable coffee in the area, not to mention free WiFi, a few choice sidewalk tables, and a great

location in a secret beach neighborhood in Playa del Rey.
WHAT Tanner's is the community hub for this great little beach
village, which has resisted the glam gentrification of neighboring
towns. It is serious about its coffee but is otherwise relaxed.
WHO Surfers, LMU students, Playa residents. 🍷 ☕ ☼

[UnUrban Coffee House] 3301 Pico Blvd., Santa Monica,
310.315.0056, unurban.com. Mon.-Sat. 7 a.m.-midnight, Sun. 8
a.m.-8 p.m. **WHY** A decent double-shot cappuccino and highly
entertaining evening performances. **WHAT** "Death Before Decaf"
is the motto at this neighborhood café. As for the décor, think first
apartment for theater majors—walls painted red and purple, old
movie-theater seats and velvet drapes in bold colors. There's also
free WiFi, plentiful tables, and evening music and spoken-word
performances. **WHO** Young hippies, stoners, artists. ☕

[Urth Caffé] 2327 Main St., Santa Monica, 310.314.7040,
urthcaffe.com. Sun.-Thurs. 6:30 a.m.-11 p.m., Fri.-Sat. 6:30 a.m.-mid-
night. **WHY** Organic coffee, excellent teas, and good food with a
vegetarian/vegan emphasis. **WHAT** Robust coffee, loose-leaf teas,
and tasty café fare for health-conscious, environmentally aware,
Prius-driving westsiders. On sunny days the outdoor tables are as
prized as seats at the Oscars. A quintessential L.A. place.
WHO Hip Match.com blind-daters, girlfriends catching up, and all
sorts of beautiful Santa Monicans. ☼

SOUTH BAY TO SOUTH L.A.

[Aroma di Roma] 4708 E. 2nd St., Long Beach, 562.439.7662,
aromadiroma.com. Mon.-Thurs. 5:30 a.m.-10 p.m., Fri. 5:30 a.m.-11
p.m., Sat. 6 a.m.-11 p.m., Sun. 6:00 a.m.-10 p.m. **WHY** Good coffee,
perfectly foamed lattes, breakfast pizza, lunchtime panini, a locals'
vibe, and Italian soccer on TV. **WHAT** Second Street's best coffeehouse is a neighborhood hub, where friends are always running
into one another while ordering a latte or a gelato. Expect good
Italian caffé food, very good coffee, and an appealing atmosphere
both inside and on the sidewalk patio. **WHO** Neighbors who can
walk here from their adorable Belmont Shore bungalows. ☼

[Bambu Desserts & Drinks] 11408 South St., Cerritos,
562.991.5263, drinkbambu.com. Fri.-Wed. 11 a.m.-10 p.m., Tues.
noon-10 p.m. **WHY** A tidy Vietnamese café that will keep you
caffeinated and sate your sweet tooth. **WHAT** Bambu is best ex-

perienced during Southern California's endless summer. Sure, the chain prepares hot coffees, but most everyone comes for the tropically flavored milk teas (think lychee and taro), iced and blended coffees, and rich smoothies (try the soursop). Plus there's all manner of fruity, jellied Vietnamese desserts. **WHO** Asian-American teens and tweens from Cerritos and Artesia. ⑤

[Berlin Bistro] 420 E. 4th St., Long Beach, 562.435.0600, berlinbistro.com. Mon.-Thurs. 6:30 a.m.-9 p.m., Fri. 6:30 p.m.-10 p.m., Sat. 7 a.m.-10 p.m., Sun. 7 a.m.-9 p.m. **WHY** For coffee, café culture, and good food in the heart of Long Beach's arts district. **WHAT** Adjoining the ultra-cool Fingerprints record store, Berlin is part coffeehouse, part restaurant. But you can visit only for coffee if you like. There's nothing wrong, however, with adding a Greek omelet or a seared ahi salad to your coffee order. **WHO** Students, creative types, foodies, record-store browsers. ☼

[Catalina Coffee Company] 126 N. Catalina Ave., Redondo Beach, 310.318.2499, catalinacoffee.com. Mon.-Sat. 7 a.m.-9 p.m., Sun. 7 a.m.-6 p.m. **WHY** Roasted-on-site coffee, a decent selection of teas, and an inviting, hang-out-for-a-while vibe. **WHAT** Outside is a sunny patio with thatched umbrellas, but inside it's more literary than beachy, with a fireplace, lots of books, comfy high-backed armchairs, and a flea-market-chic look. Even though Redondo's star indie coffeehouse has free WiFi, not everyone's on a laptop; many read, chat, or even play a board games. **WHO** Everyone who's anyone in Redondo. ☼

[Class 302] 11446 South St., Cerritos, 562.924.1315. Sun.-Thurs. 11 a.m.-midnight, Fri.-Sat. 11 a.m.-1 p.m. **WHY** A uniquely nostalgic Taiwanese café that serves all manner of sweet drinks in what's meant to look like an old, aging classroom. **WHAT** If you've ever wanted to go back to school, Class 302 is for you. Take a seat at a desk and feel like a kid again with a slushy peach smoothie, a fruity milk tea, a blended mocha with boba, or an iced pudding green tea. Then have dessert for dinner with one of Class 302's mountains of shaved snow. Cash only. **WHO** Young Asian-American families and partiers beset by the munchies. 🐫

[The Flea Espresso Bar] 2023 E. 4th St., Long Beach, 562.704.0990, fleaespresso.com. Mon. 7 a.m.-3 p.m., Wed.-Thurs. 7 a.m.-7 p.m., Fri. 7 a.m.-8 p.m., Sat. 10 a.m.-8 p.m., Sun. 10 a.m.-5 p.m. **WHY** A tiny third-wave coffeehouse attached to the Art

Theatre. **WHAT** The Flea is one of Long Beach's more serious coffeehouses, sourcing mostly locally roasted beans and serving Kyoto-style drip coffee, a summery lavender steamer, and potent espresso. Owner Jordan Pinches also takes great care to stock the place with locally made pastries and sweets—all the better to go with a nice foamy latte. Cash only. **WHO** Indie moviegoers, coffee connoisseurs, and vintage shoppers needing a pick-me-up.

[Hojas Tea House] 1201 N. Avalon Blvd., Ste. B, Wilmington, 310.818.9454. Mon.-Fri. 7 a.m.-9 p.m., Sat. 9 a.m.-9 p.m. **WHY** A serene and serious teahouse in hard-working Wilmington. **WHAT** Hojas is a remarkably friendly place where the WiFi is free and the tea is exclusively loose leaf. There's something for everyone here: peppermint-lemongrass herbal blends, flowery jasmine teas, rich coconut infusions, and more. **WHO** Nine-to-fivers savoring their lunch breaks, tea enthusiasts looking for something different, and teens studying for their next test. 🐾 🏠

[Hot Java] 2101 E. Broadway, Long Beach, 562.433.0688, hotjavalb.com. Daily 6 a.m.-11 p.m. **WHY** A relaxed and friendly vibe, very good brewed coffee (lattes and cappuccinos are unexceptional), pastries from Rossmoor Bakery, and free WiFi. **WHAT** Two airy rooms and some sidewalk tables provide lots of space for regulars to hang out, but even then, it can get full, especially in the evening. Improv and standup comedy are extras. **WHO** Beach people, gay neighbors, and the laptop-obsessed. ☼

[Library Coffeehouse] 3418 E. Broadway, Long Beach, 562.433.2393, thelibraryacoffeehouse.com. Mon.-Fri. 6 a.m.- midnight, Sat.-Sun. 7 a.m.-midnight. **WHY** Perfectly fine coffee, respectable pastries and light meals, free WiFi, and a comfortable funky-chic setting in a great neighborhood. **WHAT** A longstanding Belmont Heights hangout, the Library is large and rambling, stuffed with pleasantly shabby Victorian furniture and bookcases stocked with used titles for sale. **WHO** The young 'n quirky, often with a goth-literary bent. 🐾 ☼

[Lord Windsor Roasters] 1101 E. 3rd St., Long Beach, 562.901.2111, lordwindsor.com. Mon.-Fri. 6:30 a.m.-7 p.m., Sat.-Sun. 8 a.m.-7 p.m. **WHY** One of the hubs of Long Beach's emerging coffee culture. **WHAT** Lord Windsor isn't so much regal as it is rustic: an airy, artfully worn space that brings third-wave coffee to the heart of Long Beach. Beans are roasted in-house and brewed into fine macchiatos and lattes. There are excellent (and local) pastries for the hungry. **WHO** Bearded coffee geeks, hip loft dwellers, young families out for a stroll.

[Makai Coffee] 2771 E. Broadway, Long Beach, 562.376.1980, makaicoffee.com. Mon.-Fri. 6 a.m.-6 p.m., Sat.-Sun. 7 a.m.-7 p.m. **WHY** Unassuming excellence from a humble but gifted coffee shop. **WHAT** Good (and sometimes even great) coffee doesn't require an uptight attitude. Makai proves that with a simple, trendy space that's more about the coffee and less about the scene. Order a gibraltar—a four-ounce cup that splits the difference between a latte and a macchiato. **WHO** Belmont and Bluff Heights locals lounging in the sun and catching up over a cup.

[Portfolio Coffeehouse] 🌴 2300 E. 4th St., Long Beach, 562.434.2486, portfoliocoffeehouse.com. Mon.-Fri. 5:30 a.m.-10 p.m., Sat.-Sun. 6:30 a.m.-10 p.m. **WHY** The coffeehouse that helped make caffeine hip in Long Beach. **WHAT** A landmark in Long Beach coffee culture, Portfolio (and now its sister coffeehouse, Berlin) helped usher in a more urbane style of café. Drinks and snacks are very good (fuel up with an espresso laced with brown sugar and a warm pressed sandwich), but the place is probably best known for its comfortable setting, which attracts what sometimes seems like the entire city. **WHO** Vintage-minded hipsters, Bluff Heights locals, middle-aged friends playing catch-up. 🎵 🏚 ☼

[Tierra Mia Coffee] 🌴 4914 Firestone Blvd., South Gate, 323.563.3948, tierramiacoffee.com. Mon.-Thurs. 6:30 a.m.-11:30 p.m., Fri.-Sat. 6:30-midnight, Sun. 7 a.m.-11:30 p.m. **WHY** Authentic Cuban café con leche, heavenly mochas, lattes infused with horchata, and all-around superb coffee. **WHAT** This suave and handsome spot, with comfy leather chairs and intoxicating aromas, takes its coffee—and its beans—very seriously, buying them from organic, artisanal roasters and handling them with care. But there's a sense of whimsy that cancels out any pretension, as witnessed by the Rice and Beans, an horchata-flavored blended espresso drink sprinkled with crushed coffee beans. **WHO** The coolest people in South Gate by a long shot.

[Tierra Mia Coffee] 6706 Pacific Blvd., Huntington Park, 323.589.2065, tierramiacoffee.com. Mon.-Thurs. 6:30 a.m.-10 p.m., Fri.-Sun. 6:30 a.m.-11 p.m. **WHY** Coffee heaven in a former McDonald's, not that you'd ever recognize it as such once you're inside.

🌴 ESSENTIALLY L.A.   ⬎ DIVE   🎵 QUIET   💰 VALUE

Authentic Cuban café con leche and heavenly mochas. **WHAT** This suave and handsome spot, with comfy leather chairs and intoxicating aromas, takes its coffee—and its beans—very seriously, buying them from organic, artisanal roasters and handling them with care. But there's a sense of whimsy that cancels out any pretension, as witnessed by the Rice and Beans, an horchata-flavored blended espresso drink sprinkled with crushed coffee beans. **WHO** Huntington Park hipsters, and yes, they exist.

[Two Guns Espresso] 🌴350 N. Sepulveda Blvd., Manhattan Beach, 310.318.2537, twogunsespresso.com. Mon.-Fri. 6 a.m.-5 p.m., Sat.-Sun. 7 a.m.-5 p.m. **WHY** The best coffee in the South Bay. **WHAT** Two Guns is sleek without being sparse, a modern coffeehouse that still feels casual and comfortable. Pastries are sourced from local bakeries and the coffee beans from Seattle's venerable Caffe Vita. Two Guns's owners are from New Zealand, which is why the menu bears some Kiwi influence. Try the flat white, a creamy but not at all frothy twist on the latte. **WHO** The South Bay's hippest teens and coffee connoisseurs of all ages.

[Viento y Agua Coffeehouse] 4007 E. 4th St., Long Beach, 562.434.1182, vientoyaguacoffeehouse.com. Mon.-Wed. 6 a.m.-7 p.m., Thurs.-Fri. 6 a.m.-10 p.m., Sat. 7 a.m.-10 p.m., Sun. 7 a.m.-7 p.m. **WHY** Long Beach's artiest hangout. **WHAT** Skip the cappuccinos at this funky shop and get a Mexican mocha while you browse the adjoining gallery space, or sidle into one of the kooky vintage armchairs for a quiet chat. Thursday night open-mic nights are locally famous. **WHO** Cool college students and hip moms picking up their kids from the elementary school across the street.

INLAND EMPIRE

[Klatch Coffee] 🌴806 W. Arrow Hwy., San Dimas, 909.599.0452, klatchroasting.com. Mon.-Fri. 6 a.m.-9 p.m., Sat.-Sun. 7 a.m.-9 p.m. **WHY** Who needs Stumptown or Blue Bottle? L.A. has Klatch. **WHAT** Mike Perry's roasting skills have earned many awards, and his wife and daughters have also won acclaim for their barista skills and their several cafés. The closest to L.A. is this one where the 210 meets the 57; if you're headed to or from the Inland Empire or the desert, stop for an espresso, a pour-over brew, and/or a pound of beans. **WHO** Locals and pilgrims coming from all over L.A. to buy beans and get a cappuccino while they're at it

Juice Bars

Sick of the cold-pressed juice craze yet? Apparently most Angelenos aren't, because new juiceries are opening at a furious pace in L.A.'s most upscale neighborhoods, where ginger and chia seeds are even more popular than crossfit and mindfulness meditation. Here are some of the best places for cold-pressed juices and cleansing juices, as well as good, old-fashioned smoothies and aguas frescas.

Juice Bars

[ESSENTIALLY L.A.]

Juice Bars

🏠 GROUPS 🎤 KARAOKE ☼ PATIO ♥ ROMANTIC

CENTRAL CITY

[Beverly Hills Juice] 8382 Beverly Blvd., Beverly/Third, 323.655.8300, beverlyhillsjuice.com. Mon.-Fri. 7 a.m.-6 p.m., Sat. 9 a.m.-6 p.m. **WHY** Cold-pressed apple-juice blends that are totally delish—try the apple strawberry or apple ginger. Plus these guys get snaps for doing the cold-pressed thing years before every other hipster in town. **WHAT** It's not really in Beverly Hills, but a harmless bit of false advertising is no reason to shun this teeny place, which specializes in cold-pressed fruit juices, wheatgrass, carrot juices, and smoothie-like banana-based creations. **WHO** People just back from a hike or a spinning class.

[Clover] 8384 1/2 W. 3rd St., Beverly/Third, 323.609.3903, cloverjuice.com. Mon.-Fri. 7 a.m.-7 p.m., Sat.-Sun. 9 a.m.-7 p.m. **WHY** Not just cold-pressed juice blends and cleanses but also coffee and vegan and/or gluten-free baked goods. **WHAT** A super-cute walk-up counter, where you can get the tasty, prepared Clover juice blends, which are a bit more affordable than the competition, as well as snacks, sandwiches, and lattes. **WHO** Après-Pilates folks and people trying to resist the temptations at neighboring Joans on Third.

[Juice Served Here] 8366 W. 3rd St., Beverly/Third. Mon.-Sat. 7:30 a.m.-7 p.m., Sun. 8 a.m.-6 p.m. **WHY** For the $20 juice, when your ship comes in. **WHAT** Yet another artisanal pressed-juice place, Juice Served Here sets itself apart with its glass bottles, its generous tasting policy, and its very good flavor blends. The juices aren't made here, alas. And they're expensive, but they're damn tasty. **WHO** Bougie health buffs pulling up in Mini Coopers.

[Juices Fountain] 6332 Hollywood Blvd., Hollywood, 323.464.8986. Mon.-Fri. 8 a.m.-5 p.m., Sat.-Sun. 10 a.m.-4 p.m. **WHY** For an all-fruit smoothie with a side of Hollyweird, with none of the pretension of all those cold-pressed places. **WHAT** At this tiny, family-run juice joint, a hand-painted menu covers one wall, bananas hang everywhere, and the place smells fresh and fruity. The cantaloupe smoothie is surprisingly great, but the Pink Cloud (strawberry, banana, milk, and honey) is a sure bet. Stick around with your beverage and they'll let you hang on to the blender with the leftovers in it. **WHO** Locals, most of whom know the girls behind the counter, and the occasional loiterer. 🍹 ☼

Juice Bars

[Liquid Juice Bar] 8180 Melrose Ave., Melrose, 323.300.8070, liquidjuicebar.com. Mon.-Fri. 8:30 a.m.-7:30 p.m., Sun. 10 a.m.-5 p.m. **WHY** Beautiful acai granola bowls and tasty juices and smoothies that are a little less expensive than the competition. **WHAT** During peak hours (weekend mornings) this place can get quite crowded as it's located in the heart of Beverly Grove. If time is not an issue, grab an immunity-boosting C Splash with cayenne pepper, or the Maca Shocka, made with goat's milk yogurt, coconut water, various fruits, and a satisfyingly obscure-yet-trendy root, maca. Prices are on the low side, but the produce isn't all organic. **WHO** Commuters running in before work, families after school, post-workout folks. 🐷

[Naturewell] 🌴 7261 Melrose Ave., Melrose, 323.988.1119. Daily 7:30 a.m.-10 p.m. **WHY** The legendary coconut-kale smoothie, the acai chocolates, or the allegedly cold-busting "Facemelter" shot. **WHAT** With a slightly more reasonable price tag than some other juice bars, this popular spot on Melrose is the place to feed your smoothie habit, counteract that hangover, or beat that pesky flu bug. They've also got bulk bins of nuts, grains, and beans, and the friendliest juice makers. **WHO** Young actors, older yoga teachers, and the mindfulness crowd.

[The Punch Bowl] 4645 Melbourne Ave., Los Feliz, 323.666.1123, lapunchbowl.com. Mon.-Fri. 7:30 a.m.-8:30 p.m., Sat. 9 a.m.-10 p.m., Sun 10 a.m.-8 p.m. **WHY** Inventive flavor combinations, shakes with goofy names, and hippie staff members who are always happy to talk juicing. **WHAT** In the heart of Los Feliz Village, this hippiest of the juice bars serves up some seriously expensive and delicious shakes (read: smoothies), juices, shots, and "adaptogenic milks." Unlike other, grab-n-go juice bars, this is a place to sit and relax in the warm, pillow-filled seating area and chat with the close-knit, friendly staff. **WHO** Sweaty Hollywood hikers, moviegoers, spillover folks from nearby brunches.

[Silver Lake Juice Bar] 1753 Hillhurst Ave., Los Feliz, 323.284.8115, silverlakejuice.com. Daily 7:30 a.m.-8 p.m. **WHY** Because the Second Date smoothie will make you want a third. **WHAT** The list of ingredients is enormous and annotated— with every drink you know exactly what you're getting and what its health benefits are. Everything is 100% organic, and you can either choose from the list of smoothies and juices or design your own drink. While on the pricey side ($9 for a small juice), the drinks are flavorful and energizing. **WHO** Vegheads, cleansers, Los Feliz yoga moms.

EASTSIDE

[Moon Juice] 2839 W. Sunset Blvd., Silver Lake, 213.908.5407, moonjuiceshop.com. Daily 7 a.m.- 7 p.m. **WHY** A sleek, utterly LA juicing experience. **WHAT** This minimalist and modern juice bar is stocked with crystals and candles for sale alongside both packaged and fresh juice options. Go here for the juices, not the smoothies (the $16 green smoothie is a disappointment). Not all are made to order. **WHO** Only the fittest post-reservoir jog crowd.

[Naturewell] 🌴 3824 W. Sunset Blvd., Silver Lake, 323.664.5894, naturewell.me. Daily 7:30 a.m.-10:30 p.m. **WHY** The legendary coconut-kale smoothie, or the cold-busting "Facemelter" shot. **WHAT** With a slightly more reasonable price tag than neighboring juice bars, this hippie haven on Sunset is the place to feed your smoothie habit, counteract that hangover, or beat that pesky flu bug. They've also got bulk bins of nuts, grains, and beans, and the friendliest juice makers around. **WHO** Athletes, hippies, actors, and the mindfulness crowd. ☼

[Oaxacalifornia Juice Bar] 🌴 Mercado La Paloma, 3655 S. Grand Ave., USC, 213.747.8622, oaxacali.com. Daily 8 a.m.-8 p.m. **WHY** Delicious, fresh licuados, agua frescas, smoothies, and tortas. **WHAT** In Mercado La Paloma, a nonprofit community center with restaurants, shops, and meeting spaces, this Oaxacan stand makes delicious juice drinks that go beautifully with the food from the superb Chichen Itza. Homemade ice creams, too. **WHO** Latino families and USC students from the neighborhood. 🖲

[Pressed Juicery] The Cooper Building, 860 S. Los Angeles St., South Park/Fashion District, 213.688.9700, pressedjuicery.com. Mon.-Fri. 8 a.m.-6 p.m., Sat.-Sun. 11 a.m.-5 p.m. **WHY** Where else should figure-conscious folks want healthful pressed juices but in Downtown's Fashion District? **WHAT** Downtown folks seeking a super-healthy smoothie-type drink or a longer-term cleanse are happy that this local chain has found a home at a small stand in the Cooper Building. Best of all is the happy hour from 3 to 5 p.m., when juices are discounted 15%. **WHO** Fashion-industry workers, discount shoppers, FIDM students.

Juice Bars

🌴 ESSENTIALLY L.A.   ⬋ DIVE   🎵 QUIET   🖲 VALUE

[Silver Lake Juice Bar] 2813 W. Sunset Blvd., Silver Lake, 310.994.7240, silverlakejuice.com. Daily 7:30 a.m.-6 p.m. **WHY** Because the Second Date smoothie will make you want a third. **WHAT** The list of ingredients is enormous and annotated—you'll know exactly what you're getting and what its health benefits are. Everything is 100% organic, and you can either choose from the list of smoothies and juices or design your own drink. While on the pricey side ($9 for a small juice!), the drinks are flavorful and energizing. The spacious courtyard next door, filled with artisan wood furniture and bohemian light fixtures, is a perfect place to enjoy your juice. **WHO** Vegheads, cleansers, Silver Lake hipsters. 🍸 ☼

[Sustain Juicery] 548 S. Spring St., Downtown, 213.488.1989, sustainjuicery.com. Mon.-Fri. 7:30 a.m.-6 p.m., Sat. 8:30 a.m.-6 p.m., Sun. 10 a.m.-4 p.m. **WHY** Cold-pressed juice blends made to order, instead of from a premixed bottle, plus good whole-fruit smoothies. **WHAT** High-quality, organic fruits and vegetables go into these cold-pressed juices and smoothies, and the results are almost always delicious. Try the Green Monkey, with pineapple, kale, banana, orange juice, and spirulina. The hungover like the power shots, and the cleansers like such trendy combos as coconut water, kale, and burdock. The little café is in the heart of Downtown's historic core. **WHO** Downtown workers and lofties.

SAN GABRIEL VALLEY

[Freshly Squeezed Juice Bar] 390 E. Colorado Blvd., Pasadena, 626.577.5001, freshlysqueezedjuicebar.com. Mon.-Fri. 7 a.m.-6 p.m., Sat. 9 a.m.-6 p.m., Sun. 10 a.m.-6 p.m. **WHY** Made-to-order juices, smoothies, and "wellness shots" prepared in a chic setting fronting the Paseo Colorado. **WHAT** Perfect for those hot Pasadena afternoons, this charming shop lives up to its name with refreshing blends of fruits and veggies, made on the spot. Some favorites are the Bloody Beet, Cucumber Sour, and Pink Lady Pitaya. **WHO** Shoppers and moviegoers who'd rather have a beet juice than a burger.

[Juice Farm] 🌴 36 E. Colorado Blvd., Old Pasadena, 626.844.7555, juicefarmcoldpressed.com. Mon.-Sat. 8:30 a.m.-6 p.m., Sun. 9 a.m.-3 p.m. **WHY** 100% organic ingredients mixed together "gently" with 15,000 pounds of pressure. **WHAT** Despite its power, the cold-press juicer used for the concoctions here is quite friendly

Juice Bars

to the fruit and veggies it crushes. By avoiding the heat that's generated by many conventional machines, it makes a finished product that keeps most of the enzymes, vitamins, and minerals. And if you like this sort of thing, they're tasty, too. **WHO** True believers in the power of a wellness shot.

[Pressed Juicery] 59 E. Colorado Blvd., Old Pasadena, 626.696.3593, pressedjuicery.com. Mon.-Fri. 7 a.m.-9 p.m., Sat. 8 a.m.-9 p.m., Sun. 8 a.m.-7 p.m. **WHY** Beat the heat and break up the shopping trip with delicious and not horribly overpriced cold-pressed juice right on Colorado Boulevard. **WHAT** You can get pie or sausages from the other businesses in this foodie courtyard, but you'll feel so superior walking out with a cold-pressed juice. We love sampling a few different blends before settling upon a full serving. It also sells shot-size tinctures that claim to boost immunity, liver function, and weight loss. **WHO** Cleansers, people fresh from a workout at Breakthru or Equinox, shoppers just coming from Lululemon down the street. 🐨 ☼

EAST VALLEY

[Orchard Flats] 312 N. San Fernando Rd., Burbank, 818.842.5590, orchardflats.com. Mon.-Thurs. 7 a.m.-8 p.m., Fri.-Sat. 7 a.m.-9 p.m., Sun. 9 a.m.-8 p.m. **WHY** Cold-pressed juices and cleanses in the heart of beautiful downtown Burbank. **WHAT** Some cold-press places promise bottled juices that aren't more than three days old, but Orchard Flats presses every day. Honey from a local farm is the only non-fruit sweetener, and they donate to the effort to save the disappearing honey bee. More locations in Studio City, Santa Monica, and on Melrose. **WHO** Seekers of the antioxidant, the purifying, and the invigorating.

[Pressed Juicery] 13033B Ventura Blvd., Studio City, 818.784.8255, pressedjuicery.com. Mon.-Fri. 7 a.m.-8 p.m., Sat.-Sun. 8 a.m.-7 p.m. **WHY** How many ways can you work kale into a juice? A lot! **WHAT** Valley folks seeking a single super-healthy cold-pressed juice blend or enough for a longer-term cleanse are happy that this local chain has found a home at a little storefront. The blends are already pressed and bottled, and none are more than three days old. New branches are opening at a rapid pace. **WHO** The cleansing crowd.

WESTSIDE: CENTRAL

[Kreation Juicery] 9465 Charleville Blvd., Beverly Hills, 310.247.8110, kreationjuice.com. Daily 7 a.m.-7 p.m. **WHY** Quality juices in the heart of Beverly Hills. Try the Green Dream, with apple, banana, kale, parsley, and almond milk. **WHAT** This fast-growing chain makes good smoothies and "cleanse" juices; you can even choose your own veggies from a buffet to be juiced. There are a few tables for sitting and sipping. **WHO** Cleansers, yoga buffs, actors, moms, none of whom are budget-conscious. ♥

[Juice Crafters] 🌴 11682 San Vicente Blvd., Brentwood, 424.442.0555, juicecrafters.com. Daily 6:30 a.m.-7 p.m. **WHY** Raw, organic, cold-pressed juices, tasty smoothies, and healthy shots. **WHAT** A definitive step above the chain juice joints, this quaint shop in Brentwood has a laid-back tropical vibe and an ultra-friendly staff with good recommendations. Look for parking near the yellow cruiser bike parked out front. **WHO** Health-conscious young adults, Brentwood moms in workout wear, and aging hippies who swear by the cleansing and detoxifying benefits of liquid meals.

WEST OF THE 405

[Kreation Kafé] 🌴 1202 Abbot Kinney Blvd., Venice, 310.314.7778, kreationjuice.com. Daily 7 a.m.-10 p.m. **WHY** A fun hangout with quality juices in the trendiest part of Venice. **WHAT** Abbot Kinney is ground zero for L.A. artsy-beach culture, which means it has more juiceries per capita than any place on earth. Despite its silly name, Kreation is one of the best. The patio, with its Astroturf and umbrellas, is a great place to sip 'n' chill, but it's the juice made inside that keeps visitors returning. **WHO** Hipsters, scenesters, trendsetters, and any other "-ters." ☼

[M.A.K.E. Santa Monica] 🌴 Santa Monica Place, 395 Santa Monica Blvd., Santa Monica, 310.394.7046, matthewkenneycuisine. com. Sun.-Thurs. 11 a.m.-9 p.m., Fri.-Sat. 11 a.m.-10 p.m. **WHY** A convenient takeaway counter for sampling Matthew Kenney's lauded raw creations. **WHAT** Located in the Market inside Santa Monica Place, this raw restaurant concocts juices and smoothies from ingredients freshly foraged from the neighboring farmers' market. Our favorites are the Carrot Punch and the slightly spicy Thai Green. **WHO** Advocates of the raw lifestyle and fans of the celebrity chef.

[Moon Juice] 507 Rose Ave., Venice, 310.399.2929, moonjuice-shop.com. Daily 7 a.m.-8 p.m. **WHY** A sleek, utterly LA juicing experience. **WHAT** This minimalist and modern juice bar is stocked with crystals and candles for sale alongside both packaged and fresh juices. Come here for the juices instead of the smoothies—the $16 green smoothie is a disappointment. Not all are made to order. **WHO** Only the most beautiful post-boardwalk-jog crowd.

[Pressed Juicery] 23503 Malibu Rd., Malibu, 310.433.7541, pressedjuicery.com. Mon.-Fri. 10 a.m.-5 p.m.; at Zuma Beach Sat.-Sun. 10 a.m.-5 p.m. **WHY** Nothing says Malibu more than a ginger detox juice. **WHAT** A super-cool, eco-friendly truck outlet of this fast-growing chain makes their most popular juice blends, most of which are pre-packaged. The truck parks at Zuma on weekends. **WHO** Surfers, beach bunnies, beautiful people.

[Rejuice] 🌴 3238 Pico Blvd., Santa Monica, 310.399.0001, rejuice-california.com. Mon.-Fri. 7 a.m.-8 p.m., Sat.-Sun. 8 a.m.-7 p.m. **WHY** A charming juice bar with generous samples and customized cleanse regimens. **WHAT** The crew behind Rejuice love their product, and it shows. Service is always friendly and high spirited, and the drinks are excellent. The house mixologist knows how to blend for both flavor and health. Bring your glass bottle back for a nice discount on the next drink. **WHO** Westsiders who visit ayurvedic doctors, doulas, and herbalists.

[Renovo Organic Juice & Smoothies] 2200 Colorado Ave., Santa Monica, 310.828.7267, myrenovo.com. Mon.-Fri. 7 a.m.-8 p.m., Sat. 9 a.m.-3 p.m. **WHY** Tasty blends of fruits and veggies at a price that's hard to beat. **WHAT** Located in an unassuming storefront in eastern Santa Monica, Renovo doesn't try to impress with fancy décor. It does, however, mix a delicious and affordable smoothie, with "classic blends" starting at $6 for a large. **WHO** A post-workout crowd and ardent students of superfoods. 💲

SOUTH BAY TO SOUTH L.A.

[Aguas Tijuana's Juice Bar] 8744 Washington Blvd., Pico Rivera, 562.949.7333, aguastijuanas.com. Mon. 9 a.m.-9 p.m., Tues.-Thurs. 7:30 a.m.-9 p.m., Fri. 7:30 a.m.-10 p.m., Sat. 9 a.m.-10 p.m., Sun. 10 a.m.-8 p.m. **WHY** For wonderful juice drinks—try the strawberries and cream made with fresh berries, the piña, or the escamocha. **WHAT** This friendly juice and smoothie bar makes 11

Juice Bars

🌴 ESSENTIALLY L.A.　╲ DIVE　🔈 QUIET　💲 VALUE

drinks daily (papaya, watermelon, strawberry/banana, horchata), plus mixes smoothies and custom drinks to order. Ingredients are fresh, and the place is spotless. Tortas are offered, too. **WHO** Local Latino families and workers on a lunch break. 🐷

[Natureba] 2415 Artesia Blvd., Redondo Beach, 310.597.4517. Mon.-Fri. 9 a.m.-7 p.m., Sat.-Sun. 10:30 a.m.-5 p.m. **WHY** A Brazilian juice bar that adds a tropical twist to your monthly cleanse. **WHAT** Natureba is a bright place with even livelier flavors, a juice bar that offers a taste of South America and the Amazon. There are pre-blended drinks for your post-workout cool-down, but even better are the cups of guava, acai, and cashew fruit (a curiously mango-like oddity) juices. **WHO** Yoga moms and health nuts avoiding the artisanal cold-pressed craze.

[Naturewell] 4725 E. 2nd St., Long Beach, 562.434.9400. Daily 7 a.m.-9 p.m. **WHY** The legendary coconut-kale smoothie, the acai chocolates, or the cold-busting "Facemelter" shot. **WHAT** With a slightly more reasonable price tag than some other juice bars, this cool spot in Belmont Shore is the place to feed your smoothie habit, counteract that hangover, or beat that pesky flu bug. They've also got bulk bins of nuts, grains, and beans, and the friendliest juice makers. **WHO** Surfers, yoga teachers, triathletes, and the mindfulness crowd.

[Rainbow Juices] 246 E. 3rd St., Long Beach, 562.708.7517, rainbowjuices.com. **WHY** For tasty cold-pressed juices with a lower price tag than their L.A. counterparts. **WHAT** Health-conscious Long Beach couple Dawna Bass and Chrissy Cox serve up an extensive menu of organic, raw, cold-pressed juices that changes with the seasons. Grapefruit Riot, a blend of grapefruit, blood orange, and mint, is a refreshing winter standout, while the Local (kale, cucumber, celery, orange, carrot, and lemon) is available year-round. Customized cleanses are also available. Bonus: Each juice comes in a cute reusable jar. At this writing, the business is based on free delivery around Long Beach, but by the time you read this, the shop will be open. **WHO** Long Beach hippies. 🐷

Juice Bars

Retailers

Here's where to look when you're ready to DIY: stock your own wine and/or beer cellar, craft your own cocktails, pull your own espressos. To find great coffee beans and teas, explore the Coffee, Tea + Boba chapter; beer lovers take note of the Breweries + Tap Rooms chapter, because breweries sell their goods to take home, not just drink onsite.

Retailers

[ESSENTIALLY L.A.]
Bar Keeper, Silver Lake (PAGE 197)
Beverage Warehouse, Marina del Rey (PAGE 204)
Emilio's Beverage Warehouse, Bellflower (PAGE 206)
Galco's Soda Pop Shop, Highland Park (PAGE 198)
Greenbar Collective, Downtown (PAGE 199)
Lou Wine & Provisions, Silver Lake (PAGE 199)
Silver Lake Wine, Silver Lake (PAGE 200)
Wally's, Westwood (PAGE 204)
Wine Expo, Santa Monica (PAGE 206)
Wine House, West L.A. (PAGE 204)
Woodland Hills Wine, Woodland Hills (PAGE 203)

CENTRAL CITY

[Cap N' Cork Junior Market] 1674 Hillhurst Ave., Los Feliz, 323.665.1260. Daily. **WHY** The best selection of local and imported beer in the Los Feliz/Silver Lake area, not to mention a fine array of liqueurs and wines and a knowledgeable staff. **WHAT** There are few fancy gourmet trappings here, just a bounty of alcoholic liquids. A deep selection of Belgian and British beers are complemented by plenty of California craft beers and ciders. Spirits are also strong, especially bourbon, Scotch, and Japanese whiskey.

[Domaine LA] 6801 Melrose Ave., Melrose, 323.932.0280, domainela.com. Daily. **WHY** If you want bottles from the wine producer everyone is talking about, you'll find them here. **WHAT** Former Hollywood exec Jill Bernheimer puts the spotlight on natural and boutique wines at her shop, as well as offering informative tastings every weekend. **WHO** Larchmont and Melrose residents finding the perfect bottle of wine for a special occasion.

[Du Vin Wine & Spirits] 540 N. San Vicente Blvd., West Hollywood, 310.855.1161, du-vin.net. Closed Sun. **WHY** For its selection of French and Italian wines as well as a surprisingly large number of half bottles. **WHAT** Tucked away behind an office bungalow is this tiny cottage, a Mecca for lovers of European wines. This is the spot to find a big-ticket gift for a wine aficionado, as well as to snag esoteric varietals and regions that will spark cocktail-party chatter. Picpoul, anyone? There's a nice selection of upscale spirits, too, as well as a handful of gourmet foods. **WHO** Design professionals (it's around the corner from the Blue Whale) and wine lovers from WeHo and Beverly Hills.

[K & L Wine Merchants] 1400 Vine St., Hollywood, 323.464. WINE, klwines.com. Daily. **WHY** Great location, competitive prices, and a parking lot. **WHAT** This terrific shop, a branch of the Bay Area–based retailer, sits in the shadow of the ArcLight and offers a superb selection of imported and domestic wines. It also boasts a well-edited shelf of single malts, small-batch bourbons, craft vodkas, aperitifs, and digestifs. **WHO** Collectors who trickle in from the Hollywood Hills and Hancock Park.

[Larchmont Village Wine & Cheese] 223 N. Larchmont Blvd., Hancock Park, 323.856.8699, larchmonthvillagewine.com. Closed Sun. **WHY** Savvy wine picks, delicious sandwiches, and Mi-

Retailers

chel Cordon Bleu smoked salmon. **WHAT** This tiny shop on pricey Larchmont Boulevard stocks a well-chosen array of bottlings at a fair markup. Wine guy Simon Cocks offers trustworthy advice and doesn't hesitate to steer customers toward the best values (the "wine of the month" is always a great buy). The deli's sandwiches are justifiably renowned. **WHO** Hancock Parkers catching up with each other about kids, vacations, and remodelings.

[Venokado] 7714 Fountain Ave., West Hollywood, 323.850.1600, venokado.com. Daily. **WHY** You need the perfect wine or the perfect gift, and you don't have a vast budget or time to wander through a mall. **WHAT** The trio of women who run this chic shop sell a well-edited selection of wines and gifts (for yourself or for others, including babies) relating to food, wine, entertaining, and the good life. The name says it all—a mashup of the Italian word for wine (*vino*) and the French word for gift (*cadeau*). The ladies have gained a following for their clutch gift, a sleek box containing a bottle of wine and an intriguing, fun assortment of other items, for $45 and up. We always leave with an armful of interesting bottles, many under $20. **WHO** Style-conscious WeHo regulars and savvy commuters who regularly take Fountain across town.

EASTSIDE

[55 Degree Wine] 3111 Glendale Blvd., Atwater, 323.662.5556, 55degreewine.com. Daily; tastings Tues.-Sun. **WHY** A terrific array of Italians and a brick-walled, candlelit basement tasting room that's the hippest spot in Atwater every night from 5 to 10 p.m. **WHAT** This eastern outpost of Santa Monica's Wine Expo is an oenophile hot spot in suddenly hip Atwater. As in Santa Monica, the specialty is small-producer Italian wines at very low prices; Champagnes are also a focus, and you'll also find some good choices from Spain. **WHO** Young wine buffs from Atwater, High-land Park, and Silver Lake.

[Bar Keeper] 3910 W. Sunset Blvd., Silver Lake, 323.669.1675, barkeepersilverlake.com. Daily. **WHY** When you need not just one kind of absinthe spoon, but several. **WHAT** Given his name (and his gregarious personality), it was probably destiny that Joe Keeper would someday open a store called Bar Keeper. In the Sunset Junction 'hood that is Silver Lake's foodie bull's-eye, he's put together a drinker's head shop of wonderfully curated gifts and essentials, from glassware and shakers to books and vintage bar

gear. You'll also find an impressive selection of booze from artisanal producers, including Batavia Arrack, Willett bourbon, Del
Maguey mescal, and Crème de Violette. **WHO** The sort of people
who know that there is such a thing as an absinthe spoon.

[Buzz Wine Beer Shop] 460 S. Spring St., Downtown,
213.622.2222, buzzwinebeershop.com. Daily (open late). **WHY** A hip,
urban wine bar for people who don't like traditional wine bars.
WHAT A lot of places use the word "curated" to describe their
wares, but Buzz really earns it. The vast selection of organic and
biodynamic wines (4,000 bottles, they claim) is mind-boggling.
And we'd be remiss if we didn't mention the mouthwatering selection of craft beers. After operating mostly as a carryout wine store
for the last few years, Buzz managed to modify its liquor license
so you can now take any bottle you purchase to the wine bar at
the rear of the store, where a staffer will crack it open for a small
corkage fee so you can sip and mingle. **WHO** Oenophiles with a
penchant for obscure varietals, suds seekers.

[Colorado Wine Co.] 2114 Colorado Blvd., Eagle Rock,
323.478.1985, cowineco.com. Closed Mon. **WHY** Fun and surprising
wine bargains in an appealing, un-snooty atmosphere, with a great
wine bar to boot. **WHAT** The slogan here is "Wine for everyone,"
and that's refreshingly evident in the selection of bottles for less
than $25 and the fun and reasonable tastings. (Bonus: First-rate
food-truck appearances.) **WHO** Attractive, friendly people in an
attractive, friendly space in the hip heart of Eagle Rock. 🄢

[Galco's Soda Pop Shop] 🌴 5702 York Blvd., Highland Park,
323.255.7115, sodapopstop.com. Daily. **WHY** Because it's a vast
wonderland of fizzy drinks of every conceivable flavor, color, and
container—plus a seriously old-school candy counter. **WHAT** For
underage drinking, no place in the world beats Galco's, which
stocks more than 250 kinds of soda (as well as a good selection
of global beer). Looking for coffee soda, authentic Kickapoo Joy
Juice, or Guayaba from Brazil? Boy, have you come to the right
place. You'll also find a strange and wonderful array of near-for-
gotten regional candy, including Owyhee Idaho Spuds, Mallo
Cups, Chick-O-Sticks, and bubblegum cigarettes. And it ships.
WHO Hipster kids, nostalgic baby boomers, immigrants seeking a
fix of homeland carbonation.

Retailers

[Greenbar Collective] 🌴 2459 E. 8th St., Downtown, 213.375.3668, greenbar.biz. By appt. only. **WHY** L.A.'s only distillery is housed in a groovy warehouse space that hosts tours and special events. **WHAT** Greenbar makes organic whiskey, gin, vodka, rum, and tequila as well as uniquely flavored liqueurs and bitters. A tasting room should be open by the time you read this; call to inquire about tours and cocktail events.

[Intelligentsia Coffee] 3922 W. Sunset Blvd., Silver Lake, 323.663.6173, intelligentsiacoffee.com. Daily. **WHY** Gleaming home espresso machines to drool over, and maybe even buy. **WHAT** Pasquini's got some competition now that Intelligentsia is selling gear for the home barista. The range isn't large, but it's smart and thoughtful, from $7,500 hard-plumbed La Marzocco espresso machines that are sturdy enough for a small café, to simple little machines that go for as low as $500. It also has good burr grinders, knock boxes, and other accessories. **WHO** Amateur baristas with ambition and deep pockets.

[Lou Wine & Provisions] 🌴 720 N. Virgil Ave., Silver Lake, 323.305.7004, louprovisions.com. Closed Mon. **WHY** Fans of Lou Amdur's eclectic wine tastes will find plenty to love here. In the curated selection of 25 or so wines, there's always something surprising and enchanting. **WHAT** Located next door to the popular Sqirl café, this bare-bones wine shop is run by beloved former wine-bar owner Lou Amdur, who's a whiz at discovering great bottles for less than $30. **WHO** Silver Lake couples looking to grow their wine knowledge and find something interesting to drink on a budget. 🐝

[Pasquini Espresso Co.] 1501 W. Olympic Blvd., Pico-Union, 213.739.0480, pasquini.com. Closed Sun. **WHY** For serious home-kitchen espresso machines—but you need to have a resale license to buy here. **WHAT** If you have a resale license or are working with a contractor or designer who does, come here to get a good deal on an ultra-high-quality home espresso machine/steamer/grinder setup that will have you making espresso as good as Intelligentsia's. If you don't have a resale license, call them up to find a retailer. **WHO** Hardcore coffeeheads.

[Ramirez Liquor & Kegs] 736 S. Soto St., Boyle Heights, 323.261.2915, ramirezliquor.com. Daily (open late). **WHY** Aside from the wide selection, prices are more than reasonable, and

Retailers

the knowledgeable staff are happy to provide recommendations. **WHAT** This massive, locally owned liquor store offers a jaw-dropping selection of craft beers and spirits, including some very hard-to-find tequilas. **WHO** East L.A. residents stocking up on tequila and beer for weekend parties. 🍷

[San Antonio Winery] 737 Lamar St., Chinatown, 323.223.1401, sanantoniowinery.com. Daily. **WHY** To tour, taste, and buy at L.A.'s only remaining winery, which also happens to be a pretty good one. **WHAT** Going back to 1917, when L.A. and the San Gabriel Valley were rich with wineries, San Antonio is run with care and skill by the Riboli family. It produces wines on site under several labels, including Maddelena, San Simeon, and Riboli Family Vineyard, using grapes from Paso Robles, Monterey, and Napa. The restaurant is a fun place for a private party. **WHO** Lively groups of shorts-and-flip-flop-wearing wine tasters.

[Silver Lake Wine] 🌴 2395 Glendale Blvd., Silver Lake, 323.662.9024, silverlakewine.com. Daily. **WHY** For a well-chosen selection at every price point. **WHAT** This female-friendly, no-attitude shop showcases small-production wines from all over the world. And sometimes the best wine for your occasion might be a Pacific Northwest microbrew, or even a handmade sake. Tastings are happening events; in summer, don't miss the Friday-night wine-tasting-and-tour of the Hollyhock House in Los Feliz. One of L.A.'s best boutique wine stores. **WHO** Silverlake hipsters, but the unhip are welcome, too.

[Sunset Beer Company] 1498 Sunset Blvd. #3, Echo Park, 213.481.2337, sunsetbeerco.com. Daily. **WHY** A carefully chosen beer selection and all the accoutrements. **WHAT** This offshoot of Eagle Rock's friendly Colorado Wine Shop is smartly located in the heart of craft-beer-adoring Echo Park. Beer expert Alex Macy is in charge of the broad but carefully selected array of beers, with an emphasis on Californian and Belgian breweries. Hang out for informative tastings from the rotating tap selection and beer-friendly snacks, or get advice on which brews to pair with foods. A selection of glassware and accessories will help even the novice hophead look on top of things. **WHO** Eastside beer geeks who love to peruse the latest bottle releases.

Retailers

SAN GABRIEL VALLEY

[Chronicle Wine Shop] 919 E. California Blvd., Pasadena, 626.577.2549, cwcellar.com. Daily. **WHY** The proximity to Pie 'n' Burger adds to the eccentric charm of this wine emporium located in an old motel room. Sommelier Elizabeth Schweitzer knows her stuff but is unpretentious about it. **WHAT** The Chronicle Wine Shop is in a (quirky) world of its own. No high-end tasting room here, but the atmosphere, reminiscent of a plain-jane French *cave*, makes this place worth a trip. When the flag is up on California Boulevard, the staff is in. You can get great bargains. **WHO** Caterers, party planners, and low-key wine aficionados. $

[Everson Royce] 155 N. Raymond Ave., Pasadena, 626.765.9334, eversonroyce.com. Daily. **WHY** A beautifully curated collection of delicious wines at all price points, with great choices for less than $20, plus Friday-night tastings with the Let's Be Frank truck parked out front for sustenance. **WHAT** The friendly, savvy folks from Silver Lake Wine are behind this Old Pasadena wine shop and tasting room. Ask their advice and you won't be sorry, whether you're looking for a $12 French rosé or Argentinean Malbec or a celebratory Champagne. The spirits selection— whiskeys, tequilas, Armagnacs, bitters—is superb, and there's quite a roster of bottled beers as well. **WHO** Caterers, collectors, and low-key wine buffs.

[Gerlach's Liquor] 1075 S. Fair Oaks Ave., Pasadena, 626.799.1166. Daily. **WHY** Great buys on special wines (we've found swell Malbecs for $9), a small but thoughtful selection of French, Californian, and Oregonian wines, and a terrific choice of port, sherry, and dessert wine. **WHAT** It looks like your basic drive-up liquor store, but there's a lot more to Gerlach's than meets the eye. Brothers Lewy and Fred Fedail know their stuff, and they pack a lot of good wines into a small climate-controlled room. A devoted clientele asks for their advice and takes it. **WHO** Blue-blood Pasadenans, artsy South Pasadenans, and working guys picking up a six-pack. $

[Mission Liquor] 1801 E. Washington Blvd., Pasadena, 626.794.7026, missionliquor.com. Closed Sun. **WHY** For neighborhood-wine-shop service with bigger-store selection, as well as a

Retailers

very good roster of spirits and liqueurs, including grappas, ouzos, absinthes, and such festive liqueurs as Aperol. **WHAT** Improbably anchoring Pasadena's Armenian Row with an imposing stone front, this venerable liquor store has a bright, welcoming layout, expert advice, and a surprisingly deep selection of wines, spirits, and mixers, as well as cigars. Look for the occasional tastings. **WHO** Wine-savvy Altadenans, of which there are many.

[Mission Wines] 1114 Mission St., South Pasadena, 626.403.9463, missionwines.com. Daily. **WHY** It's a nice spot to just hang out around wine. **WHAT** Former Patina sommelier Chris Meeske runs a charming, artisan-style shop that showcases hand-made, distinctive bottlings at every price point. Wine education and pairing wine with food are specialties, and the frequent tastings have become a linchpin of South Pasadena's lively food-and-wine scene. The bargain bins are always good. **WHO** People who wouldn't be caught dead buying wine at TJs down the street.

[Red Carpet] 400 E. Glenoaks Blvd., Glendale, 818.247.5544, redcarpetwine.com. Daily. **WHY** For an impressive array of hard-to-find California bottlings. **WHAT** If Red Carpet doesn't carry it, you'll probably have to trek to the westside to find it. Staffed by enthusiasts, this venerable store has a vast selection of wine, beer, and premium spirits, as well as cigars and stemware. The tasting bar is a popular hangout on weekends and Tuesday evenings. **WHO** Collectors who don't mind paying a few bucks more for good service.

[Rosso Wine Shop] 3459 N. Verdugo Rd., Glendale, 818.330.9130, rossowineshop.com. Closed Mon. **WHY** To discover obscure vintners your tasting buddies haven't heard of, was well as good-value "country" wines. **WHAT** Although it's doubled in size since its founding, Rosso doesn't try to compete with the big guys; instead, owner Jeff Zimmitti focuses on France, Spain, Italy, and California, selecting the best-value wines that go well with food. The result is a relaxed, user-friendly shop that's a destination in Glendale's Sparr Heights gourmet gulch on Verdugo Road. Pick up a bottle to enjoy with an excellent dinner at Bashan next door. **WHO** A younger breed of collector and enthusiast, many of whom are regulars at the tasting events.

[Topline Wine Company] 4718 San Fernando Rd., Glendale, 818.500.9670, toplinewine.com. Daily. **WHY** Premium wine and spirits at not-so-premium prices. **WHAT** This no-frills shop in an industrial section of Glendale has a decent wine selection at very competitive prices. It's arranged warehouse-style, with stacks of cases, and it's worth poking through the boxes to find the buried treasures. Also check out the spirits room and the particularly good collection of aperitifs. **WHO** Price-conscious aficionados from all over. 💵

EAST VALLEY

[Flask Fine Wines] 12194 Ventura Blvd., Studio City, 818.761.5373, flaskfinewines.com. Daily. **WHY** A chic tasting bar (Thursdays and Fridays) and a smart choice of small-producer Californians. **WHAT** Excellent displays and some little-seen Californian and French wines make this a fun place to browse. There are some good values on the racks, too. **WHO** Local tasters and producers' assistants who were dispatched to fetch an emergency $250 bottle for a gift.

[Vendome Spirits & Wine] 10600 Riverside Dr., Toluca Lake, 818.766.9593, vendometolucalake.com. Daily. **WHY** For terrific wine and beer tastings, craft beers, and a great selection of harder to find beverages like French ciders, Root organic liqueurs, and small-producer sodas. **WHAT** The best all-around liquor store in the east Valley, Vendome has it all: a great wine selection, soda pops, Belgian and Californian beers, artisanal mixers, and even a solid cigar collection. If they don't have it, they'll order it for you.

WEST VALLEY

[Woodland Hills Wine Company] 🌴 22622 Ventura Blvd., Woodland Hills, 818.222.1111 or 800.678.WINE, whwc.com. Daily. **WHY** It's all about the Burgs. **WHAT** A connoisseur's Mecca, Woodland Hills Wine specializes in (sigh) Burgundies, but the selection of top wines from California, Bordeaux, the Rhône, Italy, Austria, and Spain is worth the drive to the west Valley. Woodland Hills also direct-imports many hard-to-find bottles, including some bargains. Staffers are highly knowledgeable and give good counsel. **WHO** Serious collectors as well as wine newbies.

WESTSIDE: CENTRAL

[Bar & Garden] 6142 Washington Blvd., Culver City, 310.876.0759, barandgarden.com. Closed Mon. **WHY** Owners Marissa Mandel and Lauren Johnson have assembled rows of craft

Retailers

spirits, naturally made wines, and accessories you'll notice from the city's top bar menus. **WHAT** This intimate wine and liquor shop provides wine tastings and classes for those looking to expand their knowledge, and it has one of the most well-curated selections of wine and craft spirits in the city. **WHO** Culver City couples who want an eclectic bottle of wine for their next dinner party or an interesting spirit to stock in their bar cabinet.

[Wally's] 🌴 2107 Westwood Blvd., Westwood, 310.475.0606, wallywine.com. Daily. **WHY** For the phenomenal selection of hard-to-find trophy wines and artisanal spirits. **WHAT** Steve Wallace founded his West Los Angeles wine shop in 1968 and despite cramped quarters has built it into one of California's leading wine retailers. This is the spot to find rare and small-production bottlings from Napa, Burgundy, Bordeaux, and other fine-wine regions. Partner Christian Navarro handles the care and feeding of the shop's stable of heavy-hitting collectors. The cheese collection is also fantastic, and the small roster of spirits is first-rate. **WHO** Studio bigwigs, UCLA professors, Brentwood matrons, and personal assistants picking up lavish gift baskets.

[Wine House] 🌴 2311 Cotner Ave., West L.A., 310.479.3731 or 800.626.9463, wineaccess.com. Daily. **WHY** For 18,000 square feet devoted to wine, beer, and spirits. **WHAT** Arguably the best wine shop in L.A., the Wine House has it all: great selection, good prices, informed staff, and even a little gourmet food section, so you can get a tin of caviar to go with that magnum of Cristal. A year-round program of classes makes it easy to improve your tasting skills and expertise. Also check out the cool automated tasting bar.

WEST OF THE 405

[Beverage Warehouse] 🌴 4395 McConnell Ave. #21, Marina del Rey, 310.306.2822, beveragewarehouse.com. Daily. **WHY** The best liquor store on the westside, or perhaps in all of L.A., stocking everything from Pacifique absinthe, to Thatchers organic apple-spice liqueur, to North Coast beers, to Milagro tequilas, to Poppy Pinot Noir. **WHAT** Grin your way through aisle upon aisle in this hangar-style warehouse that stocks an unbelievable selection of craft beer, wine, liquor, mixers, and accessories. Prices are fair considering the overall quality and location—and when that rare bottle happens to smile in your direction, well then, price doesn t matter much anyway. **WHO** Cocktail crafters, wine geeks, hopheads.

Retailers

🌴 ESSENTIALLY L.A.   🔨 DIVE   🌙 QUIET   💲 VALUE

[The Duck Blind Fine Wine & Spirits] 1102 Montana Ave., Santa Monica, 310.394.6705, duckblindfinewines.com. Daily. **WHY** The specials. Sometimes you can luck into a $20 wine for $7. **WHAT** Don't let the outside fool you—what looks like a standard grungy liquor store is actually beautifully stocked with whiskeys and craft beers, and the wine selection is pretty good, too, and not just on the high end. And they'll deliver in Santa Monica and west Brentwood with a $35 minimum order. **WHO** Neighborhood loyalists—this place has been around for half a century. ⑤

[Fireside Cellars] 1421 Montana Ave., Santa Monica, 310.393.2888, firesidecellars.com. Daily. **WHY** Irresistible wine selections for those who know their Alexander Valley from their Languedoc. **WHAT** This tiny shop resembles a cozy home cellar filled with boutique wines, especially those from California and France. Visions of Cakebread and Stag's Leap will have you reaching for the stemware—and your checkbook. It's not that there aren't bargains here—there are some good $15 selections—but the pricier bottles from great wineries are just too tempting. **WHO** Hybrid-driving, Viognier-drinking, Obama-voting, Whole Foods– shopping (it's next door) Montana Avenue people.

[Los Angeles Wine Co.] 4935 McConnell Ave., West L.A., 310.306.9463, lawineco.com. Daily. **WHY** Drink globally, save local- ly. **WHAT** This warehouse-style merchant has spent years scouring the world for great deals, and it lives up to its motto: "Every wine in stock, always sale priced." Whether seeking a $95 Burgundy for $80 or a $40 Italian Sangiovese for $30, value hunters love the steals and deals. **WHO** Penny-pinchers who come for the incredi- ble selection of wines for less than $12. ⑤

[Moe's Fine Wines] 11740 San Vicente Blvd., Brentwood, 310.826.4444, moesfinewines.com. Closed Sun. **WHY** Wine is more fun than software, so thank you, Moe, for quitting your day job to open this place. **WHAT** Scott "Moe" Levy's high-end neigh- borhood shop looks like a dream home cellar, with stained-wood wine racks, Riedel stemware, and a carefully chosen array of $8 to $800 wines, many from small California producers. And it is a kind of home for Moe, who quit the software business to realize his wine-merchant dream. Some international heavy-hitters are featured as well, along with delightful house chocolates and nuts.

Retailers

🏠 GROUPS 🎤 KARAOKE ☼ PATIO ♥ ROMANTIC

WHO Well-heeled Brentwood regulars, many of whom stop by for the Saturday-afternoon tastings.

[Wine Expo] 🌴 2933 Santa Monica Blvd., Santa Monica, 310.828.4428, wineexpo.com. Daily. **WHY** Educated and refreshingly honest staff members, who also know their way around tequila and beer. The Prosecco selection is worth the trip alone. **WHAT** Wine Expo started as a Champagne specialty shop and has evolved into the westside's go-to source for Italian wines. Owners Ali Biglar and Robert Rogness cultivate relationships with Italian winemakers and ship back via their own import business to keep prices low. Almost as entertaining as the vast selection are the clever descriptions posted by the cases. Ditto the newsletter, which is a hoot. **WHO** Fans of *vino italiano*. 🗫

SOUTH BAY TO SOUTH L.A.

[Emilio's Beverage Warehouse] 🌴 17251 Lakewood Blvd., Bellflower, 562.630.8683. Daily. **WHY** For a fantastic selection of tequilas, Cognacs, and strange and wonderful liqueurs. **WHAT** What looks like your ordinary liquor store is a gold mine for such hard-to-find drinks as Ole Smoky Moonshine, Pappy Van Winkle Bourbon, Torero Anejo tequila, and Kinky Blue liqueur. Its beer selection used to be so-so, but now it's carrying Stone and other craft brews. Worth a detour to Bellflower. **WHO** Cocktail geeks hunting for obscure rums.

[Off the Vine] 491 6th St., San Pedro, 310.831.1551, offthevinewines.com. Closed Mon. **WHY** For tasty, good-value bottles from the Santa Ynez Valley and the northern and southern Rhône. **WHAT** The selection is small at this tidy little shop, but it's creative and includes some very good specials. The focus is on just three regions: California's Central Coast, the Rhône, and Spain. Regulars stop by for the Friday- and Saturday-night tastings, and party-planning beer lovers order kegs of local and import craft beers (Bitburger, Allagash, Bayhawk, Green Flash, and many more). **WHO** South Bay food-and-wine buffs who are tired of Trader Joe's. 🗫

[The Wine Country] 2301 Redondo Ave., Signal Hill, 562.597.8303, thewinecountry.com. Daily. **WHY** A sprawling wine store with serious knowledge. **WHAT** Owner Randy Kemner has long championed offbeat varietals, off-the-beaten-track regions

Retailers

🌴 ESSENTIALLY L.A.   ⬎ DIVE   𝄞 QUIET   🗫 VALUE

and under-appreciated importers. The result is a shop with an eclectic array of wines selected for their ability to complement food, with particular strength in aromatic whites, including German, Austrian, and Alsatian bottlings.

Index by Neighborhood

Index

▼ Index A to Z